Academics and th Real World

CW00963020

SRHE and Open University Press Imprint
General Editor: Heather Eggins

Current titles include:

Catherine Bargh et al.: University Leadership
Ronald Barnett: The Idea of Higher Education
Ronald Barnett: The Limits of Competence
Ronald Barnett: Higher Education
Ronald Barnett: Realizing the University in an Age of Supercomplexity
Tony Becher and Paul R. Trowler: Academic Tribes and Territories (second edition)
Neville Bennett et al.: Skills Development in Higher Education and Employment
John Biggs: Teaching for Quality Learning at University
David Boud et al. (eds): Using Experience for Learning
David Boud and Nicky Solomon (eds): Work-based Learning
Tom Bourner et al. (eds): New Directions in Professional Higher Education
John Brennan et al. (eds): What Kind of University?
Anne Brockbank and Ian McGill: Facilitating Reflective Learning in Higher Education
Stephen Brookfield and Stephen Preskill: Discussion as a Way of Teaching
Ann Brooks and Alison Mackinnon (eds): Gender and the Restructured University
Sally Brown and Angela Glasner (eds): Assessment Matters in Higher Education
John Cowan: On Becoming an Innovative University Teacher
Gerard Delanty: Challenging Knowledge
Chris Duke: Managing the Learning University
G. R. Evans: Academics and the Real World
Andrew Hannan and Harold Silver: Innovating in Higher Education
Norman Jackson and Helen Lund (eds): Benchmarking for Higher Education
Merle Jacob and Tomas Hellström (eds): The Future of Knowledge Production in the
    Academy
Peter Knight and Paul Trowler: Departmental Leadership in Higher Education
Mary Lea and Barry Stierer (eds): Student Writing in Higher Education
Ian McNay (ed.): Higher Education and its Communities
Elaine Martin: Changing Academic Work
Moira Peelo and Terry Wareham (eds): Failing Students in Higher Education
Craig Prichard: Making Managers in Universities and Colleges
Michael Prosser and Keith Trigwell: Understanding Learning and Teaching
John Richardson: Researching Student Learning
Stephen Rowland: The Enquiring University Teacher
Maggi Savin-Baden: Problem-based Learning in Higher Education
Peter Scott (ed.): The Globalization of Higher Education
Peter Scott: The Meanings of Mass Higher Education
Anthony Smith and Frank Webster (eds): The Postmodern University?
Colin Symes and John McIntyre (eds): Working Knowledge
Peter G. Taylor: Making Sense of Academic Life
Susan Toohey: Designing Courses for Higher Education
Paul R. Trowler (ed.): Higher Education Policy and Institutional Change
Melanie Walker (ed.): Reconstructing Professionalism in University Teaching
David Warner and David Palfreyman (eds): The State of UK Higher Education
Diana Woodward and Karen Ross: Managing Equal Opportunities in Higher Education

Academics and the Real World

G. R. Evans

The Society for Research into Higher Education
& Open University Press

Published by SRHE and
Open University Press
Celtic Court
22 Ballmoor
Buckingham
MK18 1XW

email: enquiries@openup.co.uk
world wide web: www.openup.co.uk

and
325 Chestnut Street
Philadelphia, PA 19106, USA

First Published 2002

A catalogue record of this book is available from the British Library

ISBN   0 335 21111 9 (pb)   0 335 21112 7 (hb)

Library of Congress Cataloging-in-Publication Data

Evans, G. R. (Gillian Rosemary)
    Academics and the real world / G.R. Evans.
      p. cm.
    Includes bibliographical references and index.
    ISBN 0–335–21112–7 — ISBN 0–335–21111–9 (pbk.)
    1. Education, Higher—Social aspects—Great Britain. 2. Academic freedom—
Great Britain. I. Title.

LC191.98.G7 E93 2002
378.41—dc21   2002021403

Typeset by Graphicraft Limited, Hong Kong
Printed by St Edmundsbury Press, Bury St Edmunds, Suffolk

Contents

Introduction

The bones of this book are briefly set out. Universities are there to teach students and award degrees; and society needs a qualified workforce. Universities are places where research can seen to be done independently; and society gets the benefit. To support these activities, universities have to be extensive and complex, and so they need a proportionately large amount of administration or 'management'. This threefold division provides the core structure for the present study of the changing relationship between universities and society. Despite encouragement to universities to find resources elsewhere, society still provides substantial public funding to run universities, and that entitles it to put plain, pragmatic considerations such as these in the forefront of its thinking.

Yet there is an 'idea of a university', as John Henry Newman realized in the nineteenth century when he faced the task of 'inventing' a new one in Dublin.[1] Our starting-point in Chapter 1 must be whether there are continuities in that 'idea' which make them still central to the academic endeavour. Not to examine those would be to risk casting aside the very core of what has kept it all going century after century.

'A great deal of what I've written about education has been an attempt to recapture my own pastoral myth,'[2] admits Northrop Frye, and anyone looking backwards risks a similar charge. In defiance of that risk, and because it does not make sense to approach the present day without asking how we got here, the first part of this study is concerned with the ideas about the value of work which has traditionally underpinned the scholarly endeavour of thought and analysis and inquiry and discovery, and helped to form the first universities. Our question is how far they continue to inform them in their encounter with the changed priorities of the modern world. That is why the title of this book includes 'and the real world'. There has probably never been an era in which the world outside universities has felt so free to tell them what to do, and cited so freely in doing so the 'public', and increasingly the 'commercial', interest which currently sets the agenda. It may not do so indefinitely. It is this question whether universities face permanent change and what those concerned for their welfare can do, which presents the natural theme of Chapter 5.

Everyone has views but not everyone can get those views into general discussion. Academics have an advantage there. They are articulate, informed. They are, by profession, people who publish, who teach. They are also more *free* to speak than most. Modern English law gives a special protection to freedom of speech by the academic staff of universities.[3] It is their job to speak at the frontiers of knowledge and in the face of resistance to change of opinion. This makes universities 'free speech' environments[4] in which all kinds of talk can go on, and intellectual risks should be able (paradoxically) to be taken in safety.

The legislative protection of the still recent Education Reform Act 1988 assumed that there attaches to such 'speech' a value so supreme, or perhaps merely so 'useful to society', that it is entitled to a protection beyond that which all citizens of a free society ought to be able to claim. In effect, academics form a group which society 'pays to think'. But if society ceases to set a value on that being done so freely that 'anything may happen', the scene changes. It then makes sense to withdraw or diminish public funding and let commercial or other funders pay for the thinking. The moment that happens, the academic ceases to be free to think and has to 'think to order' and perhaps to try to find ways to think the thoughts he is being *paid* to think, and come to the required conclusions.

The teaching functions of universities are the theme of Chapter 2. The recent tendency here is for society to go beyond the vocational emphasis, the emphasis on 'usefulness' and 'relevance' which was visible in the 1990s, to the deliberate fostering of the 'entrepreneurial spirit' in students in the twenty-first century. So the students are encouraged to 'buy' the teaching, as an investment in their own (commercial) futures. At the turn of the millennium, society's expectations are visibly changing in that direction. Students are undoubtedly customers if they have to pay their own tuition fees. In order to throw the contrast of expectations into relief, Chapter 2, concentrates, like Chapter 1, on aspects of the enduring background of expectations, this time about 'teaching' in higher education.

Modern academics not only teach and seek to expand the frontiers of knowledge through scholarship, they also, increasingly, do the kind of research which has practical applications, and is funded by commercial sponsors. This is the subject of Chapter 3.

A commonly cited example of such endeavour is pharmaceutical research, where the manifest danger is the suppression of results which do not please a commercial funder. The academic researcher is presented with a dilemma. His loyalties conflict. If he does not obey the funder, he may get no more funding. If he does accept prevention of publication of the results he has arrived at, a half-glimpsed scientific truth may be lost sight of, and possibly damage done to the health of those taking a given drug or denied a better one. Will 'society' back the researcher who is 'torn'? When big corporations have influence in the innermost rooms of government, it may not. Will his university support him? It may not. Thanos Mergoupis was at work as research officer on a research project at the London School of Economics (LSE) which the World Travel and Tourism Council had undertaken, in 1998, to fund for three years. The subject of the research was the employment effects and other social aspects of tourism. According to extensive press coverage in the spring of 2001, half-way through the project the funder decided to 'change its funding priorities' and to transfer the research project to a private company. Although there were questions about the funder's motivation – early findings appeared to be tending to show that tourism did not have the huge potential for job creation the funders wanted to demonstrate – the LSE apparently did not seek to enforce its contract with the World Travel and Tourism Council. The researcher lost his job. The issue of principle which arises is the need for a university to defend the freedom of its researchers to come to independent conclusions even when their salaries are coming from sources which have an interest in a particular outcome. Chapter 3 is concerned with this, perhaps the most urgent of the contemporary test-beds of the relationship between academics and the real world.

Changes in the university world in the UK in the 1990s have appeared (to many who have taught in them for a working lifetime) to threaten universities' deep purpose, their very sense of self. Those changes have involved a movement away from respect for learning for its own sake, and towards a fear of any expertise which could not readily be seen to be applicable in manufacturing or in meeting superficially quantifiable 'social needs'. For example, a series of panels was set up in the 1990s by the UK government's Foresight project to 'encourage industry, academia and government to identify research needs and market opportunities and threats for the future'. These panels were to cover healthcare, materials, the ageing of the population, crime prevention, manufacturing, built environment, chemicals, defence, aerospace and systems, financial services, food chain and crops for industry, information, communications and media, retail and consumer services, energy and environment.[5] In a report in the *Committee of Vice-Chancellors and Principals News* of spring 1999 it was recorded with satisfaction that 'the multiplier effect from the translation of intellectual capital into products generates significant contributions to wealth and job creation locally, regionally, and nationally . . . Technology transfer covers the commercialisation of university research through patenting and licensing, spin-off companies, and sponsorships of research by companies who then bring its fruits to market.' If that is what a modern western society ought to look to, we have to ask whether the old idea of the purpose of a university needs revision. That is the question addressed in Chapter 3.

There have been recent trends in the way universities are administered which are raising profound questions about whether they can be trusted to run themselves. That is the theme of Chapter 4. It is left this late so as to point up the widening needs such administration has to meet, and their increasing complexity.

What can be done? That is the question addressed in Chapter 5. In a recent pioneering book, Donald Kennedy sets over against the notion of academic freedom a concept of academic duty.[6] His idea is that freedom requires the concomitant acceptance of some degree of regulation in the world of the university, by principles of right conduct or other means. He explores, mainly from a North American vantage-point, a series of areas – teaching, mentoring, 'serving the university', discovering, publishing, telling the truth, reaching beyond the walls, changing – in which young academics may find themselves. The book developed from sessions in which newcomers to the academic scene met to discuss their role, functions and exactly these questions of rights and responsibilities, freedoms and counterpart constraints. As an ageing generation of academics in the UK who knew an earlier world is replaced by a generation of university teachers and researchers who come without that background and with new presumptions and expectations, there is a place for similar courses or seminars in this country, and perhaps for active exchange with universities across the world.

Two centuries ago, the controversialist Robert Aspland disapproved of censorship on the grounds that it held back advance in human knowledge: 'If the distastes of the majority of a community had been always suffered to rule opinions, no improvements would have been made in the intellectual condition of mankind.'[7] He also saw that to allow censorship was to allow political control of thought and opinion: 'Truth has always been in controversy with Power, whether the human mind shall be bond or free; whether inquiry into opinions shall be permitted; whether there shall be any controversy, which on one side at least implies error and non-conformity.'[8]

It is not overstating the situation to see in recent developments a confrontation between 'truth' (defined as the proper objective of academic work) and 'power' (taken in the broad sense of the interests of the real world), for 'there is always a powerful anti-intellectual bloc in society'.[9] The pursuit of truth is not a task for cissies, and academic freedom of speech can breed a toughmindedness of immeasurable value to society.

So where does the public interest now lie in the reordering of the relationship between academe and the 'real world'? And what can academe – and individual academics and others involved in the running of universities – do to ensure that that reordering preserves and strengthens the deeper things universities stand for?

1

The Academic Project: Driving Forces

Academic values, academic habits

> More than thirty of Oxford's dons are now multimillionaires, it was announced yesterday. This is believed to be the highest number in any British University. Oxford has a share in over 32 companies which were founded to profit from ideas by academics. Their value has reached £2 billion. This makes Oxford the most enterprising university in Britain. In the past three years alone its academics have set up 20 companies worth £9.5 million. By comparison, Cambridge has a share in eight companies worth around £5 million.
>
> *The Times*, 16 April 2001

That is one kind of value. In its way it is a simple kind of value, since it is calculated by straightforward arithmetical methods. But it would of course be absurd to suggest that even the pride Oxford presumably took in that announcement is value-free. It was a statement that this was a leading university in its successful compliance with the UK government's objective of encouraging entrepreneurship.

A step further would be to say that this success was in the interests of society, since it was making Britain more prosperous and creating jobs and so on. As a 'recognized social good' this belongs to a modern western world in which having more things to consume is the highest aspiration set before most of the population. Still more recent, in the timescale of human intellectual endeavour, is the assertion that 'greed is healthy',[1] the logical next step from holding out the desire for more as the perfectly proper wish of a good citizen and consumer. This is in conflict with the value system of the West throughout the centuries during which universities came into being, when greed ('avarice') was identified without much dispute as universally a vice, and the respected 'type' of the Oxford academic was Chaucer's Poor Clerke of Oxenford, with twenty books at his bed's head and no interest in any other kind of worldly goods. In fourteenth-century Oxenford there were no spin-out companies.

The modern industrial value system is geared not only to production for sale, but to a trajectory of increase. It assumes that the more things produced, the more sales effected, the more money made, the better. It is impossible to make that compatible with the traditional ideal of academic disinterestedness, where there can be no objective but the pursuit of truth (which may turn out inconveniently not to be where the researcher was looking for it; and even when found to be not of the desired sort). Oxford has done its best to protect the interests of the University in various ways. In 2000, its Statutes, Decrees and Regulations included a *Public Interest Disclosure: Code of Practice and Procedure* (2000: 805); a *Code of Practice and Procedure on Academic Integrity in Research* (2000: 808); a *Conflict of Interest: Statement of Policy and Procedure* (2000: 811), with the requirement that 'no member of staff of the University shall hold any executive Directorship without' express approval.

The classic statement of R. K. Merton[2] is still useful. He identified a series of 'social norms' which defined science and helped to guarantee that it would pursue the truth. These are universalism, disinterestedness, scepticism, communalism or sharing. To enter an arrangement with others for whom those are not the norms may be as much of a Faustian bargain as would be the outright 'sale' of results of research and scholarship to a 'bidder' who wanted to exploit them for his own commercial benefit and keep them out of the common pool of human knowledge.[3]

C. P. Snow wrote several decades ago, on the two cultures of the humanities and the sciences;[4] he captured public imagination by pointing up a difference many recognized, long before the present internal dynamics had begun to develop. He wrote of a world where those who went to university had commonly had a general education until their mid-teens and then opted for 'arts' or 'science' subjects, and a main point of his observation was that this resulted in two educated communities whose members had little to say to one another because of their mutual incomprehension of one another's work. Even if they did not understand what each other's 'community' was talking about, academics working in the arts and sciences were still enjoying roughly similar working conditions. Academic scientists were still commonly in long-term posts, teaching as well as doing research. Funding was relatively sustained. Long-term projects and 'blue-skies research' could often be contemplated without making special arrangements to obtain special funding. There was relative freedom to go where the inquiry led, to follow things up from pure scientific interest.

New factors of recent introduction derive from shifts of funding sources and funding priorities and from the greatly diminished job security of academic scientists as a group. There has also been a sea-change in certain areas, to projects requiring vastly greater funding. This is now making the purely inward motivation a luxury for many. Yet without it is as if there were no skeleton, no 'backbone' to an academic research programme which becomes ad hoc, responsive to and creative of ephemeral market demand, and ultimately producing a society whose citizens have nothing more interesting to do than shop, 'buy' entry to recreational facilities, and 'consume' 'products'.

So we shall begin at the other extreme, with some of the ancient and inward prompters to academic work which was done in another spirit altogether, and launch ourselves first on a switchback ride, from ancient to modern and back again, so as to make the contrasts of assumption between 'then' and 'now' sharp at the outset.

Work and play

Games with words are fun. Finding things out is enjoyable. Testing and challenging are stimulating activities. Jacques Derrida takes the university to be of its essence the place for such cerebral fun:

> You can study without waiting for any efficient or immediate result. You may search, just for the sake of searching, and try for the sake of trying. So there is a possibility of what I would call playing. It's perhaps the only place within society where play is possible to such an extent. . . . This measure, this proportion of freedom, is precious, because it's the place where we can try and think what the university is. The consciousness, so to speak, of the university, may be located here.[5]

The chief *enduring* motivator of researchers and scholars and teachers in higher education has probably always been enjoyment; for the experimental, the curious, the open-ended habit of mind involves 'play' as much as work. That makes it possible to leap keenly out of bed in the morning to get back to a self-imposed task which may not even bear fruit in publication, but at which hours pass unnoticed. These are the motivations still taking elderly scholars to their desks in their seventies and eighties.

The inwardly driven inquirer of the past, the academic with his long-term job and his tenure, could look to a lifetime's accumulation of knowledge and understanding, in which there could be expected to be periods of fallowness, unexpected benefits or outcomes which could be followed up in preference to the original scheme of research, the kind of 'blue skies' exploration out of which may come a truly significant discovery, or nothing of use or long-term interest at all. This was a process of open-ended and risk-taking investment of time and effort, even of money, in projects which might go nowhere and scholars whose fallow periods might turn out to last a lifetime. For it was a system which made room for the man whose sole publication was to be a brief if excellent monograph on an antique sundial, the scholar whose great book was still forming in his mind when he reached retirement. It was what might be called the 'take the risk' model, rather than the 'targeted research' model.

The public may reasonably ask what someone whose salary comes from public funds is doing spending time in 'play', and whether the system ought to tolerate the man who never finishes his *magnum opus*. The present trend favours scientific research done on a project basis, where the funding is specific to that project, and there is a timetable and a budget (of that, more in Chapter 3).

A similar shift of fundamental expectation marks the values of teaching in UK higher education. University teachers, particularly in the 'new' universities set up by the Further and Higher Education Act 1992 from the former poly-technics, have huge burdens of teaching hours and limited job security.

University administrators, too, have priorities set by the expectations of governments and the insistent hunger for adequate resourcing, and they, too, say that they find leisure to think and the accommodation of the occa-sional 'uncertain long-term prospect' among the academic staff are unrealistic luxuries.

'I fell to wondering . . .': is curiosity 'dangerous'?

Greek thinkers of the ancient world were not working in universities, for universities had not yet been invented; nevertheless, they did understand something of the 'academy', for they were the inventors of the very idea. They are a good place to begin to get a sense of the 'motivators' of the higher intellectual endeavour which are independent of financial or political considerations and which appear to be truly common human experience. There is the danger that this is mainly a western tradition, but universities were, after all, an invention of the medieval world which was heir to the world of classical (Greek and Roman) antiquity.

The first requirement of all research is to recognize or identify some-thing which it would be interesting, or seems important, to know more about. 'I wondered why Sparta was the most powerful and famous state in Greece, even though it had the smallest population,'[6] says Xenophon, set-ting out to write about the problem. The behaviour of mirrors is 'a subject which, even considered by itself, would give scope for careful study and investigation,'[7] remarks Aristotle. That sparking of an initial curiosity strikes in much the same way more than two thousand years later. 'In the summer of 1937, when I was a young college student, I was studying calculus . . .', says one son who recollects how that gave his father the idea for the book *What is Mathematics?*, to whose second edition the son was now writing the preface.[8]

The scholar's task is to frame or identify questions. The questions do not necessarily have to be invented by the researcher. His primary task is to recognize that they exist and have a bearing on the subject in hand. Aristotle begins a book on various 'natural questions', the *Parva Naturalia*, with ques-tions in exactly this spirit. What is sleep? What is waking? What is a dream? Is it possible to have a vision of the future? We see that some creatures live longer than others. Why is this?[9] Aristotle cannot see any evident link with species or genus or even any decisive pattern within a single species, for some men live longer than others.[10] Size is not determinative of length of life. A horse and an insect both live less long than a man although one is bigger and the other is smaller.[11] The observation that all creatures' lives appear to tend to death or dissolution leads him to ask whether it is possible for any creature to live indefinitely.[12]

Then the inquirer needs the persistence to pursue the answer. What is the purpose of breathing, Aristotle asks? He reviews the theories he knows. Democritus says that respiration is necessary to prevent the soul being crushed out of the body.[13] Plato in the Timaeus sees respiration as pushing breath round and round. Aristotle goes along patiently looking at the options and dismissing or supporting them, so as the better to clear his mind. In the *Republic* of Plato, Thrasymachus becomes heated,[14] saying that Socrates has been talking rubbish and trading on the fact that it is easier to ask questions than to answer them. Socrates answers him placatingly, but with irony: 'Thrasymachus . . . if I and my friend have made mistakes in the consideration of the question, rest assured that it is unwillingly that we err . . . when we are searching for justice, a thing more precious than much fine gold.' The excitement of inquiry can generate great energy. Cicero produced a great flow of work in his 'philosophical' period of 45–44 BC. He composed *On Ends* (*De finibus*), the *Tusculan Disputations*, *On the Nature of the Gods* (the *De natura deorum*), writing from one end of the day to the other, as he told his friend Atticus in a letter.[15]

It is not simply a matter of asking and answering. It is the very nature of academic inquiry that it is open-ended. Otherwise it cannot be investigative. Ancient Greece and twenty-first century science can be seen to come to a similar view on this point. Aristotle in the *Parva Naturalia* goes on to ask second-order questions about how questions are to be answered, and in that way he begins to create a method for resolving them. A modern medical researcher admits that 'each step forward uncovers another layer of ignorance'.[16] Another comments that, 'Being a science, nutrition is more questions than answers. As answers are found . . . more questions arise.'[17] Inquiries have been undertaken with no certainty of the reward of finding an answer. On the recent modern system, there is a tendency for funders to devise projects which can promise, if not guarantee, answers, and even to seek to interfere if the 'right' answers are not produced.

This 'tames' curiosity in a novel way. Curiosity has traditionally been seen as a powerful, even dangerously strong, drive. 'Curiosity' occurs in English in a 'bad' sense from the fourteenth century, and in a good or neutral sense from perhaps a century or two later. The 'bad' sense is a direct heritage from the Latin *curiositas*, and from the early Christian and especially from the Augustinian tradition, for Augustine of Hippo (d.430 AD) had trouble with a curiosity which kept leading him in directions of which he believed he ought to disapprove as a Christian. The 'bad' sense of curiosity is connected with an undue or inappropriate inquisitiveness. Its inappropriateness may derive from its going too far, either downwards into things deemed unworthy (such as magic), or upwards into matters too 'high' (inquiring into divine secrets). This worry over the spiritual dangers of curiosity was not a concern which began with Christianity. Lucretius addresses his *On the Nature of Things* (*De rerum natura*) to Venus, as sole ruler of the nature of things. He credits human authors with the discovery of her ways, and the giving of rational explanations. He claims that it was Epicurus who first overcame supersition in this way. Such seeking after explanations is not destructive of religion, Lucretius argues. It is more likely that blind and unquestioning superstition will lead to impiety; in other words, it is the failure to think things through rigorously which is dangerous, not the thing in itself.[18] Plato asks in the *Republic*, 'are any questions forbidden?'[19] Today's western trend is to say yes, but for the new reason that the answers may not please those who are paying the bill for the research, or the salary of the teacher.

A second twenty-first century equivalent of the pervasive ancient and medieval sense that academic inquiry is associated with danger is the fear that certain pieces of research may lead to undesirable or even destructive outcomes. It may be argued to be in the public interest to prevent the making of discoveries which may be dangerous or damaging. Yet how is it to be known in advance whether a discovery not yet made will be a bad thing for humanity? The invention of the atomic bomb presumably falls into that category, but research on the fusion and the splitting of the atom has had other implications and they are not all bad. The development of genetic engineering has potential medical benefits; yet it carries dangers. The determination of the British government in the late 1990s to press on with the introduction of genetically modified crops into the human food chain before there had been opportunity to test for their effects showed that commercial interests could easily override an obvious 'public interest' in keeping the 'precautionary principle' in mind. It transpired that no lessons had been learned from the BSE scare of a few years earlier, when government reassurances had exploded into public panic as it began to be feared that 'mad cow disease' could indeed be transferred to humans: 'The public is right to be concerned about the potential – and novel – hazards of modern food-production techniques . . . The recent epidemic of bovine spongiform encephalopathy (BSE) among cattle . . . is a dramatic illustration of unanticipated dangers.'[20]

Fun and curiosity maintain interest. Persistent interest is an inward drive without which the scholar cannot keep up a lifetime of productive effort. These are the starting-points of a model of academic work which will need to be kept actively in mind throughout this book, in the face of a recent shift to the notion that the 'drivers' will be external, and involve vested interest or conflict of interest.

First of all a man must see before he can say[21]

Before there were astronomers, says one classical source, mankind lived in ignorance and did not understand what he was seeing in the universe. He did not comprehend how it all worked (what he calls the *operum ratio*).[22] 'Geographers put round the edges of their maps of parts of the earth they do not know, with explanatory notes saying that what lies beyond is water-less desert full of wild beasts.'[23] The fear of the unknown represented by the metaphorical 'explanatory notes' in the margins is conquered only by acquiring the missing knowledge. That involves either putting things in order or discovering order within them. Thales saw the great geometer Euclid's achievement as supremely one of 'ordering' (putting together the elements of the subject, arranging many of Eudoxus's theorems in order); and also in terms of completing, 'bringing to irrefutable demonstration things his predecessors had proved only loosely'.[24]

'Bringing to order' proves to be a fundamental instinct of the academic mind, and it has exactly the tendency noted here by Diodorus of Sicily to make comparisons between the patterns it observes: 'Just as providence, having brought the orderly arrangement of the visible stars and the natures of men together into one common relationship, continually directs their courses . . . so likewise the historians, in recording the common affairs of the inhabited world as though they were those of a single state, have made of their treatises a single reckoning of past events and a common clearing-house of knowledge concerning them.'[25]

The next fundamental is an 'academic ordering' of thought and teach-ing and research at a meta-level which cannot be funded or controlled on a single-project basis. 'Thinking what you are doing' is an academic task in which the scholar ought perhaps to be perpetually engaged, as he sits on a bus or goes out to post a letter. Without reflective understanding of its own processes (the *ratio*), research can give no intelligible account of itself, for it cannot explain either its purpose or what it has actually discovered. These essentials remain the same in the twenty-first century as in earlier periods. They amount to a *habit* of scholarship ingrained in the very personality and conduct of the academic.

It was Coleridge's view that 'the sole practicable employment for the human mind was to observe, to collect, and to classify'.[26] The underlying prin-ciples of classification may come to appear quite different in different ages, as assumptions about the ground-rules change, but the core task persists in being of value to clarity of thought. Theophrastus, a contemporary of Plato and Aristotle, classified plants by outward appearance. His main classes are trees, shrubs, under-shrubs and herbs. A tree has a trunk; a shrub has many branches; an under-shrub merely has many stems; a herb is identified by the fact that it comes up directly with leaves, but no stems. He recognizes that these apparently reliable differentiating characteristics can change. A shrub may grow tall and develop a trunk. He wonders whether this means that a strict classification in these terms is impossible and we should go by size, or length of life, or whether the thing to do first is to ask whether the example is a 'cultivated' plant or not.[27] He sets about classifying smells in a similar way, by looking at obvious superficial differences and then testing them, to see if his proposed principles of classification will stand up. Simple substances have no scent (water, air, fire). He suggests that smells derive from compounding of substances. Only a broad classification is proposed,

into pungent, powerful, faint, sweet, heavy, for the human sense of smell is
not as acute as that of other animals. So, although it is Theophrastus's belief
that every plant and animal and even every inanimate thing, has a scent
peculiar to itself, we are not able to distinguish them all.[28] Scientifically naïve
this may be now, yet Theophrastus is also engaged in a conscious reflection
on the mode of arrangement when he discusses how to classify plants, and
that kind of thinking may outlast its time. He asks whether they have 'parts'
in the same way as animals and what those parts are; indeed, whether the
parts of plants *correspond* with the parts of animals.[29] For example, a plant
has a capacity for growth in all its parts whereas an animal does not.[30] Then
there are the functions of parts;[31] there is the question what is permanently
'part' of a plant? For example, it may be that to call a fruit part of a plant is
like saying that the unborn young of an animal is a part of the animal.[32]
These remain not unhelpful ground-rules and among them are points of
enduring philosophical, if not scientific, importance. They are a reminder
that there are levels at which the 'ordering' activity of 'classifying' is concerned with basics so fundamental that they remain important even in an
age when technical principles have become far more sophisticated.

'I only want to make your meaning plainer,'[33] says Socrates to one of his
interlocutors. This urge to 'clarify' is also strong in academics, and it is itself
a further mode of 'ordering' the subject-matter of study, so as to know as
exactly as possible what one is talking about. This is not an easy brief. To
put it in Thoreau's words, 'it is a rare qualification to be able to state a fact
simply and adequately, to digest some experience cleanly, to say, "yes" and
"no" with authority, to make a square edge, to conceive and suffer the truth
to pass through us living and intact'.[34] This exactitude in identifying and
ordering subject-matter and deciding how to approach it is so fundamental
that not even the most precisely targeted research and development for a
commercial funder can progress satisfactorily without it.

What is a 'field' or 'discipline'?

Will so broad-brush a breakdown of academic habits really fit all? That
takes us to the questions about the ways in which knowledge is to be divided
up for purposes of study which will occupy a number of the sections which
follow. 'The knowledge of the man of science is like timber collected in yards
for public works', said Thoreau.[35] This 'collecting in yards' has historically
formed the basis of the system of working in a given 'field' or 'discipline'
within the whole span of knowledge. The recent rethinking about the nature
of a 'field' and the vogue for seeking to foster interdisciplinarity and multi-
disciplinarity has thrown the presumption into question.

The notion that knowledge comes in 'branches' or 'gatherings' or 'sections',
the 'parts of philosophy' (*partes philosophiae*), was already something of a
commonplace in the classical world. Seneca explains in his *Natural Questions*
that philosophy has a part which pertains to man and a part which pertains

to the gods.[36] In the late antique world, Augustine and Boethius have the same notion.[37] It was a pastime of twelfth-century scholars, too, to divide up knowledge ('philosophy') into its component studies.[38] These departments of knowledge had to be identified by lecturers whenever they began their lectures on a new set book, for it was the custom to provide an introduction (or *accessus*) explaining who the author was and the reason why he wrote and the contribution the book made to the sum of human knowledge.[39]

For ancient and medieval students, the question of methodology and the question of subject-matter came together in the idea that every study has its own first principles which define it distinctively. Aristotle's *Posterior Analytics* is one of the main ancient studies of this question (though Aristotle in the *Metaphysics* thought mathematical principles were general and did not apply only to the study of mathematics'[40]).

The principles of a subject may be of a practical as well as a theoretical sort. It seems to be in this spirit that Celsus in his book on medicine asks whether there is a way of finding common principles in sicknesses.[41] In the view of Cato, writing *On Agriculture*, farmers are good solid figures. He thinks merchants are less desirable citizens because it is not so certain that they will make money. So his handbook for farmers is full of practical advice.[42] Yet 'theory' has almost always been more respectable intellectually than 'practice'. In the ancient world and the Middle Ages that was a conscious preference, based on a theory that speculative science was innately higher than practical because it dealt with higher things. This is a remarkably persistent assumption, 'marking' subjects as theoretical or practical up to the present day. The novelist Henry James wanted a subject or field to yield to systematic analysis, be susceptible of rational discourse. 'Only a short time ago it might have been supposed that the English novel was not what the French call *discutable*. It had no air of having a theory, a conviction, a consciousness of itself behind it – of being the expression of an artistic faith, the result of choice and comparison.'[43] Such modern subjects studied in universities as 'sports studies' sometimes acknowledge a mild crisis of identity in their configuration, with the conscious admixture of studies of such matters as the physiology of sports injuries to give a theoretical core to a practical course, in a cluster of assorted areas of study linked only by a connection to sport or recreation.

There may arguably be subjects containing a good proportion of 'theory' so as to be capable of rational analysis which are found to be not sufficiently 'rich' or 'worthy' of academic study because they do not yield enough to persistent inquiry. A late-twentieth-century candidate for dismissal in such terms was media studies, because it studies essentially ephemeral and popular art-forms. Yet it would be dangerous to be too confident here that a proposed subject was simply shallow. Subjects have been despised before and eventually achieved recognition and respect. Henry James, trying to get the novel taken seriously, spoke of 'the old evangelical hostility to the novel, which was as explicit as it was narrow and which regarded it as little less favourable to our immortal part than a stage-play'.[44] Resistance to including the study of English literature in the syllabus of a university was a long time in fading, and yet it now counts as a respectable, 'traditional' subject.[45]

There appears to be no reliable connection between the 'respectability' of a subject and the state of development of the 'theory' of its content. 'The Cold Dark Matter theory is based on the identification of the dark matter with some hypothetical weakly interacting particle which initially has much smaller random velocities . . .'[46] 'Since we have so far detected the dark matter only through its gravitational effects, we have no direct clues as to its nature.'[47] 'It is not easy matter to obtain observational data to compare with these predictions.'[48] So in the intellectually perfectly respectable study of astronomy, large gaps remain to be filled by speculation. Quotation after quotation admits as much. Astronomy will tolerate this degree of uncertainty because it is of the nature of its experimental subject-matter that it has no alternative. Another science might not get away with so much remaining hypothesis and remain intellectually respectable. Modern astronomers recognize that they are not only working from assumptions but often resting huge edifices of inference upon them: 'Astronomical knowledge is often difficult to acquire and difficult to check. Measurements of cosmologically interesting quantities tend to be highly uncertain and dependent on a variety of untested hypotheses.'[49] 'The cosmological principle is the assumption that the large-scale universe is spatially homogenous and isotopic (that is to say, the laws of nature must appear the same to all observers).'[50] According to the perfect Cosmological Principle of Bondi, Gold and Hoyle, this applies at all times. But that is merely a hypothesis.[51] So again and again, when modern astronomy asks a question, 'the answer is rather imprecise, and may be affected by systematic errors'.[52]

Why then are scholars so respectful of astronomy and so scathing about astrology? From the Middle Ages onwards, astrology has not been treated academically in the same way as astronomy. Tamsyn Barton studied, in the context of an ancient culture, the difference between science and what would now seem pseudo-science. She noticed that the embarrassment of classical scholars against taking astrology seriously had impeded their study of ancient astrology.[53] Discomfort among such scholars in the humanities over being seen to write about astrology is based upon a history of criticism of astrology for lack of intellectual rigour and proper foundations which goes back many centuries, long before it was clear in modern terms why astrology could not be rated a science.

How do we know what to count as 'scientific' in the sense of being a proper subject for sustained academic study? Cicero notes that the Epicureans say that all knowledge is founded on sense-perceptions. But it follows from that that the sun must actually be a foot across, for without postulating another source of knowledge about it we cannot know it to be any bigger.[54] Aristotle says that it is not easy to know whether to despise, or to believe in, talk of prophetic dreams. Many believe that dreams can have significance: 'but the fact that one can see no reasonable cause why it should be so, makes one distrust it; for apart from its improbability on other grounds, it is absurd to hold that it is God who sends such dreams, and yet that he sends them not to the best and wisest but to any chance persons'.[55]

In the *Natural Questions*, Seneca makes what seem to the modern eye to be perfectly respectable scientific observations. He observes that when an oar is covered with shallow water it appears to the eye to be broken. Fruits look bigger when seen through glass. Columns standing in a colonnade seem to grow closer together as they are further away.[56] Yet within the intellectual framework in which he made the observations there was no way of taking these questions forward to solutions which would be scientifically acceptable now. Another commonplace example of the strangulation of scientific investigation by a set of pre-existing assumptions which do not lead anywhere is the classical idea that vision involves the eye sending out a ray,[57] which limited progress in optics for so long. A related problem is that starting from the wrong assumptions may actually lead to erroneous conclusions. Aristotle understands 'place' not in the modern way but as the surface which abuts on to the surrounding or contiguous place. Theophrastus sees a number of problems with this. For example, a body will be 'in' such a surface. Place will be in motion. If the surroundings alter, the things in a given place will cease to be in that place.[58]

Interdisciplinarity

A 'field' or discipline is therefore apparently marked out as much by the interestingness of the body of questions associated with it or the fashion of the moment as by any consistently identifiable or even coherent features such as Aristotle's 'distinctive first principles of every subject'. Yet if academic speech is to be 'about' something, it has to be possible to say what kind of 'something'. The 'something' becomes a moving target if the field of study does not stand still, if 'new viewpoints can . . . render old proof obsolete, or old facts no longer interesting'.[59] Dionysius of Halicarnassus, in an age when all educated men had a competence in rhetoric, bewails the decline of such studies in his own day: 'In the epoch preceding our own, the old philosophic rhetoric was so grossly abused and maltreated that it fell into decline . . . Another Rhetoric stole in and took its place, intolerably shameless and histrionic, ill-bred and without a vestige either of philosophy or of any other aspect of liberal education . . . It was altogether vulgar and disgusting, and finally made the Greek world resemble the houses of the profligate and the abandoned.'[60] But he still assumes that there is a 'real rhetoric', if only students will return to it. That kind of thinking can still appear in a form which militates against flexible reshaping of 'fields' and 'disciplines'. The classical position was Aristotle's: that all subjects are identifiable by the distinctive first principles on which they rest.

The modern form of the Aristotelian tyranny of 'given' subjects is the concept of a 'home territory'. A recent British study, commissioned by the Higher Education Funding Council and reporting in 1999 found a strong pattern of 'home territories' in the arrangement of subjects of the syllabus in higher education in the UK at the end of the twentieth century. The attempt at 'benchmarking' subjects for teaching purposes made by the Quality Assurance Agency in the late 1990s, threatened to come to grief at the outset on the difficulty of making measurements of work which does not fit conventional frameworks, or where expectations change.

When Aristotle wrote, he was thinking about a relatively limited range of subjects, what we may call 'first-order' subjects (such as mathematics, philosophy), which appeared to him to be concerned with the fundamental orientations of human inquiry. That position is not easy to sustain when the scholarly inquiry gets under way and thinkers really begin to explore, and the 'field' turns out to be different in extent or character from the way it appeared. For ancients and moderns alike, the need to orientate oneself in relation to the subject of study may appear superficially similar. Defining a subject by comparison with another in order to establish its position may be one way to make it clearer what is 'special' about each. Celsus begins his *On Medicine* by suggesting a parallel between agriculture and medicine. Agriculture is concerned with the nourishment of a healthy body, and medicine with making a sick body healthy.[61] But such relatively homely mechanisms may fail before the hugeness of questions, political as well as intellectual, which may be raised by attempts at modern boundary-changes on the one hand, and before the contemporary introduction of modern or 'aggregate' or 'conglomerate' subjects on the other. In all other subjects one goes to an expert, says the ancient agriculturalist Columella, but in country matters there is no one to consult. Columella is anxious to raise standards by bringing relevant expertise to bear.[62] Agriculture lacks students as it lacks teachers.[63] It is partly that the subject is so vast. It is not surprising if the enthusiasm of learners is dimmed by the hopelessness of mastering so many and such different branches.[64] But modern equivalents of this sense of the difficulty of knowing where to make the approach because it is hard to see *what* to approach, are not hard to find.

At the level of the very small patch, a 'topic' may limit itself by 'confining' itself by period or place: 'From all purpose anodyne to maker of deviance' (on attitudes to opiates in the USA);[65] Judy Slinn's 'Research and development in the UK pharmaceutical industry from the nineteenth century to the 1960s',[66] gives examples of very tightly focused studies. Of three 'article-sized' topics, taken from *Mental Health and the Environment*, the first two at least promise larger possibilities: 'crowding and territoriality', 'urban delinquency – ecology and education'. The last ('stress at Thamesmead'[67]) is bigger than it looks, as interpretive devices are tried out on the circumstances of this one small locality. So it is hard to say how 'small' a field should be; and it is equally hard to say how 'big' a field can be, without breaking up into more than one field.

Both the attempt to divide up the subject-matter of academic disciplines and the search for the first principles of those disciplines are complicated in the modern university by the increasing recognition that there may exist fields of study which do not lie tidily within the boundaries of the fields of study already identified. Biochemistry is now a well-established label, but it had to gain acceptance at first in an academic world recognizing only 'biology' or 'chemistry'. A work entitled *Pharmaceutical Design and Development: A Molecular Biology Approach*[68] chose to begin from the assumptions molecular biology brings to pharmaceutics. Another, *Mental Health and the Environment*, explores various ways of selecting a fresh vantage-point in another 'field': 'For architects and planners, it is the systematic analysis of human behaviour related to the settings they create; for human scientists, it is the environmental contexts of the behaviour.'[69] All this is a consideration of practical as well as theoretical importance because of the way universities are normally organized into departments and faculties, each concentrating on the teaching of certain subjects. Students who learn skills at a 'base' on a 'home territory' and in accord with 'subject benchmarks', acquire with them a viewpoint, which tends to colour their understandings of other fields. The interdisciplinary, forming new fields, threatens the 'certainties', of the very ordering of previous research and the territorial security of those who have made their names in the traditional fields of study.

Putting it all into the melting-pot

'Men are constantly dinging in my ears their fair theories and plausible solutions of the universe, but ever there is no help, and I return again to my shoreless, islandless ocean and fathom unceasingly for a bottom that will hold, and anchor, that it may not drag,' said Thoreau.[70] Are any 'specialisms' now secure? Is there any way in which we can identify expertise in a field of study about whose continuing identity or 'centre' or 'home territory' there is no doubt?

It is possible to find examples of a 'dynamic' approach to the setting of subject-boundaries and subject rationales in the ancient world as in the modern. The Roman author Varro begins his *On Country Matters* by invoking the gods, then gives an account of his conversations on rural topics with his wife. Then he lists the authors of treatises in Greek on cognate subjects.[71] Only then does he raise the question which has to be answered before he can write his book: what comes into the subject-area of agriculture? Varro sweeps an embracing arm round others' lines of study. He makes the chief divisions of agriculture four: knowledge of the farm and the soil; equipment needed for operation of the farm; operations to be carried out in tilling the soil; proper seasons. Is grazing excluded? What about managing clay-pits? What about managing silver-mines? What about pottery? What about the advice on killing bed-bugs by greasing the bed with ox-gall and vinegar? (That is good advice, even if it should not be in a book on agriculture.[72]) He comments on Theophrastus on plants: 'His books are not so well adapted to those who wish to tend land as to those who wish to attend the schools of the philosophers.'[73]

In this and other ways, new fields have attached themselves around the edges of the notions of health and disease, as the influence of circumambient circumstances had made itself felt:

In recent years the social history of medicine has become recognised as a major field of historical enquiry. Aspects of health, disease, and medical care now attract the attention not only of social historians but also of researchers in a broad spectrum of historical and social science disciplines. New bodies have been formed to address the newly-recognised questions: The Society for the Social History of Medicine . . . is an interdisciplinary body . . . It exists to forward a wide-ranging view of the history of medicine, concerned equally with biological aspects of normal life, experience of and attitudes to illness, medical thought and treatment, and systems of medical care . . . The intention is not to promote . . .[74]

Cicero discusses in his *Academica* whether it is always true that the latest discoveries are the most correct.[75] The Greeks characteristically looked to the future rather than the past.[76] The eighteenth-century English 'Whig interpretation' of history is a recent manifestation of this confidence that there is progress over time, that change is 'progress'. But it would be rash today to take it for granted that later work or understanding is necessarily to be preferred. One model of the research process takes there to be an absolute truth, which the scholar simply seeks until he finds it.[77] A second takes there to be no 'right answer', merely a succession of angles of view, one as good as another perhaps, but none barred to the inquirer who wants to test it.[78] Academics need not abandon the search for 'safe assumptions'. But they will be wise not to be too confident that they yet know what those assumptions are. Northrop Frye points out that techniques of literary criticism hitherto applied to Latin had to be adapted for the purposes of criticism of English literature, when that became a discipline in its own right in the course of the twentieth century. There was, when he made this observation in 1963, no confidence (in his mind at least), that the critical methodology to be applied to English literature was mature and free-standing and could give a robust account of itself: 'We have not yet evolved a literary criticism that is solidly based in this scholarship, which clarifies its central principles, brings its assumptions into the open, and provides a view of the whole subject giving proportion and context to its more restricted achievements.'[79] Since then there has been deconstruction, structuralism, post-structuralism, post-modernism, and still the changes of assumption come.

The same sort of thing is found in the sciences: 'Many of our current problems are not new; we have lived with uncertainty about the relative roles of environmental improvements and the scientific exploration of disease . . . for well over a hundred years,' comments David Weatherall.[80] 'The new breed of clinical scientists [between the two World Wars] were quite different from the polymaths of previous centuries. They studied their patients' illnesses in great depth by means of new tools of clinical measurement and the boundaries between patient case and research became blurred.'[81]

There may be a return to earlier priorities and methodologies. 'This textbook has a long history,' says the editor of *A Textbook of Histology*.[82] He describes how its originator, Alexander Maximov, fled the Russian Revolution and went to Chicago, how he was still writing it in Russian when he died in 1928, how it was completed by William Bloom, how it went into a series of editions in 1930, 1934, 1938, 1942, 1948, 1952, 1957. 'The book evidently met a real need,' argues its recent editor, 'for it was widely used throughout this country and students abroad have benefited from Spanish, Polish, Italian and Japanese translations.' Nevertheless, the field altered over all those years. The electron microscope was invented. It was not merely that that made it possible to gather 'valuable biochemical information on the genome and the intracellular biosynthetic pathways'; it also had the effect of encouraging the dropping of courses in histology and their substitution by new courses compounded of pathology, physiology and clinical medicine in 'so-called integrated curricula'. Fawcett says: 'I believe the pendulum will swing back from research on single cell types, isolated in vitro, and there will again be greater interest in the complex interactions of the many different cell types in their normal environment in whole animals.'[83]

What is mental health? The editor of one modern study noticed that 'in the course of our work . . . we saw many patients whose disturbances seemed amply justified by the nature and severity of the problems we had to deal with'. He concluded that it was 'better . . . for our present purpose to define mental health in common sense and pragmatic terms as the absence of identifiable psychiatric disorder, according to current norms'.[84] That is to say, they were not ill.[85] An article on attitudes to the use of opiates in the USA in the half-century from 1890 and 1940 picks up a change in the forms of advertising. At the beginning they were purveying 'nostrums', and used as evidence to encourage the buyer the grateful testimony of the cured. An alteration of approach then produced a different sort of advertising, which used laboratory findings as 'evidence' in advertisements, and this made its appeal to the purchaser in a quite different way. The effect of this shift, argues Caroline Jean Archer, 'was to replace a vision of disease as a personal and moral crisis with a view of disease as the impersonal result of natural forces'.[86] So as new viewpoints alter preconceptions about the nature of a given field, 'health' and 'disease' prove to have a wide range of defining limits.

Shifts of fashion and emphasis in the labelling of areas of study may even be traced in the changing titles of journals. *The Abolitionist*, the *Journal of the British Union for the Abolition of Vivisection*, became in 1949 *The Anti-Vivisectionist*, and then in 1969 the *AV Times*. In 1976 it changed its title to *Animal Welfare*. The *Journal of the Chartered Society of Massage and Medical Gymnastics*, 1915–44, continued as *Journal of the Chartered Society of Physiotherapy*, 1944–47, then as *Physiotherapy*. The journal *Applied Electrical Phenomena* (1970), continued as *Electrochemistry in Industrial Processing and Biology*.

Any lingering tendency to celebrate a 'history of progress', of the triumph of 'reason' and scientific method, is challenged by the hypothesis of the paradigm change.[87] Kuhn himself admitted that he could often not readily identify the field in which he was working. 'Asked what field it [*The Structure of Scientific Revolutions* (Chicago, 1962)] dealt with, I was often at a loss for a response'.[88] Since the publication of this ground-breaking work, he reflects, 'my most persistent philosophical preoccupation has been the underpinnings of incommensurability: problems about what it is for words to have meanings . . . these are the concerns which, a decade after *Structure* appeared, led me to emphasize the role played, at all levels of research, by primitive similarity/ difference relations acquired during professional education . . . Changes in one or another region of the taxonomy are central to the episodes I have called scientific revolutions'.[89] There is so much awash here that there are bound to be 'misunderstandings and distortions of a kind typical of situations in which, for the time being, only partial communication is possible'.[90]

Sextus Empiricus takes up this question in the *Outlines of Pyrrhonism*. He distinguishes the 'dogmatists' (who hold that if you look, and find what you are looking for, that will then be established as the truth), from those known as 'academics' in his day, who believe as a matter of principle that truth is not discoverable. He has a third category, of 'sceptics', those who perpetually carry on looking, being unwilling to hold either that truth has been captured or that it cannot be established.[91] This was already apparent in the ancient world.

To hold simultaneously that a discipline has first principles which are of its essence and that we do not yet know what they are, seems paradoxical, but it is a natural position for scholars to find themselves in. 'We can say that the supervisor of such a thesis has been a fathead, but in the absence of critical theory we cannot speak of academic malpractice.'[92]

If the recent lesson is still that everything is in the melting-pot, what has to happen to get a 'field' established or transformed? What is 'the relationship between the authorship of a discovery and its authorisation as a discovery'?[93] What makes it acceptable to begin to think in a different way?

We might try to answer this pragmatically, and suggest that the first stage is to see things from a new angle, making a novel juxtaposition or connection: 'The truly creative scientist spots a hitherto unrecognized identity between two items, makes them into members of a new class, and then explores the properties of this new class.'[94] The second stage is to get it said in a published form, so that it may be tested and perhaps begin to be adopted. (Here any delay or prevention of publication by a commercial funder becomes an important factor.) At the last stage of this process there is that integration of the new discovery into an existing system, or the formation of a new system for it to belong in, with which we are concered, for a discovery or new approach has to be accepted by an academic community whose members may at first be deeply resistant to, or uncomprehending of, its most fundamental manifestations. Indeed, it may require the 'old guard' to die out before a new field can be received as authentic or workable. Max Planck (1858–1947), the physicist, suggested that 'a new scientific truth does not triumph by convincing its opponents and making them see the light, but rather because its opponents eventually die'.[95]

Deliberate challenge

Sometimes, in crossing boundaries a scholar has a purpose of forcing a change of vantage-point. John J. Winkler, attempting what he describes as 'a narratological reading of Apuleius's *Golden Ass*',[96] addresses himself to three kinds of reader. The first are those 'whose focus of interest is modern fiction and its theory'; to them he does not need, he thinks, to apologize for methodological or conceptual anachronism. The second group are 'classicists', who, he hopes, 'will find that narratology, though the word and the theories it names are recent, is a good language for giving voice to the interpretive problems of Apuleius's novel'. For this group of readers he frankly identifies anachronism as a risk, but he says it seems to him a risk 'worth taking for the reward of bridge building between ancient and modern literature'. His third class is 'religious historians', whose understanding he is optimistic he can significantly alter. From each group, he says, he expects 'skepticism' and 'reluctance', but in each case for a different reason. 'Since the argument of this book draws on three kinds of expertise, even the three kinds of expert will probably find themselves sooner or later in alien territory.'[97] It is not clear whether the idea here is to bring about a fundamental change within existing disciplines or to break down the barriers between them in any comprehensive way, or to change the thinking of individual scholars, or merely to speak refreshingly about one book which survives from the ancient world. But the author certainly wants to get off 'home territories'.

Other authors go just as far as he does in challenging received viewpoints. It is not difficult to find examples: 'I draw on a number of ideas from different modern disciplines . . . the work of philosophers, historians, and social scientists who have worked in the sociology of knowledge, in particular those who have tended to relativize knowledge in relation to its social context . . . I draw on the literary–philosophical studies . . . which have used classical rhetorical theory to break down the model of value-free communications . . . I draw on the work of Michel Foucault, taking his analyses of power as cooextensive with the social to rephrase the work of the sociologists of knowledge in political terms.'[98]

Are there limits here? Could one, for example, usefully bring to bear the intellectual skills of a surgeon in the study of palaeography? Arguably, yes, if it came down to the level of exact observation and disciplined interpretation, skills which could be applied in a variety of study areas, including these two; they are 'transferable skills'.[99] At the higher levels of 'subject-specific' skills it may become impossible for all scholars working in a given field to say what it is that the skills have to be applied to and for what purpose. Tamsyn Barton says in her comments on the study of astrology that she seeks to 'break down the model of value-free communications'. That makes a value judgement about the value of being value-free. She uses Foucault as authority for the value to be placed on a 'political' frame of reference, for assuming that 'power' is co-extensive with 'the social'.[100] Whether or not that is right, such an approach unavoidably sets at naught the very notion of 'values' of a certain sort.

Even in the sciences, and even at the most fundamental level, it cannot be taken for granted that there is an established methodology. 'A clinical trial is a planned experiment designed to assess the efficacy of a treatment in man by comparing the outcomes in a group of patients treated with the test treatment with those observed in a comparable group of patients receiving a control treatment.'[101] That sounds like solid ground. The parameters are set out. It is clear what the limits of the inquiry are. But again, contrast: 'It is very unlikely that direct cause-and-effect relationships will be found between specific features of the environment and abnormal mental states or forms of psychological malfunctioning. The intervening processes must be extremely complex.'[102] Here it is being admitted that there may have to be limits to what can be inferred from 'test' situations, even that parameters cannot be set which would make possible any fully controlled test.

Is there an end-point?

Can old fields vanish altogether? Can a mine be stripped of all its ore? Can a stage be arrived at where a given subject of study really has been exhausted, everything said which can be said? It is hard to believe that it may. In *The Ancient Concept of Progress*, written in 1973, E. R. Dodds asked himself what future there was for classical studies.[103]

The classical corpus of Greek and Roman texts is finite and indeed rather small. Dodds argues that 'the questions which are central for the classical scholars today are for the most part materially different and nearly always differently formulated, from those on which attention was focussed a hundred or even fifty years ago'.[104] Thus, 'in classical scholarship, as in all the historical sciences, the more usual and more important type of progress consists in the statement and solution of problems which are themselves entirely or partly new', often 'through a change in the focus of the scholar's eye'.[105]

Suppose a field could be 'worked out' like a mine, there is still an academic task, for recovery of what is lost is itself such a task. And there are always scholars engaged in a process of recovering lost knowledge. That applies more naturally to subjects such as history and archaeology and even to literary reconstruction and the editing of ancient texts than it does to natural science. But even in scientific research it could be argued that what is going on is the unravelling of something which is already there to be discovered, and in that sense that it is a recovery, not of knowledge once had by the human race and lost, but of knowledge embedded or still hidden in things as they are.

There is a further possibility. 'Feeling as many of us do that nothing less than the future of civilization is at stake, can we afford to keep so much of our intellectual manpower employed in working the old mines?'[106] Dodds' immediate concern – and it would not have been an uncontroversial one twenty years later – is with 'the torn fabric of western European culture', and 'the moral and intellectual values by which western man has lived for so many centuries'. In that context, it could be argued that the world from which all that derived must not be lost sight of. That is, however, not the same thing as saying that there is an inexhaustible set of possibilities in the subject as originally conceived.

Dodds goes on to make a second point, which holds more securely in the self-consciously 'multicultural' period of the end of the twentieth century: 'A cultural tradition cannot be transmitted passively. Unless new minds are always at work on it, so that it is continuously reinterpreted and revalued by and for the new generations, it becomes a dead thing, an encumbrance, a pedant's burden . . . The condition of life is growth.'[107]

Resistance to disciplinary change

All this said, a sense of security about a 'patch' or 'field' is important to the innate territoriality of much scholarship. It is therefore a security easily threatened. A. W. B. Simpson reflects on the appointment of H. A. L. Hart to a Chair in Oxford in the 1950s, an appointment which 'reflected the prestige which at that time attached to a philosophical approach to legal study. For some considerable period thereafter Oxford, like other law faculties, was much influenced by anxieties as to relevance; principally these were generated by uneasy comparison with American law schools, with their close professional involvement. So legal history languished.'[108]

Safety and risk

Roses fade; the idea of a rose remains. The assumption that the elegance of an idea is always stronger than the confused particular exemplification of that idea in real life made it difficult for disciplines to change with the intake of new materials. On the same assumption, experimental evidence cannot overturn a working theory, for the theory rests on its reasonableness, whereas the evidence belongs to the realm of the contingent and corruptible. 'Some of the greatest achievements in physics have come as a reward for courageous adherence to the principle of eliminating metaphysics.'[109]

In the twenty-first century, especially in the sciences, new knowledge or a new emphasis may alter the boundaries and raise the question which of the methodological fundamentals still applies: 'The field of medical diagnostic ultrasound has expanded rapidly over the past decade,' says one author, but also: 'Although the basic physical principles are unchanged, the operator's understanding of these principles and of the factors affecting the presentation of data is more important than ever.'[110] Such transformations create moments of risk, where fundamentals may be lost sight of.

It must be the presumption of research that there is something more to know, or that what is already known can be known better or more accurately, or there is simply nothing left to do. Northrop Frye distinguishes between 'a conservative and a radical aspect of learning, a power of consolidating and a power of exploration and advance'.[111] The conservative will be confident that what he is studying is in fact there to be studied, much in the terms he is familiar with, and that it simply continues to need his steady attention to take the inquiry forward. Research may, contrariwise, be seen as essentially adventurous, risky, independent of what others think, taking nothing as given, even perhaps that there is a truth to pursue.

Patiently extending or amending by established methods what we already know is a safe path for the scholar. 'Every artisan learns positively something by his trade. Each craft is familiar with a few simple, well-known, well-established facts, not requiring any genius to discover, but mere use and familarity,' says Thoreau.[112] The 'editor' of a text written by someone else is perhaps a good example of the scholar as 'patient builder'; he presents it for the reader with explanatory apparatus.[113] On this understanding of the researcher's task, hard work and application are trusted to be productive, to be a way of making progress.[114] 'Although mathematics is still growing, it is the sort of subject in which old discoveries seldom become obsolete. You cannot "unprove" a theorem. True, you might occasionally find that a long-accepted proof is wrong – it has happened. But then it was never proved in the first place.'[115]

The truly original is, of its nature, not possible to 'plan for' in this way: 'Surely original thinking is the divinest thing . . . We should reverently watch for the least motions, the least scintillations, of thought in this sluggish world, and men should run to and fro on the occasion more than at an earthquake,' cries Thoreau.[116] Kekulé described an experience he had when travelling on the last Clapham omnibus of the day one summer evening: 'I fell into a reverie and lo, the atoms were gambolling before my eyes . . . Up to that time I had never been able to discern the nature of their motion . . . The cry of the conductor: "Clapham Road," awakened me from my dreaming; but I spent a part of the night putting on paper at least sketches of these dream forms. This was the origin of structure theory.'[117] In the experimental, risk-taking mode of enlarging learning, an idea may come unexpectedly: 'It is hard to subject ourselves to an influence. It must steal upon us when we expect it not, and its work is all done ere we are aware of it.'[118] So dark and unplumbable are the processes we are dealing with here that an answer may be 'completely formed' before the discoverer realizes it.[119] For it was Thoreau's experience too that one may have to be taken intellectually by surprise to make progress with research. He speaks of 'the novelty of impact',[120] the way in which 'truth strikes us from behind, and in the dark, as well as from before, and in broad daylight'.[121]

So is there a choice to be made, beyond a preference for a style of work which places a high value on exploratory risk-taking or one which proceeds steadily and mechanically? Can one go so far as to suggest that there can even be an abandonment of the requirement of orderliness, in the hope of making the 'eureka' experience more likely? Can scholarship deliberately become 'disorderly'? Polanyi suggests that 'to every step of scientific progress there is attached an element of uncertainty regarding its scope and scientific value'.[122] In a literary context, Gregory Orr speaks of 'disorder and order in a dynamic tension that gives us a compelling picture of the world'.[123] He conjures with the idea that 'if poetry provides numerous formal ordering principles, then life itself provides the disorder that is the raw material of poetry'.[124]

It may be of relevance here that the practice of the arts, as distinct from criticism or theory, has always sat uncomfortably as something of a guest in any academic syllabus in the UK until comparatively recently. The freedom of the artist may perhaps go even beyond that of the academic: 'Art lives upon discussion, upon experiment, upon curiosity, upon variety of attempt, upon the exchange of views and the comparison of standpoints; and there is a presumption that those times when no one has anything particular to say about it . . . are not times of development.'[125] For the scholar must be to some degree restricted by the requirements of rigour and the canons of the subject in which he works. But the artist may, and perhaps must, kick over the traces. Henry James puts it crisply: 'Zola . . . reasons less powerfully than he represents.'[126] 'Even the guides and philosophers who might have most to say to him must leave him alone when it comes to the application of precepts, as we leave the painter in communion with his palette.'[127]

That may suggest that the proper response of the critic to this stimulus is to put the order back, to get back into control. 'The human ordering response is the act of creating meaning when inspired by the assertions of disorder.'[128] Yet, paradoxically, that seems especially to press when order seems too secure. The academic becomes restless when he is not on new territory. 'As the inevitable facility comes, the conscious task becomes the rejection of whatever appears with the face of familiarity.'[129]

The proposition I want to put forward here is that for the academic there is (or ought to be) a constant motion between boldness and timidity. To withdraw an idea when it is rejected on a first hearing is to lose it. It may in the end succeed, if it is persevered with. A hypothesis dismissed as untenable when it is first floated may make its way to respectability. J. V. Luce describes how 'classical scholars laughed at Schliemann when he set out with Homer in one hand and a spade in the other. But he dug up Troy, and thereby demonstrated that it is rash to underestimate the historical value of folk memory.'[130]

In the end, however valuable teamwork may be, however indispensable to certain types of scientific inquiry, the personal driving force, 'the vitality and force of a single living man',[131] is irreplaceable. Thoreau perceives the power a single mind may have to move things onward. He also saw the vulnerability of the individual mind, its need to preserve its 'sense of self' in its encounter with others. Thoreau describes an experience at a theatrical performance when, under the spell of the action, the members of the audience were carried out of themselves. At the interval they had to return to their sense of themselves: 'We who have been swayed as one heart, expanding and contracting with the common pulse, find ourselves in the interim, and set us up again, and feel our own hearts beating in our breasts . . . In the recess the audience is cut up into a hundred little coteries, and as soon as each individual life has recovered its tone . . . it is time for the performances to commence again' (speaking of a theatre interval).[132]

This sense of the intellectual self he believes to provide a continuity, and indeed there is evidence that the individual mind has at least its stylistic imprint, distinctive as a fingerprint, and mark of a 'personal authenticity'.[133] That is not a new idea. Dionysius of Halicarnassus thought it possible to identify an author's genuine works from the unique patterns his mind formed with the words he used: 'Using as my main criterion simply that the speeches of Lysias are composed in a pleasing style, I have come to suspect many of the speeches which have been commonly regarded as genuine.'[134] Thoreau puts this in the language of personal integrity, a 'being true' to one's scholarly self. 'It is essential that a man confine himself to pursuits – a scholar, for instance, to studies – which lie next to and conduce to his life, which do not go against the grain, either of his will or his imagination. The scholar finds in his experiences some studies to be most fertile and radiant with light, others dry, barren, and dark.'[135] And 'we cannot write well or truly but what we write with gusto . . . Expression is the act of the whole man, that our speech may be vascular.'[136]

The Roman poet Horace noticed that the wandering explorative nature of research means that in the struggle to arrive at understanding, the mind goes backwards and forwards, and that when it does so it is cutting its own road.[137] 'Whatever caprice takes me, I go on my own,' admits Horace.[138] 'The interpretation given in this edition . . . supersede[s] any opinions to the contrary I may previously have expressed,'[139] says one bold modern editor, prepared to cut a swathe even through his own previous work. If all that justifies a researcher is that he should say 'what it was in him to say',[140] is scholarship, then, anything more than self-expression? Is it inherently self-indulgent? Are academics really after all only pursuing their hobbies at the taxpayer's expense? Is the interdisciplinary experiment, the taking of risks with those 'subject-benchmarks' not a good idea after all?

One answer to that question is that this exercise is not merely solipsistic. It is tested by discussion. Publishing the result of a study does not really give a picture of the study as a speech-process, and that process, or discourse, may be important, as one thing leads to another and the scholar goes more deeply into things as others challenge his conclusions. It is built into this 'continuing' character of scholarly speech, this running after a scent, that the trail may turn back upon itself, may set off in quite another direction. It is common to find in the course of a piece of research that one thinker's modest idea has become bigger or established a new pattern: 'I began thinking about how a firm grasp of the diagnosis and treatment of epilepsy could benefit a physician . . . The real challenge . . . was to create an entire series on the notions that physicians like . . . to have concrete rules to guide their diagnosis and therapy.' That particular scientist found, as he set out to put this idea into practice, that those he asked to write such books were writing in a particular way, so that a genre of medical textbook was developing, in which 'each author is forced unequivocally to say what is important'.[141]

We begin here to glimpse two further key principles of the present study. The first is the paradox that the researcher's colleagues can be expected to pull him up short if he is merely being self-indulgent. Time will tell whether the work can prove itself. The second is that this needs time and there must be room for researchers to manoeuvre while everyone finds out whether what they are doing is worthwhile. There has to be some gambling with the taxpayer's money in order to preserve the possibility that work which needs room to explore will bear fruit. That is not likely to be an immediately attractive argument at a stage where the cultural norm is increasingly to expect to be able to put down public money and know what it will buy. The same tensions are evident in the case of commercial funding. Yet there is a 'write-off' factor in much public expenditure and there is no good reason to treat expenditure on academic research any differently. On the other hand, the potential benefits are incalculable.

A great value of interdisciplinary work is its capacity to make it apparent where new questions may lie: 'Probably the greatest unresolved problem in studies of psychological effects of the environment is to fill in those considerable areas of *terra incognita* which represent the processes of interaction between individual personality and behaviour and the social structure of a community.'[142] But in a climate of impassioned resistance to experimental moves within and between established fields, those questions are less likely to be put.

Authoritativeness and the mechanisms of censorship

Multum permisit sibi[143]

The scholar who would become an 'authority' has several options. He may do a supremely reliable or solidly excellent piece of work which is referred to with continuing general respect. Or he may radically change the way things are approached in some area of scholarship. If the latter, he has to face the forces of conservatism, which are strong in academe, in consequence of the 'investment' of others in the continuance of their own work, which looks at things differently. 'A long habit of not thinking a thing wrong, gives it a superficial appearance of being right, and raises at first a formidable outcry in defence of custom.'[144] In creating or shaping a reputation, a 'group' favouring this view or that becomes popular or fashionable. Indeed, there is a 'tendency of people to acquiesce in change and then to forget that change has occurred'.[145]

When a revolution in thinking takes place very 'visibly' because someone frankly puts it forward as a challenge, there is likely to be reaction. Striking words are likely to provoke resistance. 'People who originate novel ideas need to be able to withstand the criticism of the conservative majority.'[146] The impact of what is said can be powerful. 'The words of some men are thrown forcibly against you and adhere like burrs.'[147] 'To label the whole structuralist movement as mindless and somehow wicked is the reaction, I am afraid, of those who usually do not have the faintest idea of what it is really about. "Structuralism" is an approach, or set of approaches, that cannot be simply ignored in any respectable university in Europe; and it is one that often increases understanding,' said G. D. S. Kirk. 'We have structuralists or post-structuralists in the Faculty of Classics, too; amazingly, they regard my own views on Homer, for instance, as somewhat pathetic; but I don't for that reason want to boot them into kingdom come – indeed, even as a rather feeble kind of ex-structuralist myself, I believe I can learn something from them.'[148]

'A certain plasticity in the articulation of his position'[149]

It is possible to become a leading authority even when there is visible inadequacy or incompleteness in the work: 'Kuhn has himself admitted that weaknesses, obscurities, unclarity, vagueness, confusion, real difficulties, ambiguities, misunderstandings, substantive errors, and provisional formulations grounded in metaphor and intuition are all to be found both in the exposition of [*The Structure of Scientific Revolutions* (Chicago, 1962)] and in later work, leading to a certain plasticity in the articulation of his position.'[150] Influence may continue to be strong even where the thinker exerting the influences comes to be seen to be in the wrong: 'There cannot be a page of this book untouched by his [Houseman's] influence. I differ from him more than I should once have thought reasonable, but if time has opened my eyes to his fallibility, it has also brought me to a fuller awareness of his scholarship.'[151]

Ronald Dworkin would be regarded by many as a 'big leading player' in American jurisprudence. A profile of him was written by Stephen Guest. Guest sets out 'to advance a comprehensive and coherent interpretation of Dworkin's positions in legal and political philosophy'. He does it with a sense of the need to rebut criticism, for the subject of his memoir has been attacked: 'I have considered many of the main criticisms that have been levelled against them . . . and offer . . . what I believe to be a good defence,'[152] he says. Guest admits that Dworkin's work is not without its faults and its most notable fault is its obscurity. Now, obscurity can easily give an impression of profundity: 'It is highly compressed and it is my task in this work to try to make his theory clearer and more accessible than it has so far been . . . His writing is not easy to many, including myself. And because he writes for a number of audiences, sometimes the general public, sometimes for academic lawyers, sometimes for philosophers and economists, it is an especially hard task to dig out the different strands of his thought.'[153] So extreme was this problem of incomprehensibility that it was, Guest suggests, only collaboration (with Gareth Evans, who 'forced Dworkin to be clearer') that encouraged him to be more open-textured in his writing. Evans 'had an irreverent style which exactly suited this stage of the development of Dworkin's thought'.

But he does not need to be 'loyal', for this is an author who has been controversial in a way which has ensured that criticisms are taken by the academic community as indicators of the challenging character of his work, and not as indicators of its poor quality: 'Ronald Dworkin's legal and political theories have a complexity, novelty and moral power that have excited a wide range of academic and political thinkers.'[154]

Influence of the sort that creates a presumption of authoritativeness can thus be had even – and perhaps especially – by an author mainly because he is disagreed with, even in ways which strike at the very claims of his work to be of acceptable academic quality: 'Kenneth Minogue . . . questions whether . . . Skinner's methodology has been very useful and argues that historians of political thought are better off without [it] . . . Indeed, he finds Skinner's method "pernicious".'[155] 'Nathan Tarcov . . . argues that the shortcomings of Skinner's approach can be seen most clearly by a close examination of the ways in which Skinner allegedly misinterprets Machiavelli' (p. 5). 'Skinner's account . . . is very difficult to make out. This . . . is because Skinner seems to waver from page to page in what he wants to say about Machiavelli's position' (p. 198). 'Skinner's interpretation of Machiavelli is superficial, confused and poorly documented' (p. 202). 'He substitutes an unbalanced, simply conventional, or simply counter-conventional selection' (p. 203). 'John Keane . . . argues that Skinner's method is uncritical' (p. 5). 'The form of explanation he has in mind is flaccid and uncritical' (p. 213). Joseph V. Feria speaks of 'his curious methodological strictures' (p. 175).

The 'wrongness' may indeed be the most noticeable feature and have led directly to a writer's work being a great deal noticed. For not all citations are congratulatory: 'There are well over a thousand citations of White's work in philosophy of history in . . . twenty years . . . The series . . . rises to close to a hundred per year in the late 1980s and early 1990s . . . The array includes journals in administration science, anthropology, art history, biography, communications, film studies, geography, law, psychoanalysis, and theatre. But to arrange the journals by discipline is misleading . . . because the writers are seldom readily classifiable by their own disciplines.' In this array, 'it is a good deal easier to find such comments as that the book is "irritating and pretentious"'.[156]

So, if it is true that scholars become authoritative only because of others' reaction to them, it is a truth with complex shadings. The main thing may be to get noticed, to gain an 'audience'. Attack upon the already established may achieve that. Or support by a known figure prepared to declare his faith in a hitherto obscure writer may do the same, getting an audience for someone's academic 'speech': 'Thanks to Jacob Bearman for his confidence in me when I had none and to Chris Klin for his role in developing and promoting my career.'[157]

The hall of fame

The classical world already knew the 'citation index'. Classical authors were already forming the habit of looking back to what their predecessors had said, in the 'doxographies' commonplace in antiquity.[158] For example, the late Platonist Proclus, writing on Euclid, returns to such sources so as to depict the origins of geometry as a subject of study. He looks at authors and their contributions. Thales, he says, was the first to go to Egypt and bring 'field-measuring' back to Greece. He explains that Thales himself discovered many propositions, and disclosed the underlying principles of others to his successors. In some cases, what he had to offer was something more general or abstract, in others more empirical. He goes on to discuss Pythagoras, Anaxagoras, Hippocrates, Plato and others. Leon, he says, was able to make a collection of the 'elements' of the subject, and he discovered how to determine whether a problem can or cannot be resolved.[159] When he comes to Euclid's own achievement, Thales tries to take an overview, placing Euclid's work in the larger conspectus of philosophy. (He says he was, overall, a Platonist.[160]) Diogenes Laertius is another exponent of this relatively common genre in the ancient world. He lists wise men of the past as a means of answering the question 'What is the origin of philosophy?'[161] Diogenes Laertius brought together in his *Lives and Opinions of Eminent Philosophers*[162] a collection of material which was modelled on the contemporary fashions which 'favoured personal details, anecdotes, and witty sayings . . . This encouraged in authors a peculiar species of research [which] ransacked earlier literature in order to discover anything new and startling.'[163] Cicero gives a similar doxography in his *Tusculan Disputations*, Book V. Celsus gives a list of early leading medical authors, and then he says that they had no worthy successors,[164] until literary studies began actively to be pursued.[165] This type of roll-call of names has, then, a variety of forms and purposes, but each is underpinned by the assumption that it is possible to point to those who have by their work made a permanent or important contribution to knowledge.

That does not mean that the use of a roll-call necessarily provides a *methodology* for establishing what is authoritative, as Dionysius of Halicarnassus admits: 'Who are the most important of the ancient orators and historians? What manner of life and style of writing did they adopt? Which characteristics of each of them should we imitate, and which should we avoid? . . . I cannot myself recall ever having come across any treatise on this subject, in spite of exhaustive research.'[166] But it is commonly treated as a reliable indicator. There were later versions of this approach. In the Middle Ages the *antiqui* were contrasted with the *moderni*, authors 'established' by their death, with those still alive, and with reputations still to make or to be marred. And it was the twelfth-century Bernard of Chartres who is first said to have spoken of the scholars of his own day as dwarfs standing on the shoulders of giants, with the double implication that though they were minor figures yet they could see further.

Each established area of study comes to have a hall of fame, containing those who are thought to have established or shaped it. Great minds, on *this* construction, add a brick or two to a growing edifice; they do not topple it and start to build another one. Accordingly, for such authorities, a scholarly caution is proper in the handling of earlier authorities: 'It is a feature of expository legal literature that its originality, its innovatory force, must, by the conventions of the system, be concealed.'[167] 'In the Western European legal tradition of private law successful creative work consists in a combination between intelligent plagiarism and systematisation of what is lifted from others. This is so partly because of the ramifications of the concept of authority; what the writer says appears more persuasive if it is the same as what others have said.'[168]

There is in the early twenty-first century another kind of influence at work, that of 'authority figures' identified by the importance of the positions they hold rather than by their work. 'I like to see the big leading players in, so you make sure your standards are right in where you are and where you want to go,'[169] said Cambridge's Vice-Chancellor to a House of Commons Select Committee in 1999. It is possible to become an 'authority figure' of this sort, a 'big leading player', in modern academic life by getting an important post. Authorities are listened to because of 'who they are' as well as 'what they say'. That often carries with it both influence within a university and the expectation of accolades outside it – appointments to committees making funding or rating decisions, knighthoods, seats in the House of Lords. The 'big leading player' has always been a feature of the scholarly scene. But that 'role' has not always been dependent on 'position' of a formal academic kind in quite the way it often is now: where what someone says is taken seriously when it is 'heard' to be coming from an influential or respectable or established or important or expert source.

An authority may make his name by making his point; or he may make his point by making his name. If you are famous, comments Northrop Frye, when you write 'you are continually thinking in terms of somebody who'll take this as gospel, and therefore you ought to make sure it isn't fatuous'.[170] There is obvious danger in reliance on those whose status derives principally from the posts they hold, who may have given up academic work for administration some time earlier.

Authoritativeness: the writing

We have been considering *people* as authorities. Books can be authorities too. There is a class of books which achieves an established status, becomes 'classic'. Such an opus has been variously described as 'a standard, a sub-lime truth, a rule, a master-work, an artistic model, and latterly, a book-list for educational use'.[171] But these 'stretch across some very different cultural lexicons',[172] and they appear to have in common only being respected and held to be of lasting value by the generality of readers or students. The assumptions are likely to be 'western' in Europe and perhaps still more 'local' in the USA, unless there is a conscious corrective in the direction of a wider world view. 'Until surprisingly recently, readers of very different political persuasions agreed on the liberating potential of certain works of art and aesthetic ideas.'[173] 'The acquiring of taste is probably more diffi-culty today than it ever was before . . . Johnson could defer to the ultimate authority of the Common Reader,'[174] remarks Leavis.

A book may last because it has a capacity to appeal to the reader age after age, so that twenty-first century western readers continue to appreciate Chaucer or Proust or Dante or Shakespeare or the Victorian novel as a good read, and these may also be set before students in other cultures who are learning English as the world's most useful language.

Where academic effort is spent on discussing and 'teaching' the texts to be kept in play, exposure of fresh generations to the books of the past is ensured. A book may belatedly 'arrive', even become definitive, under the critical attention of academe. So it is not necessary for a book to have been an authority from its first appearance: 'Scholars [are] always a little behind in these matters', says one critic, anxious perhaps to make more visible the candidature for greatness of the subject of his own study, Flaubert: 'This is not simply a question of fashion. Flaubert . . . has never received the full measure of his due.'[175] Conversely, the tendency to include only very modern works in literature syllabuses means that a generation may grow up unacquainted even with the names of classical authors. In an attempt to counter that, in the USA some universities run courses with titles like 'A hundred great books'. A work of modern scholarship in any field may attain something of that status, in a minor way. '*What is mathematics* has worn amazingly well. Its emphasis on problem-solving is up to date, and its choice of material has lasted.'[176]

'Authoritative criticism'

Much of the routine criticism of academic speech, at least in the humanities, takes the form of reviews of books. Coleridge already saw that as creating a licence to be cutting. 'In times of old, books were as religious oracles; as literature advanced, they next became venerable preceptors; then then descended to the rank of instructive friends; and as their numbers increased, they sunk still lower to that of entertaining companions; and at present they seem degraded into culprits to hold up their hands at the bar of every self-elected . . . judge, who chuses to write from humour or interest, from enmity of arrogance.'[177]

When I review a book, I try to be fair. I ask myself whether the book makes its case; I bring to bear what I know, and I look for gaps and imbalances. But I usually also know something about the author. It would be surprising if I did not after thirty years in the same small field. I shall be saying in my review, consciously or not, what I think of him as a rival. I shall want it to be understood that had I been writing the book, I would have done it rather differently. I polish the review; one likes to be stylish. But sharp prose is rarely kind. The review is published and the author gets to know what I have said. We may not be such good friends next time we meet at a conference. But at least I have said it to his face. And all our fellow scholars can see what I think of him, and judge me as well as him if they think I have been spiteful or unjust. Imperfect though it is, that is real peer review: the free-speaking mutual assessment of experts prepared to put their money where their mouth is and risk their own reputations as well as that of the reviewed by going into print.

In the cut-and-thrust of this kind of thing, there can be attempts to remove apparent fixtures from the landscape. 'The view . . . that new books can drive old ones out, and that everyone ought to bend his best efforts towards making sure that this happens . . . seems to me entirely wrong,' says Frank Kermode.[178] One reason Kermode gives for his distaste for the clearing of the literary forests, is that, whatever its enduring value in its own right, a book can so embed itself in a culture that it alters the course of intellectual history. This can be true even of a book which has had the impact of the Christian Bible. The content of the Biblical canon depends on 'canonical decisions made by people long ago, for reasons that you don't understand and can't reconstruct. . . . The reason why the Apocalypse is in the New Testament is really pretty obscure, but there is no doubt that not only the history of literature, but the history of politics, would have been quite different if it hadn't been included.'[179] This way of thinking tends to shift what defines a classic from the 'content' of the work to the 'effect' it has had, an effect which may arguably be a quite distinct matter from its merits.[180] The *Golden Ass* of Apuleius is a 'déclassé classic',[181] suggests one critic (though that does not discourage him from writing a lengthy book on it nonetheless, which he says he hopes will be ground-breaking).

Authoritativeness and power

Peer review is a notoriously inexact science. Mental test theory suggests that the referees brought in to assess a grant proposal (or a manuscript submitted for publication or the work of a candidate for promotion) will be so profoundly affected by the presuppositions brought to the matter by the reviewer that there will be a correlation between their views so unsatisfactory that no judgement can rest on it. 'Of 58 tabulated correlations, 4 fell short of 0.18 and only 4 exceed 0.40. So a referee's report is typically 70 per cent referee and only 30 per cent paper/grant proposal.'[182] Where 'expert evidence is *allowed* to be challenged, it proves eminently challengeable. For example, expert witness evidence can prove insecure in courts: 'Studies of US regulatory proceedings are ... deconstructed, disclosing areas of uncertainty and interpretive conflict, when evidence is developed in accordance with adversarial procedures.'[183] It becomes apparent that 'the adversary process may succeed in exposing the unacknowledged and untested presumptions concealed within a seemingly robust scientific claim, field or technique'.[184]

Factors other than pure expert judgement are unconsciously taken into account by those weighing such evidence. Judges and juries lack scientific expertise themselves, so they may have simple faith in the expert, which they judge by the way he presents himself and an impression formed 'through a multitude of informal, often invisible negotiations'.[185] 'All the factors that go into establishing a witness's credibility – not only knowledge but also social and cultural factors such as demeanour, personality, interests, and rhetorical skills – are simultaneously open to attach when scientific testimony is subjected to the adversary process. Critics accordingly worry that the non-epistemological determinants of credibility may carry the greatest weight with lay juries and judges.'[186]

In C. P. Snow's fictional account of the investigation of an alleged scientific fraud in a Cambridge college, it had to be admitted that the judges were taking almost everything on trust. F. R. Leavis said sharply, 'a judgement is a real judgement, or it is nothing ... I cannot ... have my judging done for me by someone else.'[187] Here is Snow's account: 'One of the younger Fellows had been caught out in a piece of scientific fraud. Without any notice at all, he had been got rid of ... It had been done, of course, after something like a judicial investigation.'[188] 'It was on ... technical opinion that the Court of Seniors had acted. "Of course," said Francis, "they had to go on what the scientists told them. Nightingale's the only one of them who'd have any idea what a diffraction photograph was." '[189] ' "Remember, I'm totally unqualified to analyse the evidence myself, and so are most of the people in the college. That's one of the difficulties of the whole proceedings. If I were there, I should just have to believe what Francis Getliffe and the other scientists told me." '[190]

One of the ways in which the person who becomes an 'authority' can exert control over what others say is thus to ensure that things can be said behind the scenes without the subjects of such remarks having access to them and being enabled to comment. In this way, one category of academics can keep another out of influential positions by adroit (or even unconscious 'use') of the 'referee' system. There have always been deemed to be men 'whose honour demanded that their names be kept secret'.[191] The problem with that is that 'the rules controlling the dissemination of secrets held between two parties always tended towards asymmetry ... the impossibility of dissociating confidential relationships from relationships of authority'.[192]

Scholars in the humanities are always to some degree rivals of any referee familiar with their work who might be invited to comment on an application for promotion or for a job. The University of Keele in 1999 made provision for candidates for promotion to state in detail whether they had collaborated with a given referee, been invited to contribute to volumes edited by that referee, or perhaps issued such invitations to the referee, been a research student of the referee, or conversely examined a research student of the referee. This may not be adequate protection, but it at least constitutes recognition that there is a problem. The writing of references differs from the composition of reviews because sometimes I am writing about my protégé and sometimes about my prey. My former doctoral student in search of a job has my hearty backing. I have a lifetime responsibility to help him on his way; and my reputation is on the line as well as his, especially in these days when one gets brownie points when a graduate student lands an academic job. For one's senior fellow scholars being considered for promotion or for a post applied for, one writes from much more mixed motivation. A parent may be truly pleased to find its child more able than itself. But what senior scholar is big enough to say, 'Dr Bloggs has outstripped us all'?

Anonymity used to protect even the reviewers of books. The monthy reviews of Victorian England did not give names of reviewers until the middle of the century. *Macmillan's Magazine*, which began in 1859, used signatures, and *Blackwood's* began to do so in the 1880s, but reviews in the *Spectator* and the *Athenaeum* remained anonymous throughout the century. The *Saturday Review* remained anonymous into the 1890s. The custom was changed by the argument that 'the honesty and competence of the reviewer should be vouched for by his signature'.[193] 'The man, who, in the genuine spirit of criticism impartially distributes praise or blame to the work he reviews, has no . . . need to hide his name.'[194] But against that had to be set the recognition that in reality 'signature does hamper and cramp honest and frank criticism'.[195] It also hampers spite and the destruction of reputations with the pen.

The types of 'authority' with which we are concerned here are those conferred by high office or high place in academe, and those in which the asymmetry is created by the presumption of 'special expertise' on one side which outweighs the expertise on the other and makes it possible for one scholar to do down (or puff up) another. Both are inimical to the real free-for-all exchange of academic debate.

The rise of the mediocrity

In experimental work of the late 1940s and early 1950s Solomon Asch drew startling conclusions about the average subject's limited capacity for independence of judgement in the face of an 'accepted' view. Subjects were asked whether or not they agreed with a group of people who had been instructed to falsify their answers in response to a simple perceptual test. The group would agree on what was manifestly absurd. Only 20 per cent of the subjects 'proved capable of independent judgement in the face of an absurd consensus'. 'Faced with a consensus – especially one endorsed by authority – modern individuals show an extreme tendency to conform; that is, to think and do as others do, or as others tell them to do, without question.'[196] This finding takes 'judgement' (even in an academic expert) to be an essentially social rather than an intellectual act. R. J. Johnson goes so far as to ask whether there may be 'really no discipline of geography, only a group of academics who have been socialized to believe that there is.'[197]

One result is that those who reach the top are not necessarily the most able: 'The establishment leaders in a field are elected from this relatively unthinking majority and are very often mediocrities themselves . . . They spend most of their professional lives seeking leadership roles, from which it is relatively easy to snipe at anyone in their profession who makes a significant . . . advance.' The implication is that 'science is as much a competition between people as ideas.'[198]

The loss of common culture

To juxtapose the contention that there can be a tendency within the system to advance to positions of seeming authoritativeness individuals who are really rather ordinary, with the lament for the loss of a common culture, is really to say no more than that both are illustrative of the immense importance of critical skills in the widest sense. The academic world rates criticism as an academic skill and gives posts to literary critics in universities. With rare exceptions, it does not give such positions to the authors of the works of art the critics criticize, 'the critic rising as the author sunk,' as Coleridge puts it.[199] Coleridge was keen to see those who were to form judgements set out the principles on which they would do so: 'I should call that investigation fair and philosophical, in which the critic anounces and endeavours to establish the principles.'[200] A first requirement of the weighing of 'authoritativeness' would appear to be a system of criticism, a method of speaking about academic speech. If it is true that 'we have not even evolved a theory of criticism that can distinguish the genuine from the useless in scholarship itself',[201] academe is in a poor way to protect itself.

The academic critic must be self-consciously a critic, be aware of his criteria and the method by which he is forming his judgement and not be too easily pleased. In *How to Read*, Ezra Pound spoke of 'maintaining the very cleanliness of the tools, the health of the very matter of thought itself . . . The individual cannot think or communicate his thought, the governor and legislator cannot act effectively or frame his laws, without words, and the solidity and validity of these words is in the care of the damned and despised *literati*.'[202]

F. R. Leavis perceived that criticism is so demanding that it requires a high degree of prior commitment and habit: 'A man will hardly justify time and energy spent in reading the works of Aristotle . . . unless he is committed to an intensity of sustained frequentation and to a study also of the works of the relevant specialist, that will make him something of a specialist himself.'[203] But that has the drawback that it requires the academic to be a *specialist*. That is to say, it is a drawback in that it creates a place in which realities may become detached from other sorts of reality. 'We are irretrievably committed to specialisation and no man can master all the specialists. The problem is that of educating a . . . kind of mind . . . that will give the different special-isms a humane centre.'[204] That raises a second requirement: not only must critical principles be to some degree held in common (or there can be no conversation) but there must also be a knowledge of what is to be discussed, in this instance, of the texts which are to be talked about.

Leavis found a generation ago that there were already relatively 'few who can talk intelligently about Stendhal, Proust and Henry James'.[205] The old common cultural world is being replaced by a different and culturally narrower expected 'knowledge-base' or 'content' of degree courses. This is becoming perhaps the greatest barrier to critical assessment of claims to 'authoritativeness' and the confidence to cry that the emperor is wearing no clothes. This is a 'negative' note on which to conclude the chapter; the position is not of course irretrievable. That takes us to 'teaching', which is the subject of Chapter 2.

2
Teaching

The education of a good citizen

Making good citizens

If public money is to be put into higher education – and higher education is very expensive, so it is likely to be substantial public money – should there be some expectation that it will create better citizens? And if so, in what should that 'better citizenship' consist? For it is not necessarily the case that the 'real world' always has the same expectations of academe.

There has been a change of expectation in recent years. The present idea is that the good citizen is a go-getter, an entrepreneur who will use his education to make money and create jobs and generally assist the national economy to flourish. Those are the signals sent out by the UK government and they are backed by policy decisions about the allocation of funding. There is talk of 'transferable skills', but no longer (much) about the creation of humane and intellectually accomplished people. Practically speaking, the overheating and subsequent widespread collapse of the dotcom companies showed that it was premature to be so confident that the main lines of an exciting and quite different new world with different priorities could be descried. In any case, the question goes much deeper than 'Will this work?'

Good citizens, on the model universities worked with for at least the last two centuries, were understood to be people who inhabit well-stocked minds and can think for themselves. Varro, according to Cicero, sees philosophy as a guiding principle of life and as an intellectual pleasure; it is both serious (useful) and an adornment.[1] It is, in short, 'good for people' and a former of 'good citizens', too.

Where matters of conscience or religious requirement have entered into the equation, there have been interruptions to that genial presumption. Samuel Johnson describes in his *Life of Milton* a difficulty Milton had with the taking of the oath of canonical obedience which would have been required of him if he had held a living as a cleric in the Church of England: 'He thought it better to prefer a blameless silence before the office of speaking, bought and begun with servitude and forswearing.' 'The thoughts of obedience, whether canonical or civil, raised his indignation,' comments Johnson.[2] Milton was not prepared to buy the *licentia* to preach (or teach) at so high a price. Milton the scholar was potentially Milton the controversialist.

But this kind of thing was far from the mind of John Henry Newman when he and others set about taking seriously their duties as university teachers in mid-nineteenth-century Oxford. We learn from his *Letters and Diaries* that his emphasis was pastoral as much as intellectual. He wrote to a parent: 'I have much pleasure in taking up my pen to inform you of the marked improvement which has taken place in your Son's conduct since I last felt it my duty to address [you] on the subject . . . He has shown his good sense and resolution . . . in rousing himself from the indolent habits to which he was then giving way, and has discovered an energy of mind the apparent absence of which was the chief defect of his character.'[3] But he understood well enough that teaching involved an intimate intellectual engagement with the pupil. He contrasts 'the office of Tutor' with that of 'mere lecturer [in which] teaching was not an act of personal intercourse, but an ungenial and donnish form'.[4] The chief objective here was not to liberate the student and make him critical, but to make him industrious to be well-informed.

This is particularly interesting, in the light of Newman's later active involvement in the setting up of the University of Dublin. In *The Idea of a University*,[5] he displays a startling lack of understanding of the realities of medieval universities, but he does put forward a modernized concept of the ancient Roman ideal. His 'idea' of a university is that it is a place for the formation of gentlemen, by which he means educated men who are also morally upright and in both those senses 'civilized'. It was, in short, to form the kind of citizens his society looked for (given that there was as yet no notion of widening access to create an educated workforce as a whole).[6] These are to be graduates who are humane, with a sense of duty and a willingness to engage in public service, and in that sense they are latter-day 'Romans'.

Newman makes other comments which chime with his experience of the Oxford of the 1820s and 1830s. He sees the need in a university for intellectual space and sufficient leisure to think. 'The common sense of mankind has associated the search after truth with seclusion and quiet.'[7] For Newman a university is above all for teaching. It 'is a place of teaching universal knowledge . . . Its object is . . . intellectual, not moral . . . The diffusion and extension of knowledge rather than the advancement.'[8] He does not rule out research (and indeed he did a good deal of it himself as a young don), but he is clear that 'to discover and to teach are distinct functions; they are also distinct gifts, and are not commonly found united in the same person'. 'He who spends his day in dispensing his existing knowledge to all comers is unlikely to have either leisure or energy to acquire new.'[9] He is probably more right in the latter observation than the former, but for our purposes the point is that he put the emphasis upon teaching, and teaching intended to 'form' the person, intellectually and as a civilized human being.

Compare for the twentieth century this view of the purposes of teaching in higher education: 'Education must be understood as producing not only knowledge but also political subjects . . . creating a public sphere of citizens who are able to exercise power over their own lives and especially over the conditions of knowledge production and acquisition. This is a critical pedagogy defined, in part, by the attempt to create the lived experience of empowerment for the vast majority.'[10] The 'style' and the assumptions here are quite different. The jargon (or technical terms) include words Newman would not have used, or indeed perhaps understood. We need to keep this sharp contrast in mind in an age when older assumptions have faded from view, and it is for this reason that there is a good deal in these pages about the 'traditional' scene.

'Empowerment' need not be seen only in terms of enabling citizens to be agents and not mere recipients of the events of their lives. It also arms the educated with the equipment to test what they are told. Northrop Frye writes in the mid-twentieth century: 'I should think . . . that the doctrines of Mr. Buckley or Senator Goldwater would have little appeal to a society in which the high school graduates knew something about the working of pastoral myth in the political imagination.'[11] But the reality is that the empowerment is likely to be less where the student is put in command of a less rich intellectual heritage by being taught a stripped-down and pragmatic syllabus, and where any attempt to exercise the skills of criticism is likely to prove disastrous to career advancement.

That has been the effect of the redefinition of the notion of good citizenship under the pressure of commercial imperatives, and with the basic idea that education must be practical, and immediately applicable in the circumstances of the passing moment. There is an enormous difference between setting the educated free to roam anywhere intellectually, and merely equipping them for the employment task in hand: 'The disinterested pursuit of knowledge acquires, for its very virtues, the reputation of being unrelated to social realities . . . and what this particular cliché points to, rightly or wrongly, is the insufficiency of detachment and objectivity as exclusive moral goals.'[12] Frye's 'detachment' and 'objectivity' belong with old ideals of the disinterestedness of high learning.

In a telling acknowledgement of the consequences of throwing out almost all the traditional fixed points of reference, Michael Kearns reflects on the way in which 'especially during the past two years, other actual-world plots were threatening this verbal world I was trying to craft', while his students would ask 'the hard questions, especially time and again "How can I apply this in my eleventh-grade (or tenth or twelfth) classroom?"'. He is left trying to explain why he chose certain books as his working guidebooks; he can speak only of 'my almost intuitive privileging of these two books'.[13] The 'real world' which was intruding upon him as a teacher was still expecting something useful in some of the old ways.

Let us look, then, at 'transferable skills' (or 'cross-curricular skills', 'core skills', 'key skills'). It is admitted that this debate is 'bogged down' in 'conceptual mud'.[14] But the poverty of the conceptions is clear enough from the contents of the usual lists of these skills and the fact that they are seen as basic. They include 'communication skills' (conversation, writing, all the subtleties of language and meaning reduced to putting over a sales pitch?); 'numeracy' (again, a world of philosophical and mathematical elegance or a practical ability to do the sums necessary for success in commerce?); 'the use of information technology' (being able to operate manmade computers, which seems scarely a more enduring achievement than being able to program a video recorder); 'learning how to learn' (research or merely study skills in acquiring the information required to fill in a multiple-choice examination paper?). In addition there is an increasing emphasis on 'teamworking' (disadvantaging the solitary thinker and the individual who seeks time for private reflection at his own pace) and 'understanding the world of work' (shaping the student for business).[15] At the least, if it succeeds, this scheme can be expected to create citizens of narrow vision, to discourage public service (the difficulty of recruiting to underpaid professions where there was no longer assurance that there would be pride and satisfaction and autonomy to make up for the poor salaries was already visible in 2001), to lower the expectation that graduates will have certain built-in intellectual assets and competences. It substitutes for the teaching of 'subjects', in which the content is deemed to be important in itself and mastered only by acquiring and practising the skills, an attempt to teach the skills themselves in comparative isolation.

The impact of a 'real world' motivated by greed has therefore been rather different from that of the former 'real worlds' for which university students were being turned into citizens, and it has, arguably, 'disempowered' new graduates by denying them some of the richness of the heritage of the traditional 'university' way of doing things.

The truthful teacher

In one of his letters the Emperor Julian the Apostate writes on the purpose of education as it appeared to him at the end of the fourth century AD: 'I hold that a proper education results, not in laboriously acquired symmetry of phrases and language, but in a healthy condition of mind, I mean a mind that has understanding and true opinions about things good and evil, honorable and base.' Julian the Apostate identifies informed good judgement honestly embraced, as both an intellectual and a social virtue: 'when man thinks one thing and teaches his pupils another, in my opinion he fails to educate exactly in proportion as he fails to be an honest man'.[16]

A certain disinterestedness, at least as to financial reward, has traditionally gone with academic openness and honesty of speech. According to Northrop Frye in the twentieth century, a university is 'a community, where truth and learning are pursued as such, though not necessarily for their own sakes . . . I sense this kind of respect for the university and I see the loyalty of the alumni . . . I think that what the university wants to give society is not really very different from that. They realize that what they are doing will perhaps be oblique in its social impact, but that doesn't necessarily undermine its genuineness.'[17] He, too, perceives an integrity in the purposeful and orderly pursuit of knowledge for its own sake: 'Whenever you're discussing something and attending only to the truth of the argument; whenever your conversation turns from news and gossip to serious issues and real principles; whenever you find yourself looking at something beautiful just because it's beautiful; whenever you answer hysterical prejudice with a firm and quiet voice, there the university is at work in society.'[18]

Disinterested pursuit of truth belongs, too, with detachment and objectivity: 'A scholar is supposed not to write or read an unfavourable review with any personal application . . . students are instructed that "failure" means only not meeting an objective standard, and does not refer to them as human beings.'[19]

Is this realistic? In that it requires its academic staff and students to live, intellectually at least, by such laws, membership of a university can be seen as 'a withdrawal from ordinary society',[20] in order to consider critically what society is saying. It is asking a lot. It may be asking things deemed inappropriate in the West at the beginning of a new millennium. It did not seem so at the beginning of the 1960s, when the Robbins Report on higher education was published and when it could be said to be self-evident that 'the advancement of truth is an essential function of institutions of higher education'.[21]

Utility

Our question now is whether that still holds in a UK university world where the government is keen to pay not for the encouragement in students of a love of truth or an open-ended curiosity, but for practical skills applicable in the industrial and business context of the moment. 'While emphasising that there is no betrayal of values when institutions of higher education teach what will be of some practical use, we must postulate that what is taught should be taught in such a way as to promote the general powers of the mind. The aim should be to produce . . . cultivated men and women . . . a plane of generality that makes possible application to many problems. It is this that the world of affairs demands of the world of learning,'[22] said the Robbins Report. Should education, especially higher education, now change its primary purposes and gear itself to a notion of usefulness directed either to the provision of a merely general education for citizens, or to training for jobs in industry and the creation of more industrial applications? Is that compatible with sharpening critical faculties, breeding joyous cynics, making citizens who will not necessarily wish to 'fit', and who will have the courage and resilience to refuse to 'fit' society's expectations throughout their lifetimes?

The British Dearing Committee of the 1990s saw teaching in universities primarily as a means of creating an informed, trained workforce,[23] able to pick up its intellectual equipment and move elsewhere, to 'get up' new subjects and new skills as 'society' has need of them (that is, driven from without rather than from within). Embedded within this notion of the purpose of university teaching is an attitude already inculcated in the USA at a rather earlier date by business investment in schools. There, 'the mainstream of the business community concluded that employers needed to create an educational climate more favourable to business and the capitalist system'.[24] 'Advocates of business aid to education contended that companies gave without strings but suggested that government funding implied outside control'; nevertheless, 'employers hoped that their gifts to higher education would help to create among educators feelings of obligation and indebtedness to business'.[25]

It is a correlative that the government funder, like the commercial one, may 'properly' have its aims other than the pursuit of truth or the 'fostering of education, learning and research', aims which may not be disinterested, indeed may even be politically driven like the fashion for 'education for entrepreneurship'.

Under such an imperative, research and teaching emerges as a process in which university teachers 'manufacture' knowledge, or 'process' it into forms in which it can be 'consumed' by students. Thus the prospective audience or readership or student body may shape a study by being, in a sense, the 'customer base' for it: 'Originally the idea for this book evolved from a half-day workshop . . . Pharmacologists and pharmaceutical scientists and managers ranging from those in R and D activities to those involved in clinical studies and regulatory affairs, formed the initial group to whom this work was addressed . . . I have also aimed to make this book useful to . . .'[26]

This new dual 'social' and 'commercial' priority has been having visible impacts by way of planned or proposed change. The Dearing Report encouraged the framing of 'benchmarks', to maintain teaching standards. Benchmark reports for chemistry, history and law were sent out to 'heads of institutions' by the new Quality Assurance Agency on 16 April 1999. Standards were being linked in this project with the development of 'programmes of study', and the media signalled the danger that this might lead to a National Curriculum at tertiary level. The curriculum would become hard to alter. Learning would not easily move on. The scholar who had just made a discovery might be discouraged from mentioning it, if that would require revamping of a sequence of instruction, let alone require a wholesale revision of the syllabus. The academic cannot 'question and test received wisdom' (s. 202) if he is in future to be contractually obliged to peddle it uncritically to his students as part of their standard curriculum.

Another trend potentially restrictive of freedom of speech for the academic is teaching through the Internet, in so far as that involves set 'lessons' and working in teaching teams to the detriment of the 'exploratory' pedagogy of individuals who possess that knack for teaching which is more a matter of style and personality than of systematic arrangement of the content. Something may be lost by way of the memorable and inspiring in this way.[27]

At the time of writing, the direction of development of the 'e-university' project is not yet clear, but the general idea appears to be to offer, by way of the Internet, teaching which would naturally not involve face-to-face contact and which would not necessarily be specific to an individual university or linked directly to the award of its degrees.

In the *Bulletin of the Association of Commonwealth Universities* 138 (April 1999), Sir John Daniel, Vice-Chancellor of The Open University, put forward a plan for a transformation of the teaching assumptions on which universities have been working, in response to 'the opportunities presented by technology'. He stated: 'Although universities specialise and divide labour as between disciplines, the habit in teaching is for the same individual to do everything: develop the curriculum; organise the learning resources; teach the class; provide academic support; and assess student learning.' He suggested reforming this 'cottage-industry model' along the lines of 'the working practices that underpin the rest of today's modern industrial and service economy; division of labour, specialisation, teamwork and project management', so as 'to reconfigure the eternally challenging triangle of cost-access-equality'. That would take the 'organisation' and 'systematisation' of teaching still further. A university teacher could be asked to teach in one or more slots or modules at a particular time, and in a particular way, alongside others covering similar delimited sections. On this proposal, someone else would 'develop the curriculum'. This would lead to a divorce between the personal process of learning what the scholar then goes on to teach, with some possibility of creative play with ideas as new to the teacher as to those who are taught. The relationship of teacher and taught in universities has traditionally had an element of shared exploration which it would be hard to maintain in such a structure.

A privilege for a few?

Elitism was a sensitive issue before the late-twentieth-century drive towards mass expansion of higher education. There continues to be a lingering sense among politicians that there are no votes in investment in universities, because universities do not serve the whole population. That is statistically far less the case than it was. Yet there is another core 'teaching' question here. Can there, by definition, be true higher education for everyone, or does the type of education offered have to alter to bring it intellectually within the reach of a high proportion of a population not all of whom can realistically be expected to become active 'intellectuals'? Northrop Frye argues that 'the only guarantee that a subject is theoretically coherent is its ability to have its elementary principles taught to children',[28] and university teachers too may be most fully tested by the task of making themselves clear to student beginners in their subjects.

In Plutarch's period of the Roman world, only those who were well born were allowed to speak their minds freely.[29] One of the political driving forces of the late-twentieth-century expansion of access to higher education has been a sense that it is socially unacceptable to keep a privilege for a mere few, and especially for a few already enjoying exceptional advantages of wealth and parental support. This notion that higher learning gives entry to a select circle, an intellectual elite, was well established even in the ancient world. The *disciplina arcani*, secret knowledge kept for initiates, is a feature of a number of ancient religions, even, in some degree, of an early Christianity, although its founder was ironic about the idea (Jesus' remarks on the themes of the casting of pearls before swine and the children's bread to the dogs).

In Cicero's *Academica*, Varro explores the theory that there is no point in writing what the unlearned would not be able to understand, and the learned would find too simple for them and so not bother to read.[30] The modern political dilemma is the not dissimilar one, that if an ever-wider body of citizens enters higher education, in the nature of things there is likely to be some diminution of the levels of attainment required to get a degree. Or at least it will be suggested that there may, and that is in itself damaging to public confidence.

One way of dealing with this, which was being attempted at the end of the 1990s, was the initiation of a project under which 'benchmark' standards would exist for subjects taught at degree level and to seek to 'even up' the qualifications on offer so that 'a BA was a BA' wherever it was obtained. But it still left out of account the factor of that very 'public perception' which was the problem. It required the general acceptance of a fiction by the people of the UK and the students who applied to UK universities from elsewhere, that the facilities and teaching available at all institutions was equivalent, and that was manifestly not the case. A former polytechnic turned university only in 1992 could not offer the library resources of a London college a century old, let alone those of Oxford and Cambridge, with collections amassed over 800 years.

Another feature of this 'levelling up' was a body of rumours the other way, of a process of 'dumbing down'. For a student, 'to fail' easily becomes 'to be a failure'. Political pressure grew, not only to take in larger numbers of students, on lower levels of school examination success, but also to ensure that as many as possible graduated and graduated well. Graphs began to show an upward trajectory in the numbers of first-class degrees. The consequences for perceptions outside the UK of a drop in excellence in teaching in UK universities were not thought through. There were scandals about 'franchising' of courses. That was symptomatic of a readiness to sell or hire out higher education, with universities touting for students on visits abroad.

Writing for beginners[31]

Let us explore, then, the implications of a simplification of the content of a university education. A need is met by the academic writing for a general reader or a student just beginning, for even the serious student will need a guidebook when first finding his way about an area of study. Cicero exclaims that he and his friends were wandering about their own intellectual city like tourists without a guidebook until they were given such an orientation. Then it was as though they were shown the way home and they knew who and where they were.[32] Cicero suggests that some technical terms will be necessary,[33] but the general thrust of the 'middlebrow' book is that it ought to make its case to the non-specialist. That can have its value for the specialist, too, for even the leading medical practitioner (to take a modern example) may not always be hobnobbing intellectually with those at the frontiers of research: 'All too often the most valuable discussions in texts and journals presuppose a scientific and technical training greater than that undergone by the practising cardiologist.'[34] But of its nature, such provision of starting-places for beginners will not be likely to 'challenge and test received wisdom'. The teacher arguably has a duty first of all to pass on to his students what is already known. He need not be pushing forward the boundaries of knowledge, even if he teaches at university level. But he must never lose sight, or allow his students to lose sight, of what lies beyond the elementary stage, and he is not engaged in any traditional sense in 'higher education'.

Freedom to teach

The Institute for Learning and Teaching was a proposal of the Dearing Committee. At one stage, in spring 1999, there were plans to make membership conditional upon being able to show competence in a number of areas. University teachers were to plan for 'outcomes' of their teaching, under four heads: Design and plan a course; Teach and support learning in the subject; Assess students' learning achievements; Contribute to the maintenance of student support systems (*Times Higher Education Supplement*, 9 April 1999). With the aid of *Roget's Thesaurus* I wrote the following for the *Oxford Magazine*.[35] '*Specify the learning outcomes*': Am I engaged in 'instruction, edification, pedagogy, tuition, tutelage, direction or guidance'? If I want identifiable 'outcomes', I suppose (and here I lick my pencil) I am undertaking 'persuasion, proselytism, propagandism, propaganda, indoctrination'. It would be best to avoid 'sharpen the wits, enlarge the mind, give new ideas, open the eyes, bring forward, improve', because their outcomes would be unpredictable so I could not specify them. '*Plan a structured programme of content and learning activities*': Is this a 'qualification, preparation, training, schooling, discipline, exercise, drill, practice'? The repeating of multiplication tables when I was a small child had plenty of content and learning activities, including raps across the knuckles with a ruler. For a child to die from his schoolmaster's discipline in a medieval monastic school was considered by some to come close to martyrdom and to secure him a place in heaven. So I need not fear to go too far with the content and structure, particularly if I am going to have to achieve the 'persuasion, proselytism, propagandism, propaganda, indoctrination' to meet my outcomes target. Besides, there is 'dry-nurse, breed, rear, take in hand, break in, tame, initiate, inure', to support that approach, so it must be on the right lines. *'Plan the separate learning activities/teaching sessions and the associated student work assignments'*: Here we are at 'explanation, lesson, lecture, sermon, homily, parable, discourse, prlection, disquisition'. It says in the 1562 preface to the book of *Homilies* of the Church of England that 'Her Majesty's pleasure is, that the same be repeated and read again, in such like sort as we before prescribed', so 'homily' must be the right thing to write in here. It has the expectation of keeping on the predetermined tracks. *'Design and select a range of learning resources for the course'*: I suppose the books I have written will not do, because they were not written as course materials.

Let us try *Roget* on learning. He seems to have found two kinds of words. One will do very well. There is 'grind, cram, learn by heart, learn by rote, pore over, dip into, wade through, consume the midnight oil'. I can make sure my students do that by giving them plenty of specified learning resources. But there is also 'scholarship, erudition, learning, self-instruction, inquiry, reading', and if I let them get into all that I shall have to risk their wandering away from the selected learning resources and perhaps coming to unspecified learning outcomes, and then I shall get a professional rap over the knuckles and lose my 'registration' and have my 'professional development record' annotated. I see that I am to 'encourage and support students' active learning', but it had better not be too active, or they will get intellectually out of hand. *'Design ways of informing students of the outcomes and standards expected of them'*: Well, we have always just talked about their essays and discussed the progress of their theses. Perhaps I should have been firmer all these years. There is a tempting list of stances. I could 'domineer, bully, dictate, hector, lord it over, bulldoze, exact, snub, beat, intimidate, trample, tear down, dragoon, ride roughshod over, terrorize' them, and then they would know exactly what was expected of them and not go off to the library and read things which are not on the list of learning resources. *'Anticipate and respond to changes in the learning environment'*: Today my research student is late for our meeting. She usually is, but I 'anticipate and respond to' that by meeting her in the university library tea-room. It is a good 'learning environment', and I can have a cup of coffee and get on with some of the letters I have no secretary to write for me, while I wait for the breathless apology at my elbow. The hum of scholars exercising their 'transferable skills' in gossiping about one another is environmentally friendly, provided one cannot hear what they are saying too clearly, for that would distract from one's future ability to 'maintain professional relationships and work productively with colleagues'.

It is all very dynamic and developmental. I used to have a colleague who supervised his research students on top of a bus, another who could do it from a bicycle. That would be frowned upon now, but the students will not forget their unusual 'learning contexts' and the admixture of amusement might well make the teaching stick.

Teaching in universities has a style and a set of assumptions to hand which is not easily reduced to categories and predictable patterns. Its freedom is of its essence. Something has to be conveyed about the passions which drive scholarship, about its perpetual characteristics, which cannot be captured in descriptions of 'learning outcomes'. Coleridge understood that principle. He wrote scathingly about 'Modes of teaching', designed to create prodigies or performance instead of seeking to awaken an enduring love of learning: 'instead of awakening by the noblest models the fond and unmixed LOVE and ADMIRATION, which is the natural and graceful temper of early youth'.[36] This was a way of putting in the late eighteenth and early nineteenth century an idea which in the medieval West would have been described more naturally in terms of 'formation'. The idea is that teaching ought not only to instruct the mind but also to 'form' or alter the person. It may be thought to be enough for that to have no other end in view than making the most of the possibilities of that individual. If that is the assumption, growth must not only take its own time, but also find its own way: 'The slow growth which develops accurate taste in the arts cannot be taught, however much it may be encouraged.'[37]

None of this traditional freedom and flexibility is incompatible with simplicity, or with helping the less able student. It may indeed be the best way to do it.

Quality assurance

In the 1990s a series of bodies was concerned with academic audit and the quality of university teaching. The Higher Education Quality Council (HEQC) (1992) was an 'organ' of the Committee of Vice-Chancellors and Principals. It undertook the academic audit which had been carried out since 1990 by the CVCP's Academic Audit Unit. In other words, it was 'owned' by the universities themselves. Its successor, the Quality Assurance Agency (QAA), also 'owned' by Higher Education Funding Council for England (HEFCE), continued the 'scores' for individual inspected subjects, introduced by HEFCE, which had formerly conducted the Teaching Quality Assessment (TQA), modified in 1995. The Dearing Committee called for benchmarking, programme specifications, qualifications frameworks, and the QAA began to create a new regime.

This brought about what looked like a culture of compliance, as departments strove to appear to be doing what was expected of them, and paper trails were created which had not been maintained with such vigilance before. There were benefits in the form of a general waking-up throughout the country to the need to have adequate procedures and to police the way they were followed, to create student complaints procedures and to run them properly. A great many socks were pulled up, at least for a time.

But the whole business was extremely onerous, taking over the time and effort of a department for months before a visit and sometimes distorting the actual teaching, so that it appeared to 'fit' the perceived brief. For example, a system in which students in some universities had been free to agree essay titles with their tutors or supervisors became a formalized list of stock topics, with a similar straitjacketing of the examination papers which followed. Lecturers lost something of the old liberty to introduce into a lecture a recent discovery or insight. Lecture courses spelt out their contents in advance with more 'hand-outs' and more bibliographies. There was even talk of a National Curriculum for higher education. 'Subject-benchmarking' made some headway, despite the impossibility of using it for the assessment of interdisciplinary teaching.

In 2001, the more powerful and richer universities began to call for a 'lighter touch', for exemption from future inspections for the top-scoring departments. It began to be argued that the cost in time and effort of this teaching quality assessment greatly outweighed its benefits, although 'universal visiting' had, ironically, been started at the sector's own wish.

In July 2001, a consultation document (Quality Assurance in Higher Education) was distributed by the Higher Education Funding Council for England, the Quality Assurance Agency, Universities UK and the Standing Conference of Principals (SCOP). It proposed putting a good deal more trust in the internal regulatory mechanisms of universities and other institutions of higher education, with external review taking place only on a sampling basis, and chiefly where there appeared to be some cause for concern about the quality of the provision on offer. In other words, it moved, broadly, from testing everything just in case, to testing only where there was reason for doing so. 'The presumption is,' it says, 'that every HEI approves, monitors and reviews its quality and standards through internal procedures.' The proposed external audit would then look 'on a highly selective basis' at 'the robustness and effectiveness of that internal framework' (para. 12). It would try to use 'existing information which HEIs already collect for their own purposes', so as to avoid adding to the bureaucratic burden. Examples are given (para. 15), which suggest that the material was likely to be of a statistical type inherently uninformative about the internal tensions and the internal economy of the teaching and learning process. For example, 'data on student recruitment, progression and employment', 'including consideration of widening participation and equal opportunities', would not bring to light the confusion which allows a doctoral student's admission to get lost in an episode of faculty politics wholly unconnected with the student, so that he is kept waiting for seven months to get a rejection from one quarter and encouragement to keep applying from another. 'Summary results of external examiners' reports' would not show up procedural confusion and a lack of adequate training for those chairing examining bodies. The proposal that institutional-level audit would be conducted 'on peer review principles' (para. 17) would need inbuilt protections against the kind of incestuous mutual approval by an 'Oxbridge mafia' which was strongly rumoured to have bedevilled the Research Assessment Exercise. So would the probable discrepancies between the track record of some universities in terms of standing and high-profile 'success' and the 'robustness' of their internal mechanisms (para. 31). Promised training for reviewers (para. 46) might be expected to breed in due course the kind of hard-headedness and experience of the 'dodges' practised by those being reviewed which would be needed to ensure that the new lighter regime was effective in picking up flaws in universities' conduct of their affairs.

Early in 2002 a sophisticated and practical 'operational description' was in preparation, which took forward the best elements in all this. Yet even to get such a document out for consultation proved a lengthy business in the political climate of the moment. At the time of writing it is impossible to say how it will fare in the cross-currents of politically-driven priorities which are constantly crossing and recrossing one another. There was a promising hint of a courageous change of direction (in an article by Peter Williams in the *Times Higher Education Supplement* of January 11, 2002), towards open-minded debate on the profounder purposes of quality assurance.

Teaching and research

The idea that it is necessary to pinpoint the relationship of university teaching to research is relatively new in the history of universities. The notion that the 'real world' is entitled to take an interest in that relationship is still more recent. In earlier periods, universities were mainly places where teaching went on, and teachers taught what they had learned either from their own masters or from their reading and discussion. Teaching and research ('learning') were hard to separate. The research work of universities as a distinct activity grew more central to their activities during the twentieth century, and it was only towards the end of the century that the balance of the research with the teaching became a matter of debate because it was being explicitly linked with funding. The Higher Education Funding Councils (whose terms were set out in the Further and Higher Education Act 1992), began to conduct research assessment exercises every few years, rating departments on their research output and making block funding allocations for infrastructure support accordingly. In the same stretch of time we have seen a series of 'teaching evaluation' bodies (such as the Funding Councils and the QAA) carrying out teaching quality assessment.

This dual process made institutions self-conscious as to whether institutions were to foster and reward teaching or research, whether they were to spend money first on 'buying' leading researchers, since academics of that sort seemed more likely to be 'earners' of public money than were excellent teachers. The 'new' universities created in 1992, the former polytechnics, were hamstrung in this race, since they had not had a strong research base in the past and were 'geared' chiefly to teaching.

This raised the question of the extent to which research can and should 'inform' teaching, giving students a glimpse of a world of scholarship and inquiry and investigation and of the life-long interest of their teachers in the subjects they were teaching. These were patterns at best setting research and teaching in parallel, rather than regarding them as an integrated whole, at worst separating them as though they were incompatible activities (and as though it was unlikely that the same person would be good at both).

At the end of the nineteenth century, the early issues of the *Cambridge Review* carried a good deal of debate on questions of the day about university teaching. A distinction was drawn in these discussions between the popularization of knowledge and the exactness of real scholarship. 'The short course of lectures brings one upon dangerous ground, because it is identified with the University Extension movement . . . It interests people, it may bring some few on to higher education, but [there is a suspicion that it may encourage people to] consider it the chief glory of a University to popularize knowledge, and not to make it exact.' There was also concern that even the proper serious university lecture could discourage the formation of desirable intellectual habits in students. 'There is . . . a danger lest the lecturer's opinions should be adopted without question, which, of course, destroys independence of thought.' To avoid that, says the author, 'the conscientious lecturer . . . will endeavour to shape his lecture less for giving information than for teaching method and training his pupils to work for themselves' (*Cambridge Review*, 23 February 1887, pp. 233–5).

This recognized the need for students themselves to participate actively (as they did when they read their essays to a tutor and discussed them), as distinct from sitting as passive recipients of instruction in a lecture. It also saw them as future academics themselves. For there is, in these hints of the assumptions of the late-nineteenth-century university, a strong indication that university teaching was increasingly expected to lead to new and independent work, to be at what we should now call the 'cutting edge', and to encourage students themselves to try to cut still further. In 1885 the *Cambridge Review* (11 February, pp. 195–6), carried a discussion of the implications for teaching provision of the abolition of the celibacy requirement for college fellows. This meant that most teaching was done by relatively young men, newly graduated themselves, who would get a 'living' and marry and hand on the teaching task to the next generation probably in their thirties. Some said that if fellows were allowed to marry and remain in the fellowship, this 'generation' of teachers 'will be growing old, and as science . . . progresses, these teachers will be falling behind'. Others took the contrary view that 'at fifty-five a teacher would be just beginning to give his best work . . . Few men would be able to pass for first-rate teachers till at least forty.' The underlying disquiet is derived from a sense of the importance of university teaching keeping up with its subject and breeding new generations able to make sure that the subject advances.

This makes a useful contrast with the cohorts of students in 2001, for most of whom no one envisages an 'academic career'. There was indeed some debate in the UK in the 1990s – at school as well as university level – about the desirability of abandoning the presumption that all students should be taught as though they were going to persist indefinitely in the study of their 'subject', and become professionals in it.

The university as a world of books

The book reviews of these early *Cambridge Reviews* (engagingly headed 'The paper-knife') include an enormous range, from Mark Twain's *The Prince and the Pauper*, to memoirs of life at school, *Rambles among the Hills*, the Hulsean Lectures, and serious works of scholarship. These reviews in themselves often reflect the concerns of this contemporary debate about the relationship of university teaching to the advancement of knowledge. It is possible to get from these something of the flavour of the university culture of the day, which had its bathos as well as its excellences. At one end of the scale stood such works as *Outlines of English Constitutional History*, by B. C. Skottowe, BA. This was like Cicero's *On Invention*, written just after he had left his 'school', though without its superior organization or its lasting success. The reviewer says disparagingly that 'Mr Skottowe's little book lays no claim to original merit of any kind . . . It is little more than a collection of notes . . . such as an intelligent student preparing for an examination . . . would be likely to put together for his own use.' The words 'crammer' and 'dry and dusty reading' feature, though the volume had the merit of being 'set off by type of all shades and sizes' to make it more attractive to the student (*Cambridge Review*, 26 October 1881, p. 30).

A more serious proposition, but still 'Brodie's Notes' for the examinee, was E. H. Hawkins's *The 'Nichomachean Ethics' of Aristotle*, reviewed in the issue of 7 December 1881, p. 128, 'an unpretentious little book containing such portions of the *Ethics* as are commonly read at Oxford'. 'It does not, of course, lay much claim to originality, but it is on a scale which is likely to prove advantageous for men who are not very advanced scholars.' There was admiration for the accidental gem of pedagogical value. A review of C. Elton on *Custom and Tenant Right* recognizes in this 'little treatise' (with its topical and political 'main object' of bringing 'forth reasons to show the necessity for some sort of revision or alteration in the bill now before Parliament, for the enfranchisement of copyhold tenures'), the lasting scholarly value of the accompanying 'account of the manor and its growth' and the 'essay on the nature of customary and imperfect tenures. These historical chapters . . . seem to us so clearly and concisely written that the treatise would form a very excellent handbook for the use of students' (*Cambridge Review*, 10 May 1887, p. 303).

At the other end of the scholarly scale is reviewing of books which can still be found on the serious scholar's shelves. W. Skeat's *The Principles of English Etymology* is praised as 'thorough'. Skeat himself, says the reviewer, 'disclaims any originality in the book'. 'Yet we venture to think that the highest form of originality is that which gives clearness and harmony to the dull and scattered work of others.' Its value is to be in both teaching and raising the pedagogical standing of its subject. 'In ten years this book . . . will revolutionize the present methods of teaching and learning the language and will show that English philology may be as strong a mental training as the older sciences and studies' (*Cambridge Review*, November 1887, p. 108).

A similar developing sense of the need to take a view on what constitute the hard disciplines of scholarship in universities is to be glimpsed in remarks on an issue of *The English Historical Review* for 1887 (*Cambridge Review*, 19 October 1887). This was adjudged a 'rather slow' issue, in which 'Professor Freeman discourses at inordinate length on Aetius and Boniface, taking fifty pages to cover the same ground as a page of Gibbon. His articles are apt to be like the exhibition-pen-cases at railway stations, in which all the stages of manufacture are shown, from the sheet of steel to the finished nib, only the manufacturers do not insist on our taking the whole case.'

Sloppy writing is attacked in equally lively vein in a review of C. Biggs's, *The Christian Platonists of Alexandria.* ('On p. 233 "this life" is described as "a pin-point in the boundless ocean",' mocks the reviewer.) The same book displayed startling ignorance. Biggs thought Rufinus's Latin version was Origen's own work. 'It is infatuated carelessness; an evil spirit has seized his pen, and there follow three pages of hopeless controversy with the Bishop of Durham on "Origen's rendering"' (*Cambridge Review*, 2 February 1887, p. 187). In another connection (31 March 1888, p. 336), we find a swipe at literary criticism, 'this latter-day plague of little books about great books'. In their very robustness of view about the inadequacies of others' work are signs of a developing requirement that scholarly writing should set a standard.

Towards a 'research culture'

In 1911, a Reforms Committee was set up in Cambridge, to which the departments sent in returns (Reforms Committee, 1911, Cambridge University Library, Cam.b.909.18). It makes amusing reading now, but it also raises serious questions about the relationship in the work of a university between teaching and research.

The question which began to emerge was where the balance lies between the inward drive and the externally imposed 'requirement'. The true inner urge is rare. There are perhaps more 'born teachers' than natural intellectual pioneers because the teacher has the advantage of being stimulated by the encounter with the student. It has already been suggested that teaching, or to be more exact, student demand, for an education which would be of use in furthering a career, has probably always 'led', from the medieval beginnings of the very idea of a university. Research in the subjects taught, indeed recognition that there was a need to push the subject forward, has tended to come later. That is still the pattern with 'new subjects'. Management studies did not exist in 1911. Today it is booming, but (it is admitted) with embarrassingly little strength as yet on the 'research side'. 'The Commission on Management Research had difficulty naming any significant British contributions to management research since business schools were established in the mid-1960s.'[38] The difference at the beginning of the twenty-first century is perhaps that the 'career-friendly' syllabus has altered towards the agenda of entrepreneurial 'transferable skills'.

Of course it cannot be quite true that research comes after teaching, or there would have been nothing to teach in the first place at the higher level appropriate to universities. Medieval universities taught the few set texts written by still fewer real 'originals', the *auctores*. Research which is set up and funded and conducted in an institution with or without commercial links and spin-outs may indeed be organized independently of a university's teaching, but at some risk. The early-twentieth-century figure who had gone on an expedition to New Guinea (below) was inwardly driven, not hired to work on a project. He may have been a Mr Casaubon; he may have been a real pioneer in the subject he was studying. No one could tell until the results were published. Such uncertainties may yield outcomes of importance.

To the Reforms Committee of 1911, each Cambridge department added a short note on research in the subject in question, as an afterthought to their main preoccupation, which was in every case with teaching. 'A certain amount of research work is indispensable as a preparation for all higher teaching,' remarked Mathematics.

Interested though they were becoming in the problem, those early-twentieth-century departments were so inexperienced in research that they scarcely knew how to begin to take a considered view on its relationship to university teaching. 'As to the question of research I am not qualified to speak,' said the respondent from Law. Mathematics looked to a research 'future', since it did not seem to have much of a 'present' in research. 'In the appointment of all University Lecturers, proved capacity for research should be taken into account, particularly with a view to furthering research.' Music passed it off with a jest. 'A friend pointed out that a large part of "research" in Music was done by those who "found our musical tunes".'

When it came to giving prospective students help with the learning of research techniques, the departments of 1911 were also somewhat at a loss. Classics suggests that 'with leisure for advanced study it would be known that some published work would probably be required before appointment to a University post'. It also thought that 'it is possible that something in the nature of a seminar might be held by Professors or Readers to direct research work'. History admitted that men 'who have the courage to start their research from the actual source . . . are very few indeed and they are left entirely to their own devices'.

This is entertaining reading for the historian of university teaching, but it is of more than antiquarian interest. It could begin to happen again if research goes off into centres and the 'teachers' largely cease to do research. It is significant that exactly the problems which now tend to drive teaching and research apart were visible a century ago, when the phenomenon could not be explained by an surfeit of external regulation and monitoring. One reason given for an unimpressive research performance in the department of 1911 is lack of time, apparently caused by too heavy a teaching load. 'It would be desirable,' said Economics, 'that lecturers should be able to take a term off, or a year off, and get fresh ideas and material away from Cambridge.' There is even an idea (Modern Languages) that after a period of service as a junior university teacher, a lecturer ought to be able to expect to have his time freed for research, while younger men take over the burden. 'Every fresh teacher in any of the Tripos subjects ought to set the existing teachers free to undertake independent research, and the majority of them are anxious for such opportunity and capable of availing themselves of it.' The thrust of such thinking was already to set research and teaching over against one another, as *rivals* for a university teacher's time, with research the higher calling and the privilege of the senior.

Lack of adequate finance is another impediment to doing research, which was already pleaded in 1911. Agriculture said that 'it is to be hoped that the Department of Agriculture will shortly receive large grants in aid of research from the Development Fund'. History complained of lack of funding, too. Oriental Languages asked, ahead of its time, for research studentships. 'As regards facilities for research, the greatest need is in my opinion that of studentships for post-graduate work.' Theology, too, hazarded that 'the promotion of research would be greatly assisted by the proper use of Prize Fellowships.' If the best and most money goes to research centres that, too, could happen again.

In some departments the complaint was the related one of lack of facilities. Moral Sciences had 'no doubt that Dr Myers, as representing Psychophysics, would urge that further facilities are necessary' for promoting research in that subject. Anthropology notes that when Dr G. Landtman returns 'from his expedition to New Guinea', having already at the time of writing sent nine boxes of specimens before him, 'there is no place available where he can work'. 'I do not know where I can put him,' says the author of the return. Geography thought it might be able to do research if it had 'a permanent habitation, the Department being housed at present by Professor Hughes'. Moral Sciences wanted a strengthening of the 'small departmental library'. Again, modern parallels are easily found.

In the summer of 2000, the Learning and Teaching Support Network Subject Centre for History, Classics and Archaeology circulated a Needs Analysis Survey. The three topics of most interest to respondents were developing students' study skills; using computers in teaching; and encouraging active learning.[39] Is this so different a world as to be impossible of comparison with that of a century ago? At the level at which individual academics work, trying to balance teaching and research and get access to sufficient resources for both, perhaps it is not. An awareness of local shortcomings and of the tension between one demand and another is already visible in these engaging examples of earlier academics trying to give account of themselves and accommodate their work to the new demands the 'real world' was making of universities.

The trick is still to find the 'centre' of university teaching, its place in relation both to teaching the beginnings of the subject and to its current far end, where the researcher is at work. But now the questions about the requirements of the 'real world' press in a new way. We turn to that next.

Teaching students to be businesspeople

A repeating theme of the late 1990s was the need to bring management expertise to the commercial exploitation of ideas arising from research, by, as it were, 'building it into' the students taught at universities. This became a leading concern of politicians in their dealings with universities. It has led to an emphasis on the forming of links with industry, at which we shall be looking in Chapter 3. It also led to an emphasis on including in the education of students in a variety of disciplines, but especially the sciences, aspects of management studies and a general encouragement to approach science in an entrepreneurial way. Universities were encouraged to internalize management expertise. This plan did not allow for the difficulty of finding space for it in the syllabus without evicting parts of the subject they had come to study. Yet some universities were already well ahead in this kind of activity. The *Independent* of 9 August 2001 quoted the Vice-Chancellor of the University of Manchester Institute of Science and Technology (UMIST) as saying that his university 'is very focused. We train people for jobs in a wide range of industries, commerce and the public sector. It's a good place to come if you want a good job afterwards.' 'UMIST has some 60 visiting professors,' continues the article, 'most of whom work in industry and commerce and are involved in teaching undergraduates.'

There remained unresolved contradictions among the proposed methods of achieving effective commercial exploitation of academic research ideas. Some took *experienced* management to be essential not only to efficiency, but also to attracting funding. One idea put to the House of Commons Committee on Science and Technology in 1998 was to 'marry' together 'the best entrepreneurs and managers, the innovators in a general sense, with our scientists'.[40] Another was to get 'the best of management into the smaller emerging high technology companies',[41] for 'strong management teams . . . attract investment' because of the way they are 'seen by potential investors', which has not a little to do with the fact that they are perceived to have a track-record.[42] It has been argued in government papers such as *The Innovation–Exploitation Barrier* that 'successful firms are at the centre of a virtuous circle consisting of the appropriate technology, access to the right type of finance at the crucial points in the lifecycle of the firm to allow it to grow, and a strong management team to make success sustainable'.

It is important to the planning of university courses to be clearer than the Treasury appears to have been even at this stage, in late 1998, about the difference between utilizing existing, proven and therefore attractive managers and turning scientists themselves into managers. In one paragraph (para. 26) it wanted 'to encourage high quality senior managers to join and stay with early stage high technology ventures'; in another (para. 32) 'to develop business skills in pupils and students who specialise in science and technology'. The latter is an obvious need if scientists are to succeed as businesspeople and not merely entrust their discoveries to professional managers. Accordingly, a question from the Science and Technology Committee asked 'whether the business schools should be training in innovation . . . and whether the engineering and science departments should be training in management skills',[43] but without making this essential distinction at all clearly.

It is in tune with Dearing principles for scientists themselves to be taught to be managers. In *The Innovation–Exploitation Barrier* there is discussion of the advantages of training students to start their own businesses, of devising 'a system of competence-based continuing professional development in management skills for use by engineering and other professionals'.[44] Sir David Cooksey spoke disparagingly in evidence to the Science and Technology Committee of 'scientists who believed they knew how to run a business when they did not and were often very short of marketing and general management skills'.[45]

One difficulty with this utopia of scientist-businesspeople is that not all scientists possess the intellectual bent and the traits of personality which can make those skills their own, even if training is provided. Another concern is that in such schemes, 'the cultural factors which differentiate academia and industry need to be kept in mind. Difficulties can arise where differences in language and values are not recognised.'[46]

There has been comfortable talk of 'academics who retained their academic values and their interests so that there is no question of them having to become different sorts of people. [But they have to] learn some different skills, organise their lives somewhat differently on occasions . . . work on academically satisfying but real problems so far as the economy was concerned.'[47] More of that later.

Another problem is that if we are considering not merely individual 'spin-outs' but the relation of the academic to the industrial endeavour as a whole, important questions arise about academic autonomy in the teaching of 'entrepreneurship'. The Department of Trade and Industry commented: 'We have had a very successful scheme called the Teaching Company Scheme whereby post-graduates who move from universities and actually work in projects in industry continue to be supervised by the university.'[48] There are potentially complex 'quality assurance' and 'examining' issues here for any degree-awarding institution. It is noticeable that a certain fudginess creeps in when businesses want to send their senior managers to do courses. Are they to be 'proper students'? If so, admission requirements become relevant as does competition for places with 18-year-old school-leavers who will not have the financial leverage or bargaining power of the businesses seeking places for their employees. If they are just 'enrolling' as for courses in continuing education, are they to obtain any 'qualification' from this degree-awarding body by this route. Government policy is already generating an uncomfortable degree of pressure here, for example 'programmes to enable firms to benefit from the knowledge and skills in higher and further education organisations'.[49] There is a danger that these may confuse by their very multiplicity.[50]

A further line of recent thought has acknowledged that there is no single, all-purpose version of the trained 'scientist-manager'. There may be different managerial needs at different stages of the growth of a company. Beginning with a 'start-up person' the need arrives for 'the person to manage a middle phase' and then 'the right person to run the 500-person organisation which evolves later'.[51] So the business-trained scientist seems to be envisaged as acting in that capacity chiefly at the start of his venture and then handing over to the professionals later.

It is also true that the natural gulf between academic and entrepreneur is wider in some situations than others: in a 'service company . . . so the distinction between research and projects is nothing like as clear perhaps as it is in a product company'.[52] In evidence to the House of Commons Select Committee on Science and Technology, it was pointed out that in, for example, pharmaceuticals, the scientist is 'much closer to the product' and there is a short chain. In the physical sciences there is a long chain. The UK has been more successful in generating benefits to the economy with short chains than with long ones.[53] Bringing in 'the right sort of entrepreneurial team'[54] therefore begs many questions which need to be brought out into the open.

Not the least of these is the wastage of young scientists, including those who go on to do doctoral research. They see the lack of academic career prospects for scientists. They realize that they may face a working lifetime on short-term contracts, of grant-hunting and trying not to fall foul of powerful patrons. A considerable proportion then decide that, far from becoming academic scientists who will try to discover things of commercial usefulness, or even taking their skills into industry and becoming scientific entrepreneurs, they will not continue in science at all. They go on to the law or into the City. The reasons why they do so are our next topic. But before we move to it, the culture-change implied by encouraging universities to 'teach for management', not just in management courses, but in all their courses,[55] has to be set squarely in the frame of this study. Taken seriously and allowed to pervade the university system, it would take further a shift noticeable to those who have taught in universities through recent decades. Students who, en masse, were not necessarily thinking ahead to careers, now tend to be impatient with anything not likely to appear in a foreseeable form in the examinations. The 'middle of the road' steady achievers become the norm rather than the risk-takers.

3

The Control of Research

Making research useful

'Being useful' to society has not always involved the same things. It depends on the expectations of the day; practical application or commercial potential have a claim at present which needs to be tested against a much bigger understanding of the matter, for the term 'utility' has gone through considerable evolution of meaning. In the twelfth-century beginnings of universities, *utilitas* had connotations of a benefit to soul or mind, a general 'edifying' character. By the nineteenth century, in the hands of John Stuart Mill and the Utilitarians, it had to do with constructing a political system which would benefit society in particular ways, and with a more modern notion of 'the common good'. By the Second World War, it had been debased, so as to refer to 'utilitarian' saucepans and other manufactured goods which had no pretensions to style or luxuriousness, but which simply fulfilled their purpose.

'Discoveries are commonly so serendipitous that the best plan would be to have no plan' may be taking it too far; but it is self-evident that 'a plan, by its very nature, cannot anticipate . . . utterly novel approaches'.[1] Yet the new 'utilitarianism' of commercially funded science wants finite, and to some degree predictable, results, despite the fact that even if a planned project can be delivered at the forecast rate, that may not be the best way to achieve the end in view. There are lessons in these changes of emphasis, not least that present assumptions cannot be taken to represent a settled, final position, either.

'The expansion of public funding has not taken place on the basis of cultivating young minds for their own sake. Rather, it has taken place on the basis of promoting societal, and not individual, values. Universities have been given a mission [which] is quite clear; it is to aid economic competitiveness and promote social inclusion' – thus the paper *Higher Education in the 21st Century: Some Possible Futures* (Committee of Vice-Chancellors and Principals, 1999, para. 14). This is altering the kind of graduate the universities set out to 'produce'. It inculcates a positive attitude towards greed, the notion that life is chiefly about consumerism, 'targeting' activities to profit-making ends, paying for results. Increasingly, academe is encouraged to produce marketable goods both of this 'human' sort and of the sort desired by the worlds of commerce, industry, technology. This has the dual purpose of saving the taxpayer money and improving the hitherto 'disappointing match' between high levels of research success (in terms of acclaimed discoveries), and low levels of commercial exploitation of the discoveries in the UK. A further link between the two has been the promotion of 'entrepreneurial' training for students within, or as an adjunct to, their courses.

It is more and more the case that outcomes thought likely to benefit society are looked for from academic research, and that 'benefit' coming to society from that research is construed primarily in terms of applications capable of commercial exploitation. That has a number of implications, for the directions of the search itself and for the balance of provision in higher education and in academic research in universities. 'Big business is exercising increasing control over science and the high technologies which flow from it . . . Before 1970, scientists in British universities and government labs were told not to talk to industry, but after Lord Rothschild's report in the early 1970s they were encouraged to seek industrial funding', with all the restraints of purpose and all the external controls that this imposes.[2]

In some branches of applied science, the science itself benefits from being tried out in industry or commerce; indeed it may need it. 'A science is growing up which will underpin software engineering';[3] 'some of the foundations of this science exist'; its applications, on the other hand, are already 'diverse' and cover 'a huge range'. It was being argued in 1999 that, for some research, 'controlled experiment in the academic laboratory is not enough';[4] that the task of mapping this territory could not progress without the feedback from the experience gained in attempting to make 'applications'. 'Industrial experience in these activities feeds back into the science and even leads us to modify our scientific foundations.'[5] It was further suggested that 'the strategy for developing this science' is experimental. 'It can only be developed on the basis of engineering experiment.'

So it would be a pity to suggest that all the changes of emphasis and expectation of recent decades are for the worse. But they have been dangerous because they have tended to run ahead of the creation of machinery to keep them under control, and appropriately adjusted to the needs of a university. A question put on behalf of the Select Committee on Science and Technology in December 1998 pointed up the lack of detailed planning: 'To transfer words into action does need mechanisms of some sort . . . Have you given any clues as to the mechanisms that would be used?'[6] On present showing, little thought is regularly given to such questions; it is rare for the implications of policy change to be thought through before it is put into practice and unusual for there to be any purposefully argued resistance when the government 'drives'.

Enter the 'real world': government and funders

In 1993 a White Paper, *Realizing our Potential: A Strategy for Science, Engineering and Technology*, sought to alter the priorities of research councils by insisting that scientific excellence was no longer to be the only thing taken into consideration when making an award. 'Relevance to industry and other users' was now to be a factor.[7] This White Paper began the era of systematic government insistence that public money allocated through the research councils should be distributed according to the strategy which was also fostering industrial liaison. The Technology Foresight programme went ahead, 'fostering networks and identifying priorities', and funding councils allocating project money were encouraged in a 'policy of requiring university recipients of its research grants to be responsible for the exploitation of resulting technology'.[8] Saving public money by getting universities to find their funding elsewhere has now progressed to the point where the proportions of non-public money are growing quite considerable. It was already reckoned in 1996 that 7 per cent of university funding in all subjects was coming that way and that it reached 12 per cent in the biomedical area.

The House of Commons Select Committee on Science and Technology took evidence early in 1999 for a report, namely *Engineering and Physical Sciences Based Innovation*. This project followed on from a series of responses to the Dearing Report and other documents such as the Treasury's *Report on Financing of High Technology Businesses: A Report to the Paymaster General* of November 1998.

The notion that practical benefit ought to be looked for from academic research was still being expressed in surprisingly unfocused terms as late as January 1998, in the minutes of evidence to the House of Commons Select Committee on Science and Technology in preparation for an earlier report (*First Report: The Implications of the Dearing Report for the Structure and Funding of University Research*). Question 500 asked about the 'importance of research to this country's competitiveness'. Baroness Blackstone's answer was vague and couched in terms of taking the long view: 'It will in the long term and in an indirect sense benefit the competitiveness of the UK.'[9]

By November 1998 the Treasury had concentrated its mind and produced its *Report on Financing of High Technology Businesses*. The report takes as its central assumption the idea that it is 'an apparent inadequacy of financing' which explains poor performance of the UK (especially in comparison with the USA) 'in the successful development of technology based businesses' (p. 15). It couples that with the belief that 'the natural functioning of the market' is not doing its job (p. 17). It is this natural functioning of the market whose impact has to be imported into universities in a newly purposeful manner, with a speeding and heightening of the consequential change.

There was by now a sharp focus on the importance of the academic science research base, especially in the sciences, as a source of ideas and discoveries for businesses to exploit. There was a concomitant acknowledgement that the science base in universities was insufficiently interested in making this happen. The notion that it is the market which drives did not seem unacceptable to some commentators. Sir Peter Williams said in evidence to the House of Commons Select Committee that Oxford Instruments 'is very largely market driven rather than technology driven'.[10] Sir Alec Broers commented to the House of Commons Select Committee on Science and Technology on 1 February 1999: 'Larry Sansini or one of the others was saying the other day on some programme I saw that the most important thing is the market, then the technology, then you need some people to arrange the market' (Question 1141).

The Treasury report urged the change of culture we have been sketching.[11] It spoke of the need to 'build trust and credibility between entrepreneurs and every kind of investor' (p. 6). Alongside its (chiefly financial) reflections it set the presumption that 'attitudes to making money out of science . . . are beginning to change' and that 'attitudes to technology and commercialization need to catch up' (p. 12). At this stage the funding net was being cast widely. It was held that, in any case, more money was needed and that the leading question was therefore where it was to come from. There were proposals about bringing in institutional investors and charitable funding[12] as well as venture capital[13] and specific project-related business links with academe. There was a concern with the question whether tax incentives would be effective and if so what form they should take.

In 1999 the British government had various devices designed to encourage academe to pay for itself and cost less in public funds which were in line with this trend: the University Challenge Fund (government support for commercial development of an idea for the benefit of the UK), Centres of Enterprise, of which eight were in existence, with 28 bids at stage one, involving 55 institutions. There was a Reach Out Fund, to encourage links with industry. Smart Awards – inherited from previous government – were thought to be working well and continued. Spin-out companies, university consultancy companies, incubator units were seen as the way forward. This all sprang from the now quite well-established general government policy of encouraging a broadly based entrepreneurial culture in universities, and it gave advantage to ('privileged', to use the jargon) those academic scientists and universities willing to play along.

The clash of expectations

Commerce seeks clear aims and objectives, realistic projections of results and the delivery of what has been contracted for. Academic research does not always work that way, nor should it. It is arguable that in some contexts the imposition of a framework of this sort may damage the science, that the freedom to change course or timetable or comprehensively to redefine the project, is necessary to the integrity of the scientific endeavour, and produces, in the long term, the most valuable results. 'Of the thousand or so biotech centres in the US, virtually all were financed by venture capitalists and investors whose interest in research was to create a profitable business rather than to acquire knowledge for its own sake. There was little sympathy for the usually long and always unpredictable timescale required for innovative discoveries.'[14]

Investors look for returns; governments look for benefits to the economy in the lifetime of the government, and to save spending public funds if the money can be obtained from other sources. Both governments and commercial investors are natural short-termists. The conflict of expectations with the longer-term and more open-ended academic approach was disastrous in the case of British Biotech. There was reference in that inquiry to the 'inherent difficulties for small drug discovery companies in conducting the full series of pre-clinical and clinical trials which is necessary before a drug can be brought to market without the financial and scientific backing of a larger partner'.[15] 'Concerns have . . . been raised about a possible conflict between the needs of investors for regular progress reports on drug development and the regulatory prohibitions against promotion of drugs before they are licensed.'[16] These inherent conflicts of expectations are still under no consistent regulation protecting the integrity of the science; there exist no nationally or internationally accepted guidelines to assist scientists whose work is caught up in such conflicts.

The creation of new and unregulated intimacies

'One of the most valued and enduring achievements of Foresight [no longer merely Technology Foresight] has been the creation of new networks of people drawn from sectors in business, academia, and Government that would not normally have entered into dialogue.'[17] In a 'Post-Fordist' commercial world where the old-fashioned production line is no longer the normative forum of industrial endeavour, this kind of 'networking' has a much greater power to influence things.

A new company is likely to be, at least at first, a very small company, and small companies have been held to be at a disadvantage financially. There was some unclearness about this at the stage when the House of Commons Select Committee was discussing the usefulness of tax incentives: 'On the one hand you are saying that for the small companies which are emerging from the universities and other sources like your own, like [Oxford Instruments], the fiscal stimuli do have an effect and they are critical in setting a climate. But for the GECs and the ICIs and the Zenecas, where people who have an idea may have an equally difficult job getting board approval . . . it does not work there.'[18] Little headway was made in this evidence session in resolving this seeming contradiction. Identifying it does not appear to have led to the putting in hand of work to resolve it, or any systematic further government reflection on these difficulties at all.

Considerations affecting size include the difference between projects requiring mainly thought and projects needing huge investment, such as

'British Aerospace . . . making a prototype essentially through Government help in that expensive phase'. Sir Alec Broers took the view in his evidence to the Select Committee that the large company may be helpful to the growth of the small. We must, he says, 'recognise the essential role that large companies play in nurturing small companies'.[19] Broers explained in his evidence on 1 February (in reply to Question 1131) that 'my attention is spent on making sure that we are working with BP and Unilever and with Microsoft and others'. He was interested in ensuring that these big companies were involved, because he took them to be the place where the 'leading players' were to be found. 'The small spin-out companies should be there but they have to be able to work with the big companies if they are to grow and bear fruit' (Questions 1136–7). Yet no big company is likely to assist the growth of a small rival company out of the kindness of its corporate heart, and the networks of 'working with' can easily also be networks of control, in which the big run the small. Moreover, the basic philosophy of this 'Big Daddy' approach proved to be unsound with the crash of Marconi in July 2001 and the catastrophic market slide of Vodafone and the imperilment of Microsoft's monopoly in litigation in the USA. Big does not mean solid, secure, reliable in the world of the big corporations.

The urge to 'make links with industry' is one thing; forming relationships with these big corporations is another. It is different in kind, because of their sheer clout, their international, even global, reach, and their consequent capacity to set the goals and the ground-rules. The big corporations can be bullies. 'Oil spills in California, sugar in cereals, pesticide-caused cancer, well contamination with chemicals, toxic organics in plastic manufacture, revision of the hit rate of Patriot missiles in the Gulf War are all cases where university researchers were penalized directly or where universities were threatened with the withdrawal of research funding if academics "did not toe the line".'[20]

Public feeling may well not be 'with' the big corporations, but that does not mean the government will discourage their activities. The *Daily Telegraph* of 13 January 2001 carried the story of a resentful community in Newbury in Berkshire where Vodafone has office buildings. 'Vodafone think they own the town . . . They've got their own buses, which seem to take priority over the public buses. They think they're the bee's knees. But Newbury existed before Vodafone and it'll still be there when they're gone.' To enter an arrangement of financial dependency with one of these giants is to create an unequal situation in which a university – even a government – may become unable to pull out, or unwilling to be seen to pull out, if it discovers implications it does not like.

Conflicts of interest automatically arise through the multiple reduplications of the figures from the big corporations on the committees controlling funds for academic research with the government's blessing.[21] The big corporations have now got significant representation on research councils, the statutory funding bodies which disburse public money for project research. Indeed, it has been made a point of policy to assure 'the taxpayer that industrialists are present on the research grant dispensing agencies'.[22] The big corporations which give benefactions to enable chairs to be established can also ensure that a representative from the company is on the board of electors or appointment committee or the company's scientists sit on the steering group.[23] In Cambridge's *Newsletter* of April/May 2001, there was the news that Unilever, having funded the Unilever Centre for Molecular Informatics, 'will contribute the time of some of its scientists and, through the steering committee, will work with the University of Cambridge to guide the Centre's work'. There had been no consultation in the University about the implications. It can be extremely difficult to eradicate this kind of networked influence once it has thoroughly penetrated the system, or to get rid of an individual who is 'found out' in conflict of interest.

In the face of these obvious drawbacks to the recent thrusts of government policy, governments and their statutory funding bodies may brazen it out. In the Briefing of the Higher Education Funding Council for England (No. 23, 1999) a 'links with business' piece was splashed on the front page. Lord Sainsbury, Minister for Science, travelling on behalf of the Department of Trade and Industry in the hunt for academics with research ideas which had a potential to make money, was reported as saying 'partnership with business can reinforce the values of an institution, not undermine them'. Yet it is hard to see how that can be asserted with any confidence. 'You have industry come . . . and say look we recognise what is there and we are going to put some of our crack researchers in there and work with them' (Question 1144), said Broers to the Select Committee. Much depends on the preposition 'with', in deciding 'where control ultimately resides in these partnerships'.

The Innovation–Exploitation Barrier, as early as 1996–97,[24] lists sources of finance, including government schemes, business angels, private sector funds, corporate ventures, NESTA (National Endowment for Science, Technology and the Arts),[25] and industry-specific initiatives.[26] It is not realistic to expect all these funders to keep their distance when it is government policy to encourage them to enter the university, to seek to change its culture, to grow symbiotic with it, and become cosily intimate with it in numerous ways, and when there is no provision to prevent this blurring the edges of a university's sense of its purpose and its boundaries. Universities have hitherto understood their purpose in terms which have not encouraged technology transfer. 'Universities are funded to provide education to students and to undertake research; they are not directly funded to undertake technology transfer.'[27] Now they are.

Venture capitalists want returns. They may also therefore want control of the developments they fund. 'When hi-tech companies are first launched it is often with the assistance of venture capitalists who place specialists on the board as non-executive directors.'[28] Cambridge's Vice-Chancellor conceded in evidence to the Science and Technology Select Committee on 1 February 1999 that 'most of the venture capital funders will always tell you they are actually headhunters and that is all they really look at' (Question 1138).

Venture capitalists may also want change to suit their own purposes. Herman Hauser, who has appeared on platforms with Cambridge's Vice-Chancellor, is a venture capitalist who, according to a piece in the *Guardian*, 'sees Cambridge's future in the image of Silicon Valley'.

Take your partners

A number of concepts and practices have now begun to cluster together in the area of commercial and even charitable funding of universities. The benefactors of previous centuries frequently wanted something for their money, but it was usually only the attachment of their names to a project and the hope of reward in heaven. The bids are now higher, at least in a secular sense, in that sufficiently large sums may be on offer almost to 'buy' a university. That is not an overstatement on some American campuses, where a big corporation has acquired a monopoly of patronage. The 'cola wars' in which the soft-drinks giants bid for sole franchises of campuses are a minor manifestation of the same kind of thing. America's universities have had earlier experience than those of the UK of the dangers of getting into beds with industry, and in particular with big corporations. As early as 1991 it was possible to take stock of the drawbacks on that side of the Atlantic. Irwin Feller summed it up for the Royal Society in 1991: 'The university is converted into a market-driven institution where fields of knowledge are supported in terms of perceived social utility, defined at a point in time by the expected profitability of those firms . . . willing to enter into research contracts.'[29] British universities failed to take note in any systematic way. The lure of the money and the goad of government has been leading to the piecemeal formation of innumerable individual 'arrangements', in which the university has been, more often than not, in danger of becoming the innocent dupe.

In principle, a sum of money could be given free of all further obligations, with the benefactor anxious to conceal even his name. From there stretches a spectrum of possibilities to the other extreme, where the 'benefactor' is in fact seeking to 'buy' specific 'results' of a research project. To this familiar 'linear' dimension of control must be added the third dimension of active formation of 'partnerships' between universities and funders which is relatively new to the UK. Partnerships raise immense difficulties of principle, since a university is a charity and not a business and is constrained both legally and morally by different presumptions. 'Major corporations are looking for strategic alliances with a very small number of globally significant universities . . . Companies tend to be particularly interested in recruiting and retaining Cambridge's best students, in collaborative research and in executive development.'[30]

The purpose of a university can still be stated thus: 'The University, through its research activity, seeks to promote the advancement, preservation, and dissemination of knowledge; the instruction of undergraduate, graduate and postdoctoral students; and the advancement of the public interest.'[31] Nevertheless, the new code containing this assertion continues with an acceptance that an extension into commerce is now unavoidable and it presents it as a good thing for the university and the world: 'The University considers that the establishment of links between its employees and outside bodies, whether government departments, commerce, industry, or others, is not only in the public interest but also benefits the University and the individuals concerned.'[32]

This vocabulary of 'links' is at present imprecise and requires a definition or definitions which will preserve a clear boundary between a university and an 'outside' interest. The word 'partnership' occurs in *The Innovation–Exploitation Barrier*,[33] but the thinking through of the implications has not kept pace with the rush to create such links and partnerships in practice. Yet this kind of thing potentially affects the autonomy of universities, making it unclear where the university ends and the world of commerce begins, and thus in practice taking away by stealth their right to govern themselves. This is, in essence, potentially an undermining of the identity of a university which may seriously compromise its purpose. 'A university is not a business,' said Sir Michael Davies, acting on behalf of the Queen as Visitor in his report on the Swansea affair in 1994.[34] That is becoming progressively less clear as universities and industry enter into intimate relationships on industry's terms.

Universities are also charities and receive tax benefits which go with their charitable status. The principles that charities must not make profits which are not applied to their purposes, that commercial interests may not make use of charitable premises or facilities for trading, that those entrusted with the administration of charities must ensure that all that they do serves the purposes for which the charity was created, can be got round in a number of ways. There is a good deal of 'laundering' of activities through the creation of mechanisms which appear to distance the university as charity from the spin-out company which is starting up in its publicity-funded laboratory. For this reason too, there needs to be a clarification of the boundaries of the university and those aspects of its work over which it retains control when it enters into commercial ventures or allows its employees to do so.

Here we touch on the mirror-image of the idea that universities ought to be taking their staff and students into business. Mr Thompson of Strathclyde University commented to the House of Commons Select Committee on Science and Technology in January 1999, as a representative of the community of university industrial liaison officers, that such officers 'felt it was important that our academic staff should have contact and experience of the so-called outside world, the commercial world'.[35] The cultural differences have been perceived to go deep.[36] And it has been argued that industrialists coming into universities may be better able to import their culture there than academics to take theirs out. (Sir Alec Broers commented in evidence that industrial scientists going into universities 'are very powerful because they have understood the world of industry and they can get their research groups working in that philosophy' (Question 1145).[37]) But going ahead with the marriage before the partners get acquainted is likely to work better within an established system of arranged marriages with rules that are understood, than as a social experiment.[38]

One urgent practical question illustrating the need to think through the rules before entering the arrangement, has been how far a university may legitimately bring a commercial venture on to its premises, allowing the industrial use of infrastructure facilities (especially if they are provided out of public money). A testing area here is the common sequence or cluster of science park, incubator unit, embedded laboratory. 'We are still trying to pioneer this embedded laboratory,'[39] said Cambridge's Vice-Chancellor to the Science and Technology Committee. Mr Thompson of Strathclyde University was ahead of him in his description of the evolution of a structure. He set out a series of graded options or stages by which industry moves right inside a university. The first is the science park. The second is an 'incubator unit on campus'. (In his own experience such a unit can hatch 30 companies at a time.) 'We now want incubation in amongst the university laboratories as the first step,' he suggested.[40] That means a 'use of shared facilities',[41] with all the attendant problems of determining a university's liability under health and safety legislation, of the risk of loss of charitable status, of conflict of interest, of disputes about ownership of intellectual property.

Then there is the use of the salaried time of academics. The basis on which a would-be entrepreneur can take a few days a week off from a 'full-time' university post to start up and continue a business remains uncertain. An article in the *Times Higher Education Supplement* of 17 December 1999 described an expensive dispute at the University of Nottingham, which eventually led to a landmark case. The scientist Simon Fishel earned a great deal of money as a consultant while in the university's employ and thus on its time, and the University wanted it back. He ran the Nurture fertility clinic at the University and worked with the IVF team which produced the first test-tube baby in the world. That generated a good deal of income for the University. But he also worked abroad as a consultant, where he had freedom to 'research new techniques that were forbidden in the UK by the Human Fertility and Embryology Authority'. He said this was public knowledge and that his departmental head knew of it. The University said the work was unauthorized and that in any case it owned the intellectual property rights in its employees' work. It sued him. Yet in Cambridge, the University appears to have a different view of this kind of situation. For instance, Richard Friend continued as a full-time professor while running Cambridge Display Technology as a business.

'Little' local links and 'minor' partnerships

Partnerships and links can also be formed between corporations and individual departments.[42] This may be different not only in scale but also in its potential to affect the identity of a university; yet it can still create considerable awkwardness if the partnership breaks down and there ensues a dispute about who is to have the use of the bench-space: a replacement outside partner bringing in money, or the university's own scientists.

There is also the type of 'local' partnership just referred to, in which the leading academic scientist is also a director of the company. Academics are not always clear where their fiduciary duty lies, and universities may be slow to make provision to give them adequate help.[43] (A scientist receiving funding from a venture capitalist or a charity or from big business may find himself in a complex employment situation, since the university may not be the sole employer and the other employer may have his own views on who is the primary employer and entitled to make the rules.) The holding of executive directorships should require express approval from the university and then there is no danger of confusion. Setting out clearly in published rules the steps that academics have to follow to protect both their own and the university's interest when they become involved in bargains with funders is sensible, but not all research-active universities have done it. The rules should cover conflicts of interest created by such situations as 'the use of the University's research or administrative facilities to pursue personal business, commercial, or consulting activities'; 'any attempt to restrict rights governing the timing and content of publications, save in circumstances properly approved by the University to protect privacy, commercially sensitive proprietary information, and patentable inventions'; 'involvement in externally funded activity which might infringe the right of a student engaged in the activity to complete the degree for which he or she is registered and/or to publish freely his or her findings'; 'a personal involvement in any company or commercial enterprise which is in a contractual relationship with the University' (or in process of negotiating such a contract) 'where the employee has been concerned or connected with the placing or negotiation of the contract in question or with the research or other activity which the contract might cover'.[44]

There is of course no guarantee that codes of practice will be adhered to. For example, a university keen to benefit might give its 'express approval' to a liaison quite easily. But a code of practice is an essential preliminary protection.

The consequences for the continuing identity of the university of the entry of the 'real world'

Conflict of interest would disappear if the university and the business became one. But it cannot be possible (even if it were desirable) for the university to become one with a wide range of businesses which are certainly not one with one another, and are indeed likely to be rivals. Cambridge's Programme for Industry said on its web page in early 2001 that it was 'now an integral part of the University's lifelong learning provision' and that it 'pioneers closer links with business, industry and the professions'. It was claimed that it 'draws on the rich expertise and scholarship of the University of Cambridge, and mobilizes thought from the best minds and institutions globally', that it 'operates beyond the boundaries of any particular department or subject area, allowing it to respond flexibly to its clients' needs'. This public statement potentially compromises the identity of that particular university in several ways. It may not be clear where in all this the University was acting as a degree-awarding institution, which parts of the activity are 'teaching' and which research, where the University ends and all these industrial 'partners' begin. Spokespeople for this kind of 'barnacle' on the 'hull' of the university can be remarkably unclear in their own minds when asked to comment. Supervision of what goes on a university's web page in its name is also important.

There can be an alarming degree of confusion even in a highly research-active university about the exact relationship between its commercial and its academic activities and its very identity as a university, especially where individual senior officers involve themselves to a degree which may cause some confusion as to whether they are acting 'as' the university or on its behalf or personally. 'Cambridge high tech companies . . . have university origins at some remove,' stated the University's memorandum to the House of Commons Select Committee on Science and Technology for the hearing of 1 February 1999.[45]

Speaking in evidence, the Vice-Chancellor explained that 'the Cambridge Network started with a group of about four or five of us; it now has a board of about 20 or 30'. There was some uncertainty whether the Vice-Chancellor's own involvement in this Network as chairman was deemed to be official or personal.[46] The University thought it personal; the network believed he was chair in his capacity as Vice-Chancellor. He told a House of Commons Select Committee, 'I have been acting in a private capacity in trying to see some of the negative planning decisions around Cambridge reconsidered . . . We have been working with the Government and the one in Hinxton is being reconsidered.'[47] The move from 'I' to 'we' must throw that 'private' into question and again there is the obvious danger that such inadvertent 'seeming improprieties' will be avoided only with the utmost vigilance, extending as they must far beyond the confines of the more straightforward areas of financial conflict of interest identified by the Committee on Standards in Public Life.[48] For our present purposes, the point is that when these issues of identity are fudged, a Vice-Chancellor can be seen to 'be' the university.

The guardians compromised

As in the case of direct government funding, there needs to be realism about the wish for control which comes with money from benefactions from non-public sources, whether from charitable foundations or from industry.

A truly disinterested benefactor might give money to be used entirely at the discretion of a university for purely academic purposes and would not wish even to have a name linked with the gift. But at the other extreme, such a sponsored professorship as 'The Margaret Thatcher Chair of Enterprise Studies' could easily be perceived as a safe billet for a professor of Thatcherite persuasions, unless robust protections were put in place. The difficulty is to nerve the arms of those who ought to be guardians of integrity (and give them adequate understanding of the issues) so that universities are not a 'pushover' for the interests of their new funders.

In Germany, the Frauhoffer Institutes provide 'an intermediate institution half-way between the academic world and the companies that are attracting work into them'. But evidence from the Association of Industrial Liaison Officers has indicated a preference for a direct interface between academe and industry, and where that is the model no intermediary exists to act as a watchdog of the university's faithfulness to its purpose.[49] It may be essential to place some distancing mechanism, or some person or body to act as guardian, between universities and their industrial spin-outs in the UK too, if they are not to compromise their identity and with it the very integrity of their scientific work. Research-active universities now commonly have such industrial liaison officers. It was commented in evidence to the Select Committee that 'the industrial liaison function' can be that of 'a policeman of the affairs of the institution'.[50] But a policeman who is not allowed into the inner councils cannot be effective, and industrial liaison officers are not necessarily invited into the central structures of governance of a university.[51]

The American lead

America has been ahead of the UK in making a shift of emphasis from the 'negative' concern *to protect against research misconduct* to a 'positive' concern *with the protection of research integrity*. As early as 1981 there were congressional hearings on fraud in biomedical research, with a second round of congressional hearings in 1985. The National Science Foundation and the Office of Scientific Integrity both produced definitions in 1986. By 1990 there was a training requirement, that each university train a proportion of its researchers as a condition of the receipt of public funds. In 1991 there was a public advisory committee on research integrity. There followed during the 1990s a series of reports and revisions of the definitions and the creation of Office of Science and Technology Policy National Standards. All this was embedded in the committee structure of government in the work of committees concerned with public funding of scientific and academic research.[52]

The important conceptual difference which has been emerging in the USA, but which is still missing in UK thinking at the public and political level, is between the inspection of conduct (the outward indicators of integrity in scientific research), and the inculcation of an inner integrity which discourages fraud and loose research practices alike. This constitutes a move from policing to education. Greater vigilance by journal editors also involves policing, for them; for professional societies, for those encouraging training in responsible conduct of research the task is also to educate the scientist in the ethics of research, of 'internalizing' the rules.

There has been resistance in the USA, as in the UK, to government regulation and to accepting the 'burdens' it can impose. But the breeding of internal 'regulators' in the consciences of scientists is not, of its nature, a concession to allowing government interference with the work of scientists. On the contrary, it may in the end make such interference less necessary. UK universities have done little as yet to create codes of ethics for their scientists or themselves, still less to agree such codes nationally. If they did, they would help the individual scientist by giving him something to consult when his conscience is uneasy or to point out when he wants authority to resist pressure to act against conscience.

The advisory committees

In the evidence given to the House of Commons Committee on Science and Technology in the genetically modified food inquiry, the Rowett Research Institute, Aberdeen, made two important points in response to the question on the role and framework of advisory committees. Advisory committees ought to be the appropriate bodies to keep an eye on scientific good conduct. The Institute's first point concerned the comparative passivity of role of such committees: 'The UK and EU Committees tend traditionally to be in responsive mode' in that 'they answer the specific questions put to them by Ministers . . . The system could . . . benefit from the clear acceptance that committees should be able to propose areas for further analyses.' Secondly, the Rowett Institute pointed to their slowness, to the need for flexibility, for devising a system which can 'respond to rapid scientific developments'.[53]

Even where there are protective devices, it is not easy to ensure that they work. Watchdogs may snooze on the hearthrug rather than using their teeth. In evidence before the First Report of the House of Commons Science and Technology Committee, Sir John Cadogan was asked what had become of the proposal that there would be a 'standing group of independent experts' from whom the research councils might take advice. He explained that a sensible practical point of resort had not been set up because there had come to be 'enormous pyramids of advice'. He was reassuring that 'Nolan principles now apply': advertisement, selection committees, making sure that there is the right balance and so on.[54] But as any academic scientist knows, peer review militates against independence, for those on the selection committees are likely to favour those whose work is for some reason approved, and patronage tends to rule. Any specialism is a small world of people who know one another well. Selection committees are always likely to choose 'their own'. So a standing group of 'independent experts' (could such be found) would indeed have been a valuable corrective to the natural tendency to think that there is quite enough 'advice' in the system.

That kind of smugness and lack of real requirement of independence applies, too, to the generation of names, even where there is in principle advertisement and an opportunity to apply for places on a committee. Mrs Helen Millar spoke with feeling about her own appointment to committee in her evidence to the inquiry into genetically modified foods: 'As I understand it, the committee decided they wanted a consumer representative . . . They were asked to nominate people and that is how I got there. Not a very open process . . . I would hope if the committee is restructured there would be more open advertising and a proper selection process. I have to say I just got a letter.'[55]

The journals

In *Index on Censorship*, a series of articles described the danger that 'editors who will stand up to Governments will crumble if commercial funders pressurize them'.[56] The story of bovine somatotrophin marketed by Monsanto 'contains the standard list of conflicts of interest, regulatory manipulation and back-door lobbying that are the typical stuff of . . . corporate America'. Gregory Palast quotes D. Hard, asserting on behalf of Monsanto that 'as the raw data are confidential, all subsequent analyses are as well'. Thus 'a corporation had not only claimed control over data of commercial value, but also successfully asserted control over opinions about the data', so that 'no researcher can effectively challenge Monsanto without its approval'.[57] That type of broad ban in a commercial sponsor's interest is a salutary reminder that the physical 'campus' with which we are primarily concerned in this chapter is not the only academic 'environment', but extends to the wider world serviced by the academic journals.

It is now widely acknowledged that many leading journals have been lax recently in ensuring that those who write, review or respond to articles have made it plain whether they have a personal interest involving the source of the funding for the research, or whether they are in any sense 'in the pay' of commercial sponsors who may have an interest in particular outcomes. That seems likely to change, now that there is a clearer recognition that this has been happening, as was admitted by, for example, the prestigious *New England Journal of Medicine*. Richard Smith, editor of the *British Medical Journal*, resigned his connection with Nottingham University in the spring of 2001 over the acceptance of 'tobacco money' from British American Tobacco.

The need for special vigilance on the part of senior office-holders

The higher the level of office held in the university itself, the more difficult it is for the holder to act without appearing to be doing so on behalf of the university in the ways we have already touched on and the more potentially damaging is conflict of interest. In the evidence given in February 1999 to the House of Commons Select Committee on Science and Technology by the Vice-Chancellor of the University of Cambridge and Cambridge's Regius Professor of Physic, Sir Keith Peters, there were several indicators that this sort of thing could happen. Sir Keith said: 'I have a certain amount of industrial connection through work on scientific advisory boards of pharmaceutical and healthcare companies and I am chairman of the Scientific Advisory Board of an important Cambridge biotech company, Cam.' Alec Broers was quite open that Sir Alastair Morton had been 'brought . . . on board' in University affairs because 'I was on the board of a company with him'. Broers did not quarrel with the description (Question 1124) of Cambridge University Technical Services Ltd as 'your company'. He said that 'that is a separate organisation which can act as an independent corporation . . . I am not terribly familiar with the details of the operation of that company, I would have to turn to my Treasurer.' These links were thus visibly under no regulation, controlled by no guidelines of propriety and their character apparently in large measure unperceived by the Vice-Chancellor as accounting officer of the University. 'I am not the expert on the details of how we do that,' admitted Broers. 'There seems a lack of precision in your own mind about some of these activities,' commented one of the Committee (Question 1131). These indications that there were areas of legitimate concern were never followed up and no greater 'precision' resulted from their warning remark.

It is reason for concern that an individual may be seen to speak for a university or have huge power to deploy the resources of a university, when he has to admit when pressed to explain what he understands about the constitutional and legal framework within which his university is to engage with industry: 'I would really back off here. I am a technologist. I understand where modern technology comes from . . . I work with Herman Hauser a lot and David Cleevely but I do not know about their game really. I have always been in big organisations so I am not good at that sort of stuff.'

Openness

Universities need not only codes and instruction in the implications of those codes, but also a willingness to be open in their implementation, for otherwise there is (on present showing) no way of seeing whether the will to put things right has gone beyond the mere creation of the code. 'Our group frequently raised regulatory concerns,' commented the Treasury's *Report on the Financing of High Technology Businesses* (p. 27), but their reading of the reasons was that 'the culture of the institutions and professions has been too slow to adapt' (p. 28). The select committee looking at genetically modified foods heard even from Monsanto a recognition of 'the importance of well drawn up and administered regulation' and an insistence that where there is direct negotiation with ministers or civil servants, 'all our meetings are a matter of public record' and 'there is nothing secret about them'.[58] Without an appropriate degree of openness about what is going on, potentially world-leader projects can come down with a bump in an embarrassing tangle of broken promises, debt, accidental improprieties and scientific discredit.

There are indications that the regime is not going to be capable of policing itself without hard work on the issues touched on in this chapter. There is an obvious need for the framing of regulatory provisions, guide-lines, codes of practice, for strong and effective accountability structures, to protect universities which become involved in this kind of project. There is an equal need for a will to enforce them, for policing of their enforcement and for accountability if they are not enforced. Whether there is the potential will is another matter.

'Whistling': raising a concern

It is important to distinguish between the raising of the concern that some-thing is wrong and a straightforward expression of critical or dissenting opinion. Strictly, the whistleblower does the former. But the academic critic may frequently be engaged in an exercise with some of the features of both. Dr Anthony Agathangelou became concerned in 1997–98 about the academic value and rigour of a research project on which he was employed (in a senior position, but on a short-term contract), by the University of Newcastle. The work involved testing in the field the viability of the intention under new family law legislation that couples seeking divorce should be required to seek counselling first. He realized that couples volunteering for such a study could not be typical and that the conclusions drawn might not reflect the needs of, for example, battered wives. He tried to raise his concern with the University. It would not listen. He then sought to raise it with the funder, the Lord Chancellor's Office. The University confronted him with discipline charges, among them breach of confidentiality, and although the breach of confidentiality charge was not upheld by the disciplinary hearing, he was in the end dismissed on other counts, allegations brought only after he had raised his concern. The *Times Higher Education Supplement*, the *Sunday Times* and the *Spectator* all carried the story.

At the time, the Public Interest Disclosure Act 1998 was not in force. This Act amended the Employment Rights Act 1996 to provide protection for employees who disclosed malpractice.[59] 'Worker', for the purposes of the Act, included some categories of the self-employed, such as NHS doctors. The protection extended to workers of less than two years' standing, who would not at that date normally have been able to claim unfair dismissal.

The worker claiming protection under the Act has to have made a 'protected' disclosure. The types of disclosure which qualify for 'protection' are disclosures of information which, in the reasonable belief of the worker making the disclosure, tend to show:

1. that a crime has been, is being or is likely to be committed, or
2. that there has been, is or is likely to be a breach of legal obligation, or
3. that a miscarriage of justice has occurred, is occurring or is likely to occur, or
4. that the health or safety of a person has been, is being or is likely to be endangered, or
5. that the environment has been, is being or is likely to be damaged, or
6. that the information tending to show any of these matters is being or is likely to be deliberately concealed.

There is no time limit – the matter disclosed may have happened in the past, be happening at present or be likely to happen in the future.[60]

The disclosure must have been made in good faith. The worker must show that he has a reasonable belief that the information he discloses was substantially true and that he has no purpose of personal (usually financial) gain, and that in all the circumstances of the case it is reasonable for him to make the disclosure. The last is particularly important because disclosure might well harm the employer's reputation and thus amount to a breach of trust on the part of the employees. (To rush to 'expose' something without allowing time for amendment of what had perhaps only been a slip, might be held to be unreasonable.)

These categories and criteria do not 'fit' the university scene as closely as they might. For example, students are unprotected, unless a university chooses to include them in its code, though the Committee of Vice-Chancellors and Principals (CVCP) expected it would. And confidentiality and intellectual property rights, though strictly the relationship of a university and its employees, may, as in any other employment, be affected by the rights of academic freedom of speech.

The Public Interest Disclosure Act 1998 prescribes the manner of disclosure if there is to be protection of the person making it, and here, too, there are questions about the degree to which the university resembles the 'real world' in which most employees work. The disclosure ought first to be made internally to the employer. Agathangelou would have benefited, as would others nervous of taking the plunge to disclosure, from a notion floated in Australia. Australia saw the value of a Public Interest Disclosure Agency, a safe place to try out a concern where it is not counted as having been 'raised',[61] for the difficulty with imposing a duty to begin inside the institution is that it is a rare institution which will frankly examine its own conduct. This is analogous with the need for an independent buffer on the funding front.

Disclosure to a prescribed regulatory person or body is envisaged as the appropriate first step towards external disclosure. In the case of universities, that would seem to include the Higher Education Funding Councils, the Quality Assurance Agency, the research councils, as well as the National Audit Office and the Public Accounts Committee, the Secretary of State and the relevant department of the civil service. Not all have powers to act.

It remains a not infrequent matter of dispute whether governing bodies and boards of governors count as 'external' (what about a trade union?).[62] In *Re A Company's Application* (1989) IRLR 477, the High Court refused to grant an injunction preventing an employee in the financial services sector from disclosing confidential information about his company to a regulatory body. Attempts have been made to suggest that a whistleblower may legitimately be disciplined for going to such a body but that cannot be in the public interest. The disclosure is thus expected to be made 'up a ladder' from internal to external, and to take in any prescribed regulatory body before there is any leakage to the media. External disclosure (for example to the press) may become appropriate if the internal or regulatory authority to whom disclosure is made does not take the action which might reasonably have been expected. The worker may also make external disclosure if it is reasonable for him to believe that he will be victimized if he makes the disclosure internally, or that there will be a cover-up. This is a very likely scenario. Repeating patterns of cock-up, cover-up, corruption; and delay, denial, dividing, discrediting, dismissal, are regularly reported in universities.

To whom is the duty of loyalty owed? Only to the university as employer? To the academic community? To a funder? To society? What is to be done if there is more than one employer and their interests conflict?[63] There are potentially conflicting duties here for the academic, beyond the potential conflicts of fiduciary duty which could arise from his being the employee of both a university and a company. They include duties to maintain professional standards, to protect freedom of speech, especially academic freedom of speech, to foster the advancement of knowledge. There are balancing acts to be carried out in all directions. If contracts include terms which prohibit disclosure of information acquired during employment, and if codes requiring reporting of wrongdoing are voluntary, the contract is stronger than the code.[64] On the other hand, it appears that an employee would have no contractual duty to 'tell' on himself. 'A contract of employment is not one of utmost good faith and employees have no general duty to reveal their own misconduct.'[65]

To impose a statutory duty to disclose would be unfair as long as employees can suffer retaliation.[66] The old tenure enjoyed by the academic staff of a university before the Education Reform Act 1988 was a strong protector of freedom of speech, but it is now enjoyed by only a relatively small category of academic staff, for short- and fixed-term contracts automatically curb the whistleblower.[67] Furthermore, employees may be 'exposed' to all kinds of action short of dismissal.

The presumption of the Public Interest Disclosure Act 1988 is that the burden is on the whistleblower to show that the disclosure was lawful. He does not have a presumed 'right to disclose unless good cause is shown why he should not'. Nevertheless, a category of employees has a duty to report unacceptable behaviour as part of the discharge of their duties. That would apply to internal auditors, for example. Some employees have professional codes of conduct which may go against their job description (nurses, public service accountants).[68] The Civil Service Management Code provides that if a civil servant considers that he or she is being asked to act in a manner which appears to him or her to be improper, unethical or in breach of constitutional conventions, or to involve possible maladministration, or to be 'otherwise inconsistent with the standards of conduct prescribed in this memorandum and in the relevant Civil Service codes and guides', something should be said.[69] On the other hand, there is no provision for *external* reporting in the civil service system. The matter has to be reported to a senior officer and, if appropriate, to the Permanent Head of the Department. There is a built-in assumption that managers are willing to deal with such reports fearlessly and are capable of doing so justly, which is not borne out by experience; and why should it be expected to be otherwise when it is human to protect oneself, and the manager will not wish to offend powerful colleagues?[70]

The core problem is that it remains a highly risky matter to go to an employer with a concern, even in the theoretically 'free speech environment' of a university. The employer may not only make life extremely unpleasant for the whistleblower, but also rule what he has brought up 'vexatious' so as to avoid doing anything about it. The whistleblower then suffers reprisal and no good comes of his courageous stand. It is easy to see that a small matter might not be thought to justify the use of powerful machinery, or that someone who persists in raising again and again a complaint which has genuinely been dealt with, might reasonably be rated a vexatious complainant. But it is not so clear when the vexatiousness might consist in a mistimed complaint about a real problem which will grow if not attended to. How bad are things allowed to get before the need to call to account overrides other considerations, such as this one of giving administrators time to correct mistakes when they have been pointed out to them? There have been lapses in the internal communications of Whitehall, with the result that at certain crucial times officials dealing with aspects of the affair 'were unaware of relevant information in the hands of their colleagues elsewhere in the government machine,' says Sir Douglas Wass, describing the events depicted in the Scott Report. 'There were misjudgements, for instance, in the failure to inform ministers of particular developments, and to allow a businessman seconded to the civil service to represent his private employer on a business mission to Iraq during his secondment. There were minor abuses of statutory powers, for instance over the employment of powers of inspection for VAT purposes to elicit information about suspected illegal imports. The catalogue of specific criticisms is indeed a formidable one, and to itemise them all would convey an impression of a civil service that is inefficient, rather casual and unprofessional and badly in need of reform and overhaul, if not reeducation.'[71]

Wass's point is that allowances have to be made: 'Anyone who has been involved in the sort of multidimensional operations described in the Scott report knows that administrative structures do not always operate in complex situations in the way that the rule-book requires.'[72] Sir Douglas observed that he had himself been required, before a tribunal of inquiry appointed to investigate the Crown agents in the 1970s, 'to justify my choice of words in minutes I had dictated under great stress and pressure in the interstices of meetings six years previously. These minutes were subjected to a textual analysis that they simply could not bear.'[73] There is also the factor of having too many things to do, to allow for sustained reflection upon any one of them.[74]

That is forgivable, up to a point. But it may be less forgivable when it becomes plain that the structures are not adequate for the purposes they have to serve and when nothing is done about that; when there is not some reflection upon what has happened and a good will to see where mistakes have been made and to put them right. The scandal described in the CAPSA report on Cambridge's waste of £10m on a new accounting system (*Cambridge University Reporter*, November and December 2001) was shocking for precisely that reason. Systemic carelessness and arrogance were found to be making a mockery of the University's constitutional safeguards.

Codes of practice and the protection of the climate of expectation

How well do the provisions of the Public Interest Disclosure Act 1998 fit the academic scene and what, if any, special circumstances attend the raising of concerns by academics? If statute deems it to be in the public interest to protect academic freedom of speech so that academics may 'question and test received wisdom', there is a sense in which the academic who raises concerns in that spirit may be entitled to be regarded as something of a hero. However, the notion of whistleblower as hero is more natural to the USA than to UK expectations. The Federal False Claims Amendment Act 1986 in the USA provides for the rewarding of whistleblowers.[75] In the USA, employment law takes the relationship of employer and employee to be 'at will' and so the employee cannot claim unfair dismissal. That has encouraged a more robust attitude to the legislative protection, and even the rewarding, of those who blow the whistle in the public interest.

Nevertheless, even in the USA, the academic whistleblower 'hero' may well suffer substantial professional or other detriment. Three types of case are distinguished in a recent article.[76] In the first, a medical school departmental chairman alleged scientific misconduct against an associate professor in his department. There was eventually a full investigation and it was found that there had been fabrication, falsification of data and plagiarism. But the chairman himself suffered retaliation. A fresh investigation concluded that his reputation 'had been severely damaged by the action and inaction of institutional officials, that he had been forced to step down as department head, that he was relieved of committee and teaching responsibilities, that he was accused of criminal activities as well as character flaws, and that he was ostracised in his own department'. Most whistleblowers will recognize this profile of personal damage to reputation on themes irrelevant to the matter in hand.

In a case of the second type, an allegation was made, and it was found that further investigation was not warranted, though it was not found that he had been wrong to raise the question. But the whistleblower in this case, too, complained of reprisal.

In a case of a third type, allegations were made by a biostatistician who had been dismissed by the institution which conducted the research in question. Not only was it found that his accusations were groundless but 'evidence existed that some of the allegations may not have been made in good faith, that is, that the whistleblower knew that his allegations were false when he made them'.[77] He, if that is correct, is the kind of whistleblower the legislation is designed to discourage.

A particular concern in many prospective whistleblowers is whether the raiser of concerns can be sued for defamation. There is in the USA a conditional privilege to protect the whistleblower who acts in good faith against defamation suits.[78] It can be invoked where the 'defamatory' information which affects an important public interest is disclosed to a person authorized to take action; where it is disclosed to a person who shares a common interest in the subject-matter; where it is disclosed to protect the interest of the recipient or a third person; where information which affects an important interest of the one making the defamatory statement is disclosed to a person who can protect that interest.[79] It is not nearly so clear that that applies in the UK. At South Bank University in the spring of 1999 an attempt was made to get round the existing statutory protections of trade union activity by de-recognizing the National Association of Teachers in Further and Higher Education (NATFHE) just as the Fairness at Work proposals were published. The majority of members of the full-time academic staff were members of NATFHE, but the University did its numerical reckoning so as to include part-time and contract research staff, and announced that the union was not 'representative'. NATFHE conducted a ballot to establish the support of the staff for union recognition. But in advance of the ballot the University threatened the coordinating committee with libel action over a NATFHE leaflet arguing against changes to the contract of employment.

> There have been a number of recent cases where colleagues have failed to follow University policies and procedures . . . If you are in doubt about the validity or interpretation of a specific procedure or policy you should seek advice from your line manager in the first instance . . . Exceptions will be rare and should be . . . authorised by the relevant service. However in normal circumstances breaches will not be tolerated. Failure to follow University procedures, without proper authority, may in future lead to disciplinary action being taken against you.[80]

This letter from the Vice-Chancellor of Middlesex University appears to take the University's codes of practice seriously. But it seems that they are to be strictly enforced against only those staff who are relatively junior, for their seniors may 'authorize' exceptions and there does not appear to be provision for calling them to account. This is not atypical. The situation for academic staff remains unclear. So it is by no means certain that the protection of freedom of speech will extend in any clear way into the provisions of the Public Interest Disclosure Act 1998, to give academic staff either a special right or a special duty to disclose matters of concern.

Paradoxically, equally familiar is the tendency already noted for the university to be satisfied when it has created a code and not to be equally vigilant about its enforcement.

So what is a Public Interest Disclosure 'code' in a university for? Arguably, it ought to be a breeder of new attitudes, of a climate of expectation, as much as a prescriptive manual for correct behaviour. A main reason is that 'an approach based on purely legalistic interpretation can make the holders of information extremely cautious. They may take a restrictive line not because of the merits of a particular case, but because they fear a precedent which would be binding in other more sensitive situations.'[81] Because the system of administrative law of the UK is weak, it is inadequate in its protections in comparison with that of other jurisdictions.[82] There is also the difficulty with the use of statute that when a matter goes to court, the party withholding the information will normally be more able to afford representation than the applicant, and the prospect of having to find the costs if they lose may deter ordinary academics.[83]

But at least statute secures the ground a little. What does not get as far as being formally enacted, at the stage when a government's ideals are running high, may become greatly emasculated by the time it finds its way on to the statute book. A clear example is the Freedom of Information Bill 1999, which backtracked substantially on the principles outlined in *Open Government*, most notably in closing down on the notion that the process of 'formation of policy' should be more visible, before becoming the Freedom of Information Act 2000.

Sir Douglas Wass pointed out that there is a long trail of evidence of reluctance to allow advice to see the light in British public life. 'The confidentiality of such "advice" has always been a datum of British public life.' All the ministers Scott interviewed (in the Scott inquiry on the arms for Iraq affair) took this line.[84] Civil servants appearing before select committees are instructed that 'the internal discussion and advice which has preceded Ministerial decisions should not be disclosed'.[85] What is being protected here? It is usually said to be frankness. It is uncontentious that it is necessary that there should be safe places to try out ideas in which there may reside some risk. But the same safe place may also be a place where things are covered up and where unfavoured options may be hidden away and where the very existence of certain papers may be disguised, for it is easier to get a policy accepted if the exceptions to it are not available for inspection or consideration. 'Whitehall was grudging about the supply of information to the public about its activities, regarding this as an objective quite subordinate to that of the successful implementation of policy.'[86] 'There was a lack of appreciation, when the Government was involved in legal action against the citizen, as it was in several of the cases Scott investigated, that the public interest requiring absolute fairness towards him must be given its due weight against the public interest of securing the policy objectives of the department, whether this involves the protection of sensitive information or indeed the protection of the policy itself.'[87]

Sir Douglas had long argued that those affected by a policy are too easily disregarded, when those trying to get a policy through 'focus their objectives very tightly' and seek 'to secure those objectives to the exclusion of most other considerations'. Civil servants are given the instruction that when they appear before select committees they 'should as far as possible avoid being drawn into discussion of the merits of alternative policies where this is politically contentious'.[88] It is argued in *Open Government* that the 'whistleblower' defence 'should not be necessary if internal review procedures provide effective ventilation of matters of conscience'.[89]

A culture change needs to inform the operation of a code so as to lift the process above a level which can otherwise become mechanistic. Mechanisms are needed for protection when the spirit in which things are done is not right. There is a hierarchy of delegated legislation, sub-delegated legislation and unsanctioned administrative rules, of which eight modes have been identified: procedural rules (mandatory or discretionary); interpretative guidelines; instructions to officials; prescriptive rules; commendatory rules; voluntary codes; operational rules; administrative pronouncements.[90] It has been suggested that these have valuable features, in that they can 'routinise the exercise of complex discretions' which will 'encourage consistency' and enable officials 'to operate at levels of specialisation or complexity that are high considering their training'.[91] Bureaucrats like codes, because they 'inexpensively and swiftly routinize the exercise of discretion'.[92] They are less at ease with the creative problem-solving possible through alternative dispute resolution. They are not given to owning up quickly when mistakes are made, so that problems need not escalate.

Nevertheless, badly formulated rules may be over-inclusive or under-inclusive.[93] They can be transparent but so simple as to lack the necessary nuances or refinements.[94] And the 'regulatory ratchet' tends to add to regulation to the point where one may begin to speak of 'regulatory unreasonableness'.[95] That could well happen under the understanding evinced in Michael Driscoll's letter as Vice-Chancellor of Middlesex University that a rule is a rule, especially where there is little imagination in the implementation, or the rules themselves are not in evidence when a real case arises.

It is a rare senior figure who can take overt or implied criticism of what he has been doing, apologize for mistakes and put them right. Sir Richard Scott, reflecting on his experiences while conducting the Scott Inquiry, commented: 'I learned of the tenacity with which officialdom can strive to avoid publicity for manifest mis-management'.[96] 'Public institutions exist to serve the individual, not the other way about',[97] but in practice the 'individual' seeking to raise concerns about what is happening in a public body such as a university is likely to find himself blocked.

The effect on the individual researcher

Short-term, long-term: the scientific effects of insecurity

Two 'stories' are to be heard about the ways in which individual researchers are being affected by the trends we have been looking at, and the inadequacy of the protections against them. They are contradictory. On the one hand, it has been hinted that the Research Assessment Exercise (RAE) encourages university researchers 'to concentrate on carrying out further research in order to develop the knowledge base and publish the results. They may prefer to avoid the very substantial effort required to support patents and marketing of licence opportunities without a guarantee of return. It is by definition "high risk".'[98] In other words, it seemed only a few years ago that while the professional benefits of seeking industrial liaison remain uncertain, the ambitious will tend to put their effort principally into what they know will advance them professionally, and at the moment that means academic research of a broadly 'blue skies' type. The RAE is also perceived as a disincentive to collaboration.[99] The inference drawn from this assumption was that there should be a policy change in the allocation of public money for academic research. The research councils could be encouraged to reward 'academic researchers who have undertaken basic and strategic research funded by industry'.[100]

This was coupled with a strong push in the direction of giving academic career awards to those who followed this path in the direction of techno-logy transfer and the commercial exploitation of scientific discoveries. 'The Government is aware of concern that the system of incentives and rewards for academics engaging in technology transfer and exploitation is often confused and uncertain. The CBI's 'Tech Stars' report recommended that academic career progression should give more recognition to the commercial exploitation of research and collaboration with industry'.[101]

There is an ongoing debate here. An overarching cultural consideration is the (extremely ancient) assumption that theory is of higher dignity than practice, which led one witness to a select committee to seek recognition of 'the dignity of practical knowledge'.[102] Others were frank that: 'we have a culture in Britain which essentially says pure science for its own sake is good. The application of science is not viewed to have the same significance to our culture.'[103] The question of giving RAE weighting to 'utility of research' was mooted, to try to 'correct' this presumption. But in consultation a large majority in 1997–98 'stated that they did not wish there to be additional weighting given in the RAE for the utility of research'.[104] This balancing act (when a balance is achieved), will affect the choices made by individual researchers to concentrate on 'blue skies' or basic strategic research or on project research with industrial links.

On the other side stands all the evidence assembled in this study that the second 'story' is the correct one and that there is in fact already a considerable weighting *against* the preference for non-applicable and non-entrepreneurial research.

At present, there is what has been vividly described as 'a rapid turnover of researchers at the bench'. The short-term contract renewable scientist has become the norm. Indeed, one of the most intractable problems in university science is the proliferation of short-term contracts. These are in only a few cases 'for the benefit of the post-holder or because of the research requirements of the research funder'; more commonly they reflect the 'host institutions' inability to guarantee long-term funding for posts'.[105]

Despite the comments just rehearsed about the influence of the RAE in the opposite direction, it is clear that this is happening in conjunction with a cluster of other, related phenomena. The first is an increasing short-termism in the science itself. It tends to be done in 'funded episodes', rather than open-endedly, with a long-term plan. 'Now that the researcher dances to the tunes of many pipers, research topics lack continuity because the research which is effected is dependent on a series of grant applications or on which particular industrialist is prepared to pay for what specified piece of research.'[106]

This short-termism is coupled with a foreseeable effect on the choice of topic. There is a drift towards rewarding of 'compliance with expectations', coupled with a concentration on selective research lines, an 'increased tendency to choose research topics which are easy and yield results which can be neatly presented in a report or thesis. [And] it is normally designed to conform to the dominant paradigm rather than to challenge it and establish an alternative view of the world.'[107]

The long-term academic career scientist is now a comparatively rare animal. Promotions criteria for scientists in universities often favour those who can show that they have obtained large grants. So scientists are increasingly likely to win promotion only if they can bring in the money, and the chances of doing that are likely to be increased by a willingness to do the kinds of work currently favoured by the research councils or to 'make terms' with prospective funders in industry. In some respects, then, the career scientist is as heavily limited in his freedom as a researcher as his short-term contract colleague (and it is preponderantly 'he': a higher proportion of women scientists are in short-term posts). So the insecurely funded scientist leads a life of the mind in which one effect of the impact of the 'real world' is an enforced myopia.

Then there is the wastage of time. Scientists spend a great deal of time 'making bargains' with the 'real world', to enable them to carry out research at all. In a recent list of 'research activity', 'the writing and reviewing of research papers'; 'the reading of periodicals and attendance at lectures and seminars'; 'discussions of one's own and other research topics'; work at the bench and thinking come in only a minority place in a long trail of activities *preliminary* to doing the actual scientific work. First come 'the generation of grant applications (some 50–90 per cent of which fail)'; 'the solicitation of partners to research projects to demonstrate collaborative activity and inter- or multi-disciplinarity'; 'interactions with industry or commerce to obtain associates who can demonstrate the need for the research in the "real world"'; 'the coupling up with people in other countries to demonstrate trans-nationality as for European Commission grants'; 'the production of reports replete with diagrams, tables and references'; 'the hiring (and firing) of researchers (advertisements, job description, short listing, interviewing, induction, personnel matters)'; 'attending to the career needs of the researchers and the provision of training in the specific skills and understanding for the particular project'; 'providing an account of monies spent'; 'attending committees (including grant reviewing committees) and meetings to learn of the latest in research fashions and grant application techniques'; 'the negotiation of "deals" with suppliers of equipment and materials'; 'the negotiation of space, technical support . . . and workshop activities within the university'.[108]

Restrictions on sharing work in progress

A dispute between university-based researchers and the corporation that funded their study is threatening to erupt into a $7 million to $10 million legal battle. Last week, the researchers reported that a large clinical trial of an immune system booster to treat HIV-infected people found that the drug isn't effective in slowing progression to AIDS or reducing mortality. The company that developed the drug tried to block publication of the study unless the researchers included the company's analysis of a subset of the data that suggested the drug might help some people. The researchers refused.[109]

This is unusual, mainly because it can rarely be done with the backing of the university and by the whole team. It is likely to be disastrous to the career of any individual whose values are generating a research environment fraught with pitfalls.

The dramatic silencing of a scientist who tried to signal dangers in genetically modified foods in 1999 became a focus of media interest. In the end the ban was lifted, but not before irrevocable damage had been done to this scientist: 'A Scottish research institute this week lifted a ban on one of its scientists from speaking to the press, in a bid to dampen allegations that it had tried to suppress data indicating potential health risks in genetically modified food.' But the ban had had its lasting effect. When it was lifted, he did not feel free to speak: 'Arpad Pusztai, a senior researcher at the Rowett Research Institute in Aberdeen and an authority on lectins, had been banned from speaking to the press after allegedly disclosing un-published data from his experiments on television last August... Earlier this week, Pusztai was continuing to refuse to speak publicly.' The damage to his career seemed likely to be irreversible: 'But Luke Anderson, an environmental activist and Pusztai supporter, says the researcher is angry and hurt at how a career in which he produced 280 research papers and wrote three books has been brought to an abrupt end.' And he faced censorship: 'Anderson adds that one journal was offered the data, but declined to publish it.'[110]

The presumption in academic research has traditionally been that knowledge is to be shared; that the best way for it to move on is for it to be open to testing by the research community. As these examples show, that is not easily reconciled with commercial interest in protecting exploitable discoveries, especially when the university has financial interests in keeping the money, and in preserving a long-term relationship with the funder. Even where there is no dramatic dénouement, there is subtle undermining of the freedom and security of the researcher in the very structure. A professor enters into a contract with industry to do 'research and development' of ideas developed in academic research. Perhaps he gives the work to a postdoctoral researcher to carry out. The university, the professor and the industry may or may not stake out their respective claims at the outset. It is not unusual for the researcher, especially if he is a junior researcher and dependent on the patronage of the leader of the team, to be required to sign away not only the intellectual property rights, but also his moral rights of authorship, together perhaps with the freedom to continue with research in the area; that could take away his freedom of research in his particular area of expertise for the rest of his life.

At the least this calls for training for individual research staff in basic intellectual property issues, in the way that has become a US requirement in cognate matters where public funding is involved.[111] The situation could be transformed if individual researchers were clear about their rights and the implications of signing things; if they had a code of good practice to point to and somewhere to go for support if they found themselves under inappropriate pressures. This needs to go back to the beginnings of research training, and indeed even earlier, to the undergraduate course. For example, in undergraduate essays in the humanities, it is quite usual to quote from sources without giving references. In graduate work it becomes plagiarism, a form of misconduct, to do so. The supervisor or the institution ought to have explained the difference and the reason for it. The student is in an especially difficult position because he is dependent upon the supervisor's own understanding of these issues, and his adequate guidance of the student's work to save him from falling into misconduct. A student 'learning the trade' may have no evident intention to deceive. The university's responsibility to teach students not only this kind of basic academic honesty, but also an awareness of ethical issues, is a heavy one.

The problem also demands a large-scale review of the policy questions, the statutory framework and the international legislative scene, which *allows* the personal research freedoms of academics to be set at risk over against such powerful and well-funded commercial interests.

Intellectual property

Intellectual property has been defined as 'the intangible expression of an invention, design, sign or other expression of an idea, or, more simply, information'. 'It may . . . be used simultaneously in different physical markets',[112] but that is less likely if its owner is unwilling to allow its free exploitation, for intellectual property law protects the ownership of the commercial value of abstract ideas. It embraces patents (which protect for a limited period), trademarks (which protect indefinitely) and copyright in literary and artistic productions (which covers the right to reproduce or perform).[113] The notion that mental labour is a form of property, so that the law ought to protect rights in it, was systematized in the UK from the early nineteenth century.[114] The academic whose mind's work is in question may, these days, be involved in enterprises with global implications and intellectual property law is increasingly an international concern.[115] Yet 'the fact of the matter is that we do not understand the international intellectual property system and its potential impact on the public interest'.[116] That is scarcely less true now than in 1997. And, *a fortiori*, scientists going out into 'marketplaces' with little or no expertise in the law will understand it even less, with attendant dangers to their academic freedom if their universities do not advise them and protect them.

This area of concern is not far removed from that in which industrial sponsors and funders require as a condition of funding that researchers *delay* 'sharing' their findings in the way they otherwise would, by giving papers at conferences or publishing articles. 'Of arguable propriety is the widely-practised university-industry venture . . . A survey . . . disclosed that, in roughly half of the programs, research information was delayed or withheld in order to favour the sponsors. It should be of great concern whenever an academic institution accepts industrial [or government?] support for basic research that is specified by the industrial donor.'[117]

Such questions of intellectual property involving patenting and timing of publication almost inevitably arise when academe and industry try to work together. Intellectual property is acknowledged to be a minefield of conflicting advantages. Imperial College, London, formed its own intellectual property company (IMPEL) to try to keep control in these difficult waters.

The problem here is that the industrial or commercial sponsor naturally wants to make use of the findings it has paid for, for its own advantage; and that 'selfishness' is diametrically opposed to the traditional academic presumption that knowledge is 'advanced' by sharing. The policy-tide is now, paradoxically, encouraging the view that that is no longer in the public interest. The interests of the commercial funders are being elevated above those of the academic or world community of knowledge. The push for publication is endangering the protection of intellectual property and therefore its later exploitation.[118] 'A university . . . may be tempted to believe that its best interest is served by constraining the freedom with which academics in the university develop relationships with industry', said one witness cautiously.[119] Bolder altogether in its call for restriction was *The Innovation– Exploitation Barrier*: 'universities [are to manage intellectual property] in a way that encourages partnerships with industry'.[120] 'This may involve treading a fine line between patenting and publication,'[121] sagely remarked a witness to a House of Commons Select Committee.

The present damage to the free exchange of information might in principle be prevented by prophylactic methods, such as declaration of all potentially conflicting interests, for example, editorship of journals, membership of funding council committees, membership of Research Assessment Exercise panels, consultancies, involvement in setting up commercial companies, directorship of companies, previous research supervision of doctoral students subsequently employed in commercial ventures as postdoctoral workers. But while the structures of financial control are not counterbalanced by equally powerful sanctions protecting freedom to share the outcomes of research, the sort of misconduct which consists in keeping silent or in suppression or distortion of results will be inevitable. The policing of such misconduct, if it is in the end held to be misconduct, will remain difficult or impossible. And the individual and his work remain imperfectly protected.

Conflict of interest and misconduct in research

The individual scientist is not always the 'little man', the junior who needs support against the potentially oppressive behaviour of those who have the future of his research in their gift. Sometimes he is the 'big leading player' or 'patron' of others, with 'clients' in his labs, with many irons in the fire, and much to lose at a quite different level. His scientific work is also affected in the present climate in which the 'real world' is actively at work within the very fabric of the university and priority beginning to be conceded to its interests.

The senior academic scientist faces conflicts of interest. The *Sunday Times* of 30 May 1999 carried an article on ten 'senior doctors awaiting disciplinary hearings after General Medical Council investigations into alleged research misconduct and forged drug studies'. One of them was 'believed to have received between £300,000 and £500,000'. There were also allegations of misuse of research funds to pay for foreign holidays 'in the guise of attending medical conferences'. This latter allegation is clearly one of fraud. But is this? 'One university doctor of my acquaintance often comments that it is difficult to find any research on nutrition that has not been financed by industry, and that it is almost impossible to find any "objective" opinion.'[122]

The real danger in this world of changing priorities is that the academic may now lose not only his intellectual freedom, but even his inward honesty, his honesty with himself about what he is trying to do and why, in the 'deal' which obtains him the necessary funds. 'Those who seek grants must appeal to the whims of their financiers . . . Isaac Asimov once commented wearily that if you wanted money to do research on the moon, you had better drag in the word "cancer", only to be told of one ingenious proposal that did just that.'[123] It is now widely accepted that the hold of the multinationals 'on high technology is . . . pernicious. It perverts the course of science and, more dangerously, it perverts the course of all human life and, indeed, of all non-human life.'[124] That carries through into a danger of confusion in the minds of senior scientists who may now be on the committees and in the directorships which can ensure the awarding of both public *and* private money while themselves having research in their hands, laboratories to staff and postgraduate studentships in their gift.

Ethical questions

It is not a long distance to move, as we must now do, from minor constraints and diversions of effort to something close to corruption where major ethical issues prove to be involved. There can be not only distortion of the purposes of projects at their inception, but also control by censorship of the revelations or discoveries that may result:

> Secretive censorship is familiar to anyone who has questioned orthodox views on AIDS. The result is that essential questions are debated only in lesser journals. There are, naturally, vested interests involved: many individuals receive high rewards for their work within orthodox AIDS science. Underlying much of this, the pharmaecuticals companies have their own agenda. This censorship is not unique but, in my 57 years as a professional, I have never encountered anything like it, nor did I think I ever would in the world where difference of opinion is the *sine qua non* of all advance.[125]

So much is this now the norm that it is hard to insist that it may amount to an impropriety or misconduct for a scientist to reach an agreement to do a particular piece of work, or for a particular purpose, at the funder's wish. If he does not do so, the work will not be done at all; if he does so, what he wanted to investigate may remain unexplored, but something like it will be an acceptable project, and he may prefer to settle for that.

It is not easy to sustain the position that 'science . . . should be value-free . . . Science attempts to say how the Universe is, and not how it ought to be'.[126] Are some contentious topics bound to take researchers into misconduct and, if so, does that place a restriction upon their freedom of speech? A well-trodden area of this sort is research that asks socially forbidden questions, such as whether one race is innately intellectually superior to another. Jean-Philippe Rushton of the University of Western Ontario propounded theories that different races consistently appeared in different proportions in, for example, IQ scores and crime statistics: 'The scientific study of race . . . is proscribed by a "taboo" . . . Rushton . . . has been denounced in the media and investigated by the police.' His university was disturbed but eventually 'upheld his right to freedom of enquiry and expression, but not before the state had explored the possibility of criminal charges'.[127] Here, then, society was minded to suppress. But academe in the end allowed an inquiry which not only challenged received opinion but also risked causing offence. In the public domain, the ethical balance went one way; in the academic, it went the other.

This raises the question whether a scholar is restrained from an absolutely unconstrained freedom of speech by the proprieties of his subject area. The medical scientist is bound by a professional ethic which has been described as the 'precautionary principle'. He must not do harm. If there is doubt, he must avoid putting the patient or the subject of a clinical trial at risk. If a scientist speaks in terms of 'oughts' which are in force in his 'field', he is, on this understanding, speaking not as a scientist but as an ordinary citizen.

All this throws increasingly into question what constitutes misconduct in research, for it is only if it is clear that something is in breach of an ethical standard that there comes into being a duty to do something about it, or to resist it. The main clear areas of potential misconduct seem to lie in these areas: of conflict of interest; breach of a professional ethic; betrayal of professional responsibility; misleading readers over the actual authorship of a piece of writing, such as the attribution of work to someone who has not really been involved in it; and the falsification or manipulation or suppression of data or results. Personal relationships and personal ambition may also lead to misconduct.

One approach to identifying misconduct is to see it solely in terms of an *intention* to deceive. A US Public Health Service Regulation (42 CFR para. 50.102 (1993)) defines misconduct in science (in terms quite widely found elsewhere too) as 'fabrication, falsification, plagiarism, or other practices that seriously deviate from those that are commonly accepted within the scientific community for proposing, conducting, or reporting research. It does not include honest error or honest differences in interpretations or judgements of data.' (Of these, most apply outside the sciences too, of course.) That approach attempts no value-judgements, takes the project as it is set up and running, does not ask where the money came from and why. It perhaps assumes that not reporting the results of research is not itself necessarily misleading. Yet a scientist who happens to be working in 'research and development' for a commercial enterprise may not be able to join freely in the debate with his academic colleagues working in the same area, since 'the "horizontal" transition of ideas from scientist to scientist is interrupted in many different ways; so, too, is the flow of notions out of science and to the rest of us'.[128]

Missing from the list is the *positive* duty of independence of thought and speech which may be held to lie upon the scholar or academic by virtue of the nature of the work he does. That can now be compromised by external pressures to a degree where, ironically, what began as a freedom may now be becoming a responsibility. Can we say, then, that refusing to speak out where something needs to be said amounts to misconduct? Or that partial suppression of findings, or bending of them to fit a funder's brief, is an improper limitation upon freedom of academic speech and academics have a responsibility to resist? It seems we must, but the price for the individual is high.

4

Politics, Administration
and the Real World

Quality of administration[1]

> It is a longstanding principle of our educational system that universities enjoy academic freedom. That freedom is properly constrained. They are accountable.[2]

Are they? There is evidence of confusion between academic autonomy and academic freedom here and elsewhere in the debates which took place in the House of Lords at the Committee stage, before the passing of the Further and Higher Education Act 1992. The academic autonomy of universities consists in their right as institutions to regulate their own affairs. Academic freedom is something much bigger, encompassing freedoms to teach and to engage in research and scholarship which may stretch far beyond a single institution. Research has always been an international activity, but, as we saw in Chapter 3, the freedoms at stake are growing bigger still, and now require protections against the commercial interests of funders and spin-out companies which may not be particular to a university. That 'dates', but does not necessarily make less useful, the distinction in the Robbins Report of the early 1960s (p. 229) which distinguished between the academic freedom of the individual and 'the relations of academic institutions to society and the institutions of government', in short, the academic autonomy we have been considering.

The Lords are to be forgiven some confusion. Lord Pearson suggested that 'those who oppose Clauses 53, 64, 77 do so more because they fear interference from the Secretary of State in academic matters than because they fear the proper scrutiny of the use of public funds'.[3] The perceived threat common to both academic autonomy and academic freedom was state interference,[4] and that led to the forming of a common front behind which the distinction blurred.

The present legislation provides inadequately for calling universities to account for the poor quality administration which can result from an autonomy with too little check upon it. The Further and Higher Education Act 1992, s. 70 makes provision for the assessment of 'the quality of education provided' in institutions, but not expressly for assessment of the quality of the administration which provides it.

Baroness Cox spoke darkly in the 1991 debates of comparisons with 'totalitarian regimes' and listed concerns about 'violations of freedom to pursue knowledge and truth, freedom of legitimate access to academic institutions and freedom to speak on campus'.[5] She described her own experience of standing out in the 1970s against the practice of pressurizing students to adopt a particular slant in their research. Here she touched on a concern which goes to the heart of the problem created by the autonomy of universities. 'I received numerous letters of support from academic staff in other institutions, who were so frightened that they begged not to be identified, but who described similar situations,' she said. 'Where were the guardians of academic freedom and quality then?' Her point was that 'the academic community' itself had condoned 'violations of the rights of students to freedom to pursue knowledge and truth even if it was not the ideologically or politically popular truth'.[6] Academic autonomy had worked against academic freedom, but that was not clearly drawn out as the implication. Where the House of Lords arguably went wrong in the debates before the passing of the 1992 Act was in not recognizing that the defence of academic freedom raises different questions from the defence of academic autonomy. 'I hope to hear advice . . . about ways in which academies may reassure the public about their methods of protecting this fundamental principle,' said Baroness Cox,[7] but in the helter-skelter of concern about freedom no one fixed on the need for mechanisms of 'reassurance' about the autonomy. Baroness Cox spoke of the proposed amendments as seeking 'to enshrine the principle of accountability at the level of the academies themselves'.[8] The question left in the air was whether they could be trusted.

Some requirement of training of governors and of administrators and those entrusted with authority over others seems not unreasonable. But there is strong resistance to the latter among senior figures in universities, who take 'staff development courses' to be for their juniors. Indeed, it is uncommon for universities even to offer such courses to those put into senior positions. In the USA it is recognized that 'preventive' training of staff in fair procedures and in the technical responsibilities of their positions may be a wise investment for a university.[9]

A number of danger areas were identified in 1987 and 1991, however, and we must take those next. When the House of Lords discussed academic freedom in December 1991, it recollected that it had done so when the Education Reform Act 1988 was being put together. 'It is only three years since the Chamber debated . . . the freedom or power of the Secretary of State to intervene directly in the affairs of a specific educational institution.'[10] In 1991 the question arose again whether the Secretary of State should be given powers under the new legislation to intervene directly and at his own discretion in the internal 'affairs, syllabus or workings'[11] of individual institutions.

Here the debate was clearly about the autonomy of universities, but because of the conflation of affairs, syllabus or workings, the fright expressed by the noble Lords concerned the danger to academic freedom.

A power of last resort?

The situation in which it was envisaged that direct interference with an institution might be needed was extreme. Despite the caveat entered by Baroness Young that 'the subsection gives the Secretary of State power to intervene, in detail, in individual institutions . . . It does not suggest a power of last resort',[12] it was assumed that the Secretary of State was to move in only when an institution had gone completely 'off the rails'.[13] There was a good deal of noble amusement at the unlikelihood of that, and especially at the improbability that the funding councils would go off the rails at the same moment.[14]

Here again, the hounds lost the scent. No one seems to have envisaged a situation where the funding council simply fails to intervene, or finds it does not have powers to intervene on the matter in question. In the evidence given to the Parliamentary Accounts Committee about the débâcle at the Southampton Institute in the spring of 1999, there is reason for concern on this point. Brian Fender, the chief executive of the Higher Education Funding Council for England (HEFCE), had to admit that guidance had been issued only 'earlier this month'. 'The fact that you were coming here today had nothing to do with the timing, of course,' remarked Mr Williams dryly.[15] It was plain that the HEFCE had not only failed to have codes of practice in place in a timely way, but was simply ineffectual in identifying problems through its audit processes. 'Why do you think it is that you never spotted that there was this weakness in the system, in other words, that [the director] could make decisions in cases involving himself?' asked Mr Twigg. Fender's defence was that it was the governing body's job to notice that and do something about it. 'So you left it to the governing body to call the head of the institute to account?' asked Mr Twigg.[16] 'They are autonomous bodies and they have that responsibility,' said Professor Fender. 'So you think in the use of public money it is perfectly acceptable to leave it to chance as to whether a governing body holds its head of institute accountable or not?' asked Mr Twigg.[17] 'Basically until the whistle-blowing happened you had no idea that the head of the institute was doing basically what he wanted and the governors were not performing to the required standard? . . . Basically you had no checks in place?'[18]

These exchanges illustrate a widespread threefold problem.[19] Production of guidelines and codes of good practice under the aegis of the statutory 'supervisors' and the sector's own bodies, such as the Committee of Vice-Chancellors and Principals and the Committee of University Chairmen, is slow and uncertain and there is no provision for policing their adoption and still less their observance in individual higher education institutions (HEIs). Governing bodies are commonly manned by individuals untrained for the task, often unaware of their responsibilities and not greatly interested in the nature and operation of good governance. There is no routine machinery for picking up trouble, such as might be provided by a quality audit of the conduct of administration at all levels in an HEI.

Because the theme was the – by definition – rare and extreme case of complete breakdown, the more frequent situation where the governance of an institution has become dysfunctional, where its self-regulation has broken down, where there is a lack of clear-headed, well-informed, open and fair-minded management to keep things running in the interests of the institution, had not been carefully thought through before the passing of the 1992 Act. Baroness Blackstone skated close in asking for reassurance that (where institutions had got into financial difficulties) 'in all cases those problems have been resolved under existing legislation without the need for the Secretary of State to intervene with these new powers'.[20] But the obvious gaps in the provision were not picked up.

There is a paradox here of too much and too little control. John Griffith has been proved right in his observation that, as early as the 1988 Act, the government had 'provided itself with the detailed powers ... necessary to control the activities of the universities' as it wished.[21]

In a 'scene' discussed in December 1991, the Secretary of State would have powers to intervene only when a given institution had not come to a satisfactory agreement with its staff in the annual local pay-bargaining round. Lord Belstead defended the existing formulation[22] on the grounds that the Secretary of State needed to be able to instruct the funding councils to withhold grant from institutions which did not reach a satisfactory settlement in 'pay and conditions' negotiations. The House of Lords here envisaged the relatively innocuous principle of using a financial sanction (withholding of grant) for strictly financial reasons which, although it would apply to individual universities and thus intrude upon their autonomy, would at least apply like to like by way of sanction. He accepted that there would have to be amendment to 'put beyond doubt on the face of the Bill' that the Secretary of State could not use his powers of intervention for purposes of the sorts about which the alarm had been raised. 'The basic issue is academic freedom,'[23] he said, again unclearly.

A further group of concerns raised in the House of Lords in December 1991 foresaw financial sanctions being used for academic purposes, and here we are closer to the need for defence of academic freedom itself. The fear was that the Secretary of State would take against specific courses or subjects and require them to be removed.[24] Much of the concern expressed in the committee discussion of 16 December turned on the possibility the Secretary of State might intervene on such matters as the content of courses, the examination of students, the types of student and staff to be appointed.[25] The Act as eventually passed provided that terms and conditions attached to grants 'may not be framed by reference to particular courses of study or programmes of research'.[26] So those areas of activity have largely been left under the direct control of universities.

Yet here we are at intervention in decisions in a grey area between academic judgement and political priority. Lord Russell pointed up the inherent difficulty of classifying beyond question those matters in which the Secretary of State ought not to be able to interfere if academic freedom was to be safeguarded. Let us suppose that an academic department says it has not enough books available to take on more students. 'Is the decision how many books will be needed for how many people an academic decision . . . or not? Is the decision how many undergraduates we can properly teach in one group without diminishing the quality of our teaching an academic decision . . . or not?'[27]

A sea-change has been brought about which makes it no longer as clear as it was even in 1993[28] that a university is not a business. There has been a mounting tide of quality assessment of teaching and research. But, still paradoxically, this heightened control has not been applied to the purpose of ensuring that individual universities are well run. The quality of administration in universities remains largely unregulated.

The present safeguards

It bears serious consideration ten years later whether the provisions about governance in the 1992 Act have hit it right in protecting academic freedom from what may paradoxically be the threat of an academic autonomy which allows universities to go their own way without check, to the detriment of academic freedom and quality of teaching and research. What are the weak spots in the statutory provisions?[29]

Governance structures

The governance provisions of the Further and Higher Education Act 1992 create governing bodies which are arguably at the same time too close to and too remote from the institution. Section 71 of the Act inserts the Education Reform Act 1988, s. 124, with its Schedule 7, setting out the constitution of a higher education corporation. The corporation is to consist of not less than 12 and not more than 24 members, including the person who is for the time being the principal of the institution, unless he chooses not to be a member.[30] So routinely present at the meetings of governing bodies is the head of the institution, and that will make it – did indeed make it at Southampton Institute – difficult for the governing body to discuss openly and freely any concerns which might informally be presented to them about what was afoot. The Parliamentary Accounts Committee report on the Southampton Institute brought out the surprising degree to which governors could feel themselves to be intimidated. 'One of the depressing things . . . is that the governors themselves did not blow the whistle . . . A number of the governors felt they were intimidated.'[31] These were people chosen for their standing in the world and their independence.

But was it ensured that they were 'absolutely aware of what their rights and responsibilities' were? Was there 'proper training'? Was any effort being made by the HEFCE to ensure that such guidance about good practice as there was, was being followed?[32]

Among the key principles embodied in the Schedule 7 provisions is independence. The governing body is to include 'persons nominated . . . otherwise than by other members of the corporation' (3(2)(b)) and having experience or skills in 'industrial, commercial or employment matters or the practice of any profession' (3(2)(a)). The House of Lords turned over the 'independence' question in December 1991.[33] Their chief concern seems still to have been with the prospect of government, or in this case local government, interference. They were less actively concerned to ensure a balance between independent and relevant knowledge of the academic world itself, and especially the local world of the individual institution. That would seem to require an adequate staff or student presence, to ensure that those who governed an institution had some working knowledge of its affairs. Baroness Blackstone said that she 'knew of no evidence [since 1988] that staff or student representation had been detrimental to any institution'.[34] Yet those chosen for their independence have, *ipso facto*, no intimate daily involvement with the affairs of the institution, may not be being trained and told what their powers and responsibilities are, and the members of the academic staff have a limited voice on the governing body of post-1992 HEIs under the current legislation.

Failure to obey the governing instruments or the statutes

The available machinery for dealing with a failure to follow the governing instruments of a higher education corporation is limited.[35] There have been successful judicial review applications quashing decisions as *ultra vires*.[36] Where there is a visitor, he would have analogous powers. In *Pearce v University of Aston in Birmingham (No. 2)* [1991] 2 All ER 469, Browne-Wilkinson, the Vice-Chancellor, took it that a threatened breach of the statutes of a pre-1992 Act university should go to the visitor. The visitor's powers were held to extend to ensuring 'the lawful conduct of the university in accordance with its regulating document' and to ordering the university to restore the pre-breach position after the breach had occurred.[37] Hyams argues that an act in breach of the statutes would be effective until overturned by a successful challenge by one of these routes, in line with the principle of s. 35A of the Companies Act 1989. But that means going to the visitor or courts; the latter is uncertain and expensive, and few with the standing to challenge a university will also have the money.[38] It is still unclear whether a university is a public body or an emanation of the state, and until that is clarified, public law routes are insecure. Recent testings of the water have produced contradictory results.[39] This means that an HEI will routinely get away with breach of its domestic legislation unless someone makes a huge and personally costly effort to void the act in question. That is an inadequate mechanism for ensuring that the rules are followed.

Concerned at what the Secretary of State might do, Lord Renton took up the point that a power 'needed as a last resort' is a dangerous power. 'We must not have a reserve power which might be used in an unreserved way,' he argued.[40] Yet fear of that has arguably led too far the other way.

How is it to be decided when a institution needs reining in and by whom? The first need is for a regulatory framework within which whiffs of trouble may be sniffed out. Universities cannot be expected to respond with enthusiasm to the need to explain themselves more. But they cannot expect to be allowed to go on using public money with such carelessness without being answerable, not for the conduct of their affairs, but for the quality of the conduct of their affairs. League tables of maladministrative incidents, misconduct in public office, mismanagement, cases taken to the employment tribunal, complaints and appeals from students, breaches of the domestic legislation would tell the world a great deal that universities would rather it did not know. Such 'figures' are a very different matter from the burdens of RAE and TQA. How is information to be obtained about what is really going on in an institution, so as to make it possible to get a picture of the quality of its administration? There is a real difficulty here. It is an unusual individual member of staff who is alert to anything more than a very local incident of maladministration or misconduct affecting himself.

What circumstances would trigger a duty for the institution itself to own up to an episode of 'administrative failure'? A vice-chancellor is the accounting officer, but with reference only to financial matters. That was spelled out by Lord Dainton in the House of Lords debates at the Committee stage. He said 'the Government now have all the safeguards they need through the accounting officer system'. He spoke only of 'financial discipline'.[41] The governing body of the institution has an existing duty to 'furnish . . . information' and to make available for inspection 'accounts and such other documents' as may reasonably be required for the purpose.[42] Lord Dainton commented in the 1991 debates, 'Clause 65 . . . states: "Each [funding] Council . . . may provide the Secretary of State with such information or advice relating to such provision as they think fit.' He wanted to change that 'to make it possible for the councils to proffer such advice in any manner that appears reasonable to them'.[43] But a Higher Education Funding Council does not necessarily have its finger on every institution's pulse, and if the initiative for an inquiry has to come from above, there are as many questions about political will as about ways and means.

An inspection visit might find the same tidied up and rigorous conduct of affairs encountered by those engaging in teaching quality assessment. But the Act further provides at s. 83 that a Higher Education Funding Council 'may arrange for the promotion or carrying out by any person of studies designed to improve economy, efficiency and effectiveness in the management or operations of an institution within the . . . higher education sector'.

Some shifting of the onus on to the institution, coupled with some sanction which will really bite, personally as well as institutionally, seems essential if we are to achieve a quality of administration in the universities of the UK of which we can be as proud as we can be of much of their teaching and research.

We need a much clearer idea of what would constitute poor-quality administration. It is not difficult to draw up a working list. (1) Failure to obey the law (especially to observe private contractual requirements) or the domestic legislation of the university. (2) Failure to observe the canons of fairness and lawfulness in the treatment of staff or students. (3) Failure to create codes of good practice or to observe them. (4) Failure to train those to whom responsibilities are given in the duties entrusted to them. Failure to provide for vigilant and independent oversight of the good conduct of the university's affairs. (5) Failure to provide internal avenues of recourse for staff or students with complaints, or wishing to appeal against decisions made against their interests, avenues which are followed honestly and fearlessly with no closing of ranks or fudging of issues or unreasonable delay. Only if such continuing institutional autonomy as now survives is made conditional upon continuing fulfilment of such requirements can it protect the great and undisputed good of academic freedom, rather than set it at risk.

Managers and managed

We must now consider the most difficult relationship of all: the 'dealings' between those who run things, the managers and administrators of universities (including, in some universities, heads of department who are also academics), and those who do the teaching and research but who have little or no administrative power. There are two main models. In one, there are managers and managed. This is now by far the most common in UK universities. The other is the 'civil service' model, in which there are only administrators, who remain in principle answerable to the academic community, as in Oxford and Cambridge, and who have line management authority over each other though not over academics. But these still have, in reality, considerable power. Like any 'civil service' they can outlast those who are, in theory, in charge of their activities. Ministers change; vice-chancellors change; but senior 'civil servants' and managers may continue from regime to regime, and they can await their moment and get their proposals accepted in the end by sheer attrition.[44]

Indeed, a civil service as a whole, or sections of it, may deem itself to possess a collective mind. 'The whole nature of the civil service is that it is very much a team game.'[45] Sir Douglas Wass defines 'the departmental view' as 'an opinion about policy which is widely shared at official level throughout the whole department'.[46] There is 'pressure on key advisers to avoid expressing differences of view on a critical option or decision, in other words, to present a united front'.[47] The official position is that, individually, 'civil servants are responsible to their Ministers for their actions and conduct',[48] yet they also serve all ministers collectively.

An example of the kind of thing which can happen when the administrative will rolls like a juggernaut is the episode of Newall's field. In 1931 the Financial Board of the University of Cambridge published a report (*Reporter*, 3 February 1931), in which it printed a restrictive covenant which was to be incorporated into the contract for sale of a piece of land, requiring the University, as purchaser, to ensure that 'no use will be made or permitted by the University of the land or any part thereof which in the opinion of the Directors for the time being of the [University's] Observatories shall or may be undesirable or tending to prejudice the proper and efficient use of the said Observatories'. About 1970 there was a bid to use the land to build a turbomachinery laboratory. The director of the time was at least aware that he had powers to exercise his discretion to stop any such move. In 1999 a more serious threat to the protections in the restrictive covenant arose in the form of the plan to build to accommodate what has been described as the [Bill] 'Gates empire'. This time the directors were not informed (or did not realize) that they had a duty to take a view. The director of the University's Estates Management and Building Service was not aware of this covenant either. No formal documentation seems to have been produced (or able to be produced on request) which could amount to the formal exercise of the discretion with which the director was entrusted. Members of the Finance Committee and the Council, as well as the directors with the discretion under the restrictive covenant were all acquiescing in the 'team-play' which was bent on ignoring the requirements of this covenant. Attempts by a member of the academic staff to call a halt were 'dismissed' by the Vice-Chancellor. At no point did anyone in the administration apparently look at the issue itself: the illegality of the disposal of this field.

In the civil service, 'one of the biggest crimes is to have failed to consult or to inform'.[49] This expectation of consultation 'ensures that anyone involved in the consequences of the decision, as well as those responsible for making a particular decision, is brought into the decision-making process. It involves consulting and informing a wide network of people . . . so that a . . . line of action is not subsequently upset.'[50] In *The Duties and Responsibilities of Civil Servants in Relation to Ministers*, the head of the Home Civil Service explained that he had issued a memorandum only 'after consultation with Permanent Secretaries in charge of Departments and with their agreement'. But that seems to apply only 'within' the structure, among the 'insiders' or the managerial 'team'. The same will to be open with the university as a whole about what is afoot is not often to be seen. It is frequently objected that that cannot be risked where commercial confidentiality is involved. But if there is no way of finding out what is going on, that legitimate protection is, in its turn, easily made to provide a cloak for transactions which may be unlawful or simply sloppy and not in the interests of the university. And if there is no response when procedures are involved, consultation breaks down in another way.

The authority to decide and the power to decide

One of the dangers of secrecy in the conduct of a university's affairs is that formal and constitutional authority to decide may give way in practice to the *de facto* decision-making of administrators in rather the way the Newall's field episode illustrates. This was an issue to the fore in *Carltona Ltd v Commissioners of Works* [1943] 2 All ER 560 AC. Could civil servants act on behalf of the competent authority without reference to that authority, even though they had taken no detailed instructions that could constitute delegation of that authority? The court held that no minister or his equivalent could deal with every detail of a department's work himself. The operational functions clearly had to be discharged by others. The Commissioners of Works constituted an authoritative body in this case, but it never met. Letters authorizing action were signed on their behalf. But 'the persons constituting the requisitioning authority never brought their minds to bear on the question'. It was held that 'the duties imposed upon Ministers and the powers given to Ministers are normally exercised under the authority of Ministers by responsible officials of the Department. Public business could not be carried on if that were not the case. Constitutionally, the decision of such an official is, of course, the decision of the Minister'; and only if an official of very junior standing had been chosen so that 'he could not be expected competently to perform the work' would the delegation be inappropriate. That was a special case, not only because the commissioners never met to authorize, but also because the decision fell, on the face of it, within the 'operations' and not the 'policy-making' sphere. It was, in essence, 'routine'. The *Carltona* story is also about the place of common sense. Christopher Grey commented in the *Times Higher Education Supplement* of 27 July 2001 that 'what is needed . . . is little more than simple common sense'.

Where common sense and goodwill fly out of the window and 'managers' act as though they had powers (and indeed they may have those powers) without the restraint of common sense, serious questions of accountability begin to arise. This *Carltona* issue is becoming increasingly important in the climate of secrecy in which universities are run and in which managers act on behalf of the university without there being, in reality, any force in any constraints the university's domestic laws are intended to provide.

Seeing what is going on

Ahead of the coming into force of the Freedom of Information Act, it is not easy to make a general rule as to the stage at which, in a process of decision-making, documents should become open so that as many as possible of those whose interests are affected should be able to express a view. In the USA a much stronger right of access to information exists than is promised in the UK by the new legislation. Even there, a dilemma presents itself. It is not disputed that secrecy may lead to evils in public life. 'Secrecy facilitates official lying and makes it possible to cover up embarrassment.'[51] On the other side, stands the 'inhibition of frankness' argument. Those who know that what they say will be heard will be less frank: 'Human experience teaches that those who expect public dissemination of their remarks may well temper candour with a concern for appearances and for their own interest to the detriment of the decision-making process.'[52]

Much the same reasons are given in the USA as in the UK: 'Because it is essential to efficient and effective administration that employees of the Executive Branch be in a position to be completely candid in advising with each other on official matters, and because it is not in the public interest that any of their conversations or communications, or any documents or reproductions, concerning such advice be disclosed, you will instruct employees of your Department that . . . they are not to testify to any such conversations or communications or to produce any such documents or reproductions. This principle must be maintained regardless of who would benefit by such disclosures.'[53]

This remains the central dilemma in the UK too, even in a climate which is moving towards greater openness: 'Governments and public authorities should be able to think in private . . . In the absence of such protection there would be a risk of loss of candour in discussions, and an increasing gap between what is said at meetings and on the telephone and what is recorded in files.'[54]

Yet there is an argument from informed debate which may override these legitimate concerns about the inhibition of frankness: 'The more information about government that the public has, the more informed becomes the public debate on political matters.' Lord Armstrong of Ilminster commented in his remarks about the creation of policy-records: 'It might well make for better decision-making because if it was known that such a document had to be produced . . . the likely contents of that document would be in people's mind while the decision was being processed and I think that would have a healthy effect on decision-making itself.'[55]

In universities, as in other big organizations and in government, decisions have to be made and policy framed within complex structures where such considerations of what degree of 'openness' with the documentation is appropriate are always pressing, and always under a high degree of pressure in the direction of secrecy, especially in the crucial early stages when it can be represented that everything is 'in draft'. Someone has to do the thinking and drafting, and commonly it will be administrators, even if the decisions in universities are technically taken by committees of academics or by academic deans or heads of department, or a vice-chancellor as chief executive. So subtle is this process of 'communication' of what Newman calls 'leading ideas' that it may become very difficult to retrace the steps or to reconstruct the process, especially where access to the papers in the paper-trail is denied. That makes challenge difficult, and so it works against accountability. In public life (at least in principle) this is now undesirable, if we are to take seriously recent calls for 'explanatory accountability'.[56]

In the course of the interaction between minister and civil servant are created various documents which make up what has been described as a policy-record. At the stage when Lord Armstrong of Ilminster was giving evidence to the Public Service Committee, in the wake of the Scott Report, he wanted to see 'a process whereby when a decision is announced . . . there should be made available as well to the House of Commons and to the public a much fuller account of the facts and the figures that are taken into account in making the decision and the arguments and considerations which have led to the decision being taken as it was'.[57] Graham Mather supported this notion of a policy-record. This would include all the advice leading up to the taking of a ministerial decision, so that if the decision turned out not to have been sound, 'one could look at the policy record and if the overwhelming majority of advice rejected by the Minister pointed in the right direction, the Minister would have to explain clearly why he had rejected those things'.[58] Peter Shore MP also thought it an acceptable requirement that the evidence on which it is claimed that a decision is based should be produced. He did not think it was reasonable to withhold it 'where it is simply ministerial convenience . . . if what is being held back is simply to avoid what should be legitimate criticism and to cover up on mistakes'.[59] If that is a proper concession in public life it should surely also apply in the free speech environment of universities.

Should the policy-record tell it all, the whole sequence of the decision-making including all the information reviewed in the taking of the decision? How much openness is right? There is a stage at which it may be appropriate for documents to remain inaccessible. This is at the earliest stage of sketching out ideas, unfinished business, information which is not 'information' yet, because the policy has not been framed. It is perhaps in this context, but only here, that we should set the principle that 'confidentiality is sometimes necessary to ensure the effectiveness of government decision-making'.[60] Yet even here some protection is surely needed to prevent managers and administrators merely asserting that what they wish to withhold falls into this category. They can read what they like; they control the documents. Academics cannot.

This category of early drafts aside, it is hard to justify the withholding at least from those with a 'proper interest' – itself a definition not easy to arrive at – of (1) working texts which have got to a stage where they can be circulated (that is, not experimental first drafts which may be entitled to a little decent privacy); (2) background information necessary to identifying the problem and assessing the facts; (3) completed texts (as sent out to committees or others involved in the decision-making),[61] which will affect people's interests.

At the hearing after the Scott Report (Report of the Inquiry into the Export of Defence Equipment and Dual-Use Goods to Iraq and Related Prosecutions (1996), London: HMSO) was published, Mr Booth asked Sir Robin Butler to distinguish two areas: 'One would be information and the other was opinion advice to Ministers. In the case of information, you saw no difficulty with revealing more to the public, but with advice that was an opinion you thought [that] should be subject to continued confidentiality.' Sir Robin Butler stood by what he had said. His reason was directly connected with that convenient tradition that the anonymity of civil servants is a protection of the candour with which they will offer advice: 'The problem about publishing official advice, civil servants' advice, particularly when you have a non-political civil service, is that it gets personalised and it is known that Mr X has advised this and Mr Y has advised that and great significance is attached to it, and that may make such people's position more difficult, particularly if the Minister disagrees and the opposition agrees or whatever. So I think in those ways it would be likely to curtail the candour of advice and it might indeed lead to the sort of conclusions that you mention, where such advice would then be given orally and not recorded for fear of disclosure.'[62] It was suggested that that difficulty could be overcome if the advice were published without the civil servant's name being attached,[63] but that did not meet with much receptiveness.

There is some underpinning of the protection of anonymity for civil servants in case law, which presumes that the decision-maker is the minister alone.[64] But it is not unknown for civil servants to be named as having been responsible for serious administrative failure.[65] While a similar practical protection of anonymity remains in force in universities, as it frequently does, there is a real danger that those whose actions (or failures to act) were in fact the cause of a problem cannot be prevented from making the same mistake again because their personal responsibility cannot be brought home. It is not a sufficient solution to blame departments, for that does not get to the source of any incompetence or error.[66] Taking responsibility for one's juniors is noble, but not helpful to the correction of errors. Nor is it sufficient to allow the head of the department to take the blame because that does not enable an error to be traced to its course and prevented from occurring again.[67] All in all, there is an urgent need for separation of person and office here.

The relationship between minister and civil servant as it is at present con-stituted 'is wide open both to "suppressio veri" and to "suggestio falsi"'.[68] It is incestuous. 'Officials . . . are not responsible under the Butler doctrine other than to their Departmental superiors, who may themselves have instigated or approved the course of conduct complained of.'[69] But more importantly for our purposes, it can be a power-game in which the giving or withholding of information spins the plot: 'In the Butler doctrine, Ministers' "accountability" is discharged by giving information to Parliament. Even if this information is misleading, and the Minister knows it is misleading, it seems, the view is that no liability attaches unless the information is not given in good faith.'[70]

The defence that any misleading was 'innocent' because the decision-maker was 'ignorant' throws into confusion this hierarchical picture of a delegation of powers. For the truth is that in this matter of having information in his possession, the civil servant (or in a university the administrator) is the one with the power: 'The Butler doctrine [of a distinction between responsibility and accountability] leaves an accountability gap . . . The result . . . is that Ministerial responsibility for departmental acts has been defined away almost to nothing. Ministerial accountability can be discharged by statements that turn out to have been knowingly misleading, whilst officials have no responsibility other than to Ministers, and cannot give an account independently of them.'[71] Here it is the 'knowing' that matters, and again: 'A Minister accepts accountability for actions he did not know about, but in such circumstances disclaims responsibility, at least personal responsibility; as civil servants cannot be held either responsible or accountable by Parliament, there is surely a responsibility gap, at least for a large amount of government activity' (Sir Peter Lloyd).

If we transfer all this to the university environment, it is plain that a great deal hangs upon what is open to scrutiny by way of a policy-record; and how far it is made possible to track back and discover how a decision was prompted and to what ends. That holds for university policy-making and decision-making too. It is a significant contrast that at present it would be impossible to provide for universities the sort of documentary underpinnings in the footnotes which it has been possible to include here in another area of public life.

The relevance of all this to universities and its application in academic environments needs to be explored with some urgency. That takes us to Chapter 5.

5

What is to be Done?

Values again

The public has come to feel that it has a stake in what universities do. Universities increasingly publish their procedures and guidelines on their websites, and prospective students and their parents can read them on electronic tours when they choose a university to apply to. This creates an interactive process in which universities explain themselves directly to the public. There is an appearance of accountability in this, albeit of a crude financial kind. The present trend is to try to eliminate potential 'wastage' of this public money, by publishing league tables so that the public can see what it is 'getting for its money'. In this contemporary context, the value statement of the Robbins Report (1963–64) of the 1960s no longer looks quite so straightforward:

> For the individual teacher academic freedom means . . . the right to teach according to his own conception of fact and truth, rather than to any pre-determined orthodoxy. It involves, further, freedom to publish and, subject to the proper performance of allotted duties, freedom to pursue what personal studies or researches are congenial. Freedom of this sort may sometimes lend itself to abuses. But the danger of such abuses is much less than the danger of trying to eliminate them by general restriction of individual liberty.

> The restriction is now not merely of the individual liberty of academics but a wholesale revision of priority and purpose. In a recent study, Maskell and Robinson have looked at the indicators of an intellectual poverty manifesting itself in a poverty of language. They ask how a university whose purpose is the pursuit of truth can run courses in tourism and advertising, which seem to have to teach students how to be economical with the truth or to be downright misleading in order to sell a product.[1]

All this puts our dilemma crisply. On the one hand, stand the demands of a 'real world' which is encouraged to think of value for money. On the other, stands a notion of value of quite another sort.

The paradox of the developments discussed in these pages is that this greater intrusiveness of the 'real world', the stronger sense of a right to know what is going on and to interfere, is not leading to a university system bolder and more courageous in its self-understanding and able to engage fearlessly in a frank dialogue about the public interest. It is creating a fearful, creeping, apologetic, resentful and both intellectually and financially impoverished university world. It should be possible to say robustly that the university 'is' the real world, a world of a higher 'reality', but that will convince only when it is presented with uncompromising conviction. The universities have become pusillanimous about speaking up for these larger priorities.

There seem to be broadly two reasons for that. One is a loss of clarity about the value system of a university – the kind of thing which was the subject of Chapter 1. The other is the failure to stand up to government pressure to create relationships with industry which may be potentially compromising and insist upon making terms in which universities are equal 'partners' and join in the 'delivery' of training as well as education.

Speaking clearly about academic values

It was perceptively suggested by Mike Shattock in a review in the *Times Higher Education Supplement* of 31 May 2001, that much of the development of recent decades has been driven by a power struggle between the 'monarchical' vice-chancellor and the collegial or committee structures of the university. Advertisements for senior posts in universities commonly send mixed messages, couched as they are in 'management-speak' and featuring words which could equally be used for recruitment for senior posts in business. There is talk of leadership and vision, with the prospective senior post-holder depicted as something of a hero figure with steely eyes fixed on the horizon. Teachers of management studies may consider it naïve to query the appropriateness of the term, and explain that 'leadership' in management is about 'building a team', or 'empowering' others, or something of that sort, but the recent reality has been that vice-chancellors have easily become monarchs, behaving like chief executives and hard to call to account. Potential 'leaders' who have no interest in personal power are never thick on the ground.

An older and still useful concept is that of stewardship. The vice-chancellor, as servant of the academic community, would not have seemed absurd a few years ago. Indeed, that is what he was. A return to the sending of that kind of signal would distinguish a university quite clearly from a business. He should also be visibly of high intellectual quality, able to hold his own in a fair argument. He should be able to write his own speeches. Indeed, a good performance test for a prospective vice-chancellor would be to have him up on his feet in debate. He should, in short, show himself to be in the full possession of the very mental powers the community should be able to expect in the academics employed in universities. This public test, repeatedly to be expected in the course of a vice-chancellor's tenure of his office, should demonstrate that he is not a mere diplomat, not just a 'higher civil servant', certainly not merely an effective fund-raiser. The style, the clarity, above all the visibility of his personal values should be striking, and they should include, indeed make prominent, the long-term values. Here he is not 'speaking for' the university but setting a standard, identifying an identity.

The other word likely to be in large letters in the advertisement for the post of modern vice-chancellor is 'vision'. The ancient formulation which made a university a place of teaching, learning and research is hard to better. A vice-chancellor with dollar-signs in his eyes belongs in a cartoon. The far horizons on which his eyes are fixed ought to be those of the advancement of knowledge. He should be defending things with no obvious cash value. And he should have the courage to do it in the face of government pressure to turn his university into a business whose 'product' is little future entrepreneurs. Substituting 'values' for 'vision' would significantly alter the emphasis.

The combination of a personal love of scholarship, a strong sense of the old, deep things a university is for, and with a capacity for getting to the point in practical matters is rare. But it is hard to believe that such individuals will be 'netted' by the style of advertisement currently to be seen. A recent advertisement seeks an 'academic leader' who will 'undertake a leadership and management role' in 'directing, coordinating and embedding strategic university objectives in learning, teaching, curriculum development'. 'Strategic objectives' and freedom to teach and pursue the truth do not belong in the same bed. Money is not the right incentive for the candidate who will understand that. He will want a good reason to postpone the academic research he is bound to be doing and hand over his doctoral students to someone else for a time. Setting a new course for the university to encourage it to get its priorities right may just fit the bill.

This is idealistic of course, but also perhaps a 'higher pragmatism'. Unless someone, man or woman, takes this kind of lead in the next generation of vice-chancellors, universities will not survive; they will be transmuted into something subtly but essentially different in their self-image and purpose. For it will be difficult for institutions that have allowed their priorities to be altered and their values to be compromised to assert themselves and insist on the preservation of their distinctiveness.

Restoring the balance: the bargaining power of universities

The inequality[2] of the relationship between universities and their funders proceeds in part from the cap-in-hand attitude which has been perhaps too readily adopted on the university side in recent years, in the interests of making sure of the money. That balance needs to be redressed. Universities are in a stronger bargaining position than they may realize: governments are anxious to show that an increasing proportion of the population is entering higher education; industries want to take advantage of associations with the 'brand'. Universities with a clear sense of their identity and purpose are in a better position to make terms with those who want to be in on their work and to benefit in their reputations from the association.

That used to be self-evident. On 22 October 1969, a notice by the Council of the Senate in Cambridge was published, on the *relationship between the University and science-based industry.*[3] A number of now familiar themes were already in play: the problem of finding sites for University development; the local planning consequences of any substantial increase in population consequent upon enlarging the local industrial base; the importance of 'preserving the character of the City as a predominantly University City'. In the area of relationships with industry a number of equally familiar considerations were floated without, apparently, any consciousness of the questions of principle which now present themselves. The notice was consciously 'written against . . . the need to develop teaching curricula and research programmes in a manner . . . relevant . . . to the industrial needs of this country, and establish close links through joint research programmes which may involve an interchange of staff and the shared uses of expensive research facilities'. There is talk of 'multiple use [of costly scientific equipment] by industrial and Government as well as University scientists'. It was a matter for pride that there were already collaborative research programmes with industry 'leading to direct recruitment of Cambridge scientists into these units and even to the transfer of research students for substantial periods into these external laboratories'.

Why were these developments then not a threat to the identity and integrity of the University if they are now to be seen in that light? The difference is precisely that it was then not in doubt that the University was the dominant partner. There is a description in the notice of 'the generous attitude of departments to *bona fide* external users'. Today the departments are not the 'generous givers' of free access to facilities and expertise indisputably their own, but the recipients of funding from their industrial partners, and on a scale which in itself threatens to alter the balance of control.

It was recognized – but at this date only in principle – that large-scale industrial involvement would raise questions different in kind, that there would be difficulty in establishing 'planning controls which would prevent research-based units from developing into large-scale manufacturing processes of a type which neither the University nor the County believe should be located in Cambridge'. The notice of the 1960s holds back from that and suggests that 'the type of science-based industry' which should be fostered is of the modest size which could be accommodated in a science park and 'usually' involve 'the same scientists and engineers as managers throughout the entire process'. Also unnoticed at this stage seems to have been the problem of the ownership by the University of the time and work and intellectual property of its employees.

The model was a simple, open one, of friendly, non-exploitative cooperation 'where there is a strong community of interests'. Then 'close cooperation will take place between a Department or teaching officer of the University and a firm anywhere in this country or even overseas'. In this same non-threatening way, research establishments (then mostly government institutions) 'develop links with University Departments through common interest in a particular field of study'. While the lead was intellectual and academic, that demonstrably stood to benefit the University and to assist it in fulfilling its statutory purpose of fostering education, learning and research. If the lead becomes industrial and commercial, there begins to be a potential conflict. It is thus partly a matter of scale and partly a matter of keeping distinct the role of the university and the role of the industrial partner. The 'drift' of recent years has been rapid and universities have, without necessarily always noticing it, slipped into positions where their 'core values' are compromised. The creation of many new relationships in a hurry, some of them relationships of dependency, has been destabilizing for universities,[4] particularly when some of these relationships have not been visible, so that it has been impossible to be sure where the tugs and thrusts were coming from.

The government hovers helpfully

The Treasury's *Report on Financing of High Technology Businesses: A Report to the Paymaster General* of November 1998, speaks in terms of a government 'role as enabler' (p. 3). This theme of enabling and facilitating was already visible in *The Innovation–Exploitation Barrier: The Government Response to the Third Report of the House of Lords Select Committee on Science and Technology* in 1996–97.[5] In the light of the subsequent developments we looked at in Chapter 3, it is reasonable to read into these anodyne terms something more purposeful, going beyond the kindly support that 'enabling' seems to imply. For example, it was revealed in evidence to the House of Commons Select Committee on 16 December 1998 that the government appears to favour clusters of hi-tech companies. Lord Sainsbury was to be one of the 'ministers leading clusters'.[6] It was noted that local communities, especially in historic or preservation areas, might be resistant. 'There are some massive problems, for example, in the case of Cambridge on planning permissions.'[7] 'Will they be going out to Cambridge and saying: you have got to sort out the local planning authority, or what?' it was asked. Mr Foster commented that 'ministerial clout can be pretty helpful if one is really going to address seriously issues like planning permission'.[8] So there was no apparent distaste for direct intervention.

Government policy driving the research

Government willingness to see active control of specific research projects emerged in evidence in December 1998. '[In the USA] it is government which is funding . . . research through . . . contractual obligations. I think that could work in the UK.'[9] 'In regard to using public money in situations where very high leverage is obtainable, then yes I would advocate it.'[10] It was acknowledged late in 1998, in evidence to the House of Commons Committee on Science and Technology that in the USA large companies 'receive a great deal of contract work from Government where the aim is to achieve an outcome which the defence industry, or whatever, may need'. 'I would have no problem with that [in the UK],' acknowledged Sir David Cooksey.[11] Universities might, and if they do not, they should.

The kind of dilemma which was almost bound to arise was vividly put by Northrop Frye in the late 1980s: 'The question . . . in Canada, is whether Canada should get into Reagan's Star Wars schemes or not, and whether this would be accompanied by contracts let out to universities. Well, hell, there was a time when no university that valued its reputation would even think of such a thing. It would mean classified information, and the universities are not supposed to deal with classified information. If you want to work on that stuff, you get the hell out of the university.'[12]

During the period when the Science and Technology Committee and the Treasury had been travelling this road, there had also been headway upon another which appears to run crosswise to it. The British Biotech and the genetically modified foods inquiries of the Science and Technology Committee were concerned with the problems which can arise when the interests of commercial urgency and academic scientific caution come into conflict. Yet there was no frank recognition as yet in the UK of the problem already familiar in the USA, when 'in 1994 . . . obituaries were being written for an industry over-expanded by greed for profit'.[13]

One of the most important indicators of the continuing need for a buffer-state between government money and institutional academic recipient is the (apparent) failure of this House of Commons Select Committee for Science and Technology to notice that what is sauce for industrial geese is also sauce for the government gander.

The USA-envy evident in the texts cited here made UK commentators often uncritical of the drawbacks, although those were being recognized and even attended to under other policy headings. There are frequent approving references in the literature to the success of the USA in making research pay through industrial liaison. This seemed to take the USA to be cutting a path the UK should seek to follow if it wanted similar results for the UK economy.[14] But that was only half the story, as the 'horror stories' of biotech blunders and the impending political disaster in Europe of the genetically modified foods projects illustrate. The USA experience had been not only of financial success but also of unforeseen and serious impediments to the freedom and honesty of research, which have the potential to undermine the very science base on which commerce relies. 'I was at one time Managing Director of a start-up company called Stanford Rook. This had one biological product, which was thought to have a beneficial therapeutic effect on clinical tuberculosis.'[15]

In this example (a letter sketching this story was among the materials submitted in connection with the British Biotech inquiry), there were some clinical trials and then the company was floated. The managing director was concerned that the flotation documents 'contained statements about the previous trials that were unduly optimistic and could not be sustained by the available data'. He declined to sign the prospectus and 'thus resigned as a Director and later as an employee'. Two years later, after a much bigger and better-controlled clinical trial, it was publicly announced that 'the therapeutic agent had no beneficial effect in the treatment of uncomplicated clinical tuberculosis . . . The share price of the company collapsed.'

In this situation the only regulatory process which could have controlled the growth of this company beyond the stage of listing on the stock market was the Stock Exchange Rules (requiring declaration of major changes in expectation of a company's performance). There were no publicly accepted 'Nolan-type' rules to which this managing director could point when he faced his dilemma, to ensure that commercial interest did not run ahead of the science.

It is not easy for universities to stand up to this kind of government pressure, since they must have enough money to pay salaries and maintain buildings. But with determination, cooperation and a set of vice-chancellors who believed it to be of vital importance for the future of the very survival of true universities, it could be attempted. It is notorious that politicians see few votes in backing universities (but that may change now that the children of an increasing proportion of families are adversely affected by student tuition fees and changes in what is on offer to students).

The restoration of an 'independent intermediary'

The restoration of an 'independent intermediary' might be helpful here. The tendency towards direct government as well as commercial and industrial funding of academic research involves a radical innovation with major public interest implications. It goes against the principle, established by the Robbins Report in the early 1960s that: 'Considerations of academic freedom require that autonomous institutions of higher education should draw the Government's financial support through an independent body.'[16] Since it was framed in response to the Robbins Report of nearly 40 years ago, the requirement that government money should be given to universities through an independent intermediary has been honoured in principle and in the main. In recent years, the Higher Education Funding Councils have provided the 'infrastructure'. Infrastructure funding has normally been awarded from public money, by the statutory funding councils on an untargeted block grant basis. Research councils (which were deemed to assess applications on academic not political grounds) awarded the project money. In this way, at least a notional separation continued to be maintained between the choice of specific topics of scientific and other research in universities and government funding to enable the research to be carried out. That was in line with this caveat in the Robbins Report: 'Without proper safeguards, the "necessity" for . . . coordination may easily come to be influenced chiefly by the short-term context of political considerations and pressures, and . . . the orderly development of academic institutions may thus be liable to interruption by forces quite foreign either to education or to the advancement of knowledge.'

The 'buffer' or 'barrier' is a protection which can be expected to be constantly under attack, in the rough and tumble of political life.[17] Baroness Young, speaking of the balance of power between funding council and government in the House of Lords before the passing of the Further and Higher Education Act 1992, already saw danger signals.[18] In the projected Cambridge–MIT scheme as it was at first published in late 1999, the government suddenly inserted a last-minute provision which would remove this protective shield altogether for this £68m, a considerable amount of public money. The Cambridge–MIT venture was to get government funding so direct that the government proposed to release portions of money as it approved the purpose for which they are to be used: 'the Government is willing to commit up to £68m over five years against contracts for specific programmes of activity'.[19]

Values have to be fought for against such seductive, subtle, persistent influences as these. It is an unremitting task. Even if an independent intermediary cannot now be realistically expected in every situation, it is not too late to recover the habit of always considering what difference it would make if it were still a requirement.

Nationally accepted guidelines: a committee on standards?

Are systematic protections possible?

It would not be impossible to set up a structure containing proper protections of the core purposes of universities and of the independence of their research. This would involve a series of provisions: first, an agreed code of good practice; secondly, its policing.

In 1997, Packham and Tasker made a list which might form the basis of a code, based on the experience of Yale, Harvard and other institutions.[20] It is regrouped here, under three heads:

1. *Intellectual freedom.* The university must insist that there is to be no restriction on the freedom of inquiry of their academics, or their freedom to discuss their work.[21] Similarly, there should be no restriction on publication, except for any minor delay necessary for patenting. The university should not agree to any arrangements which will restrict the free communication of ideas.

2. *No ethically dubious obligations.* In so far as that may be compatible with their duties as charities to accept benefactions offered to them, the university should accept sponsorship for research or enter into partnership for research only with business entities whose area of operations is compatible with the university's core purposes (no tobacco money?).

3. *No hidden connections.* All authors of publications should acknowledge their funding sources and any direct business associations. The academics involved should report to their university all their involvements with organizations which have any connection with their professional work.

Another way of approaching the conflict of interest problem is to see it in terms of a conflict of loyalty. The academic making a scientific discovery with commercial potential is now caught between two conflicting pressures. The first is his scholarly duty to share his knowledge. That is his primary duty as an academic researcher, arguably overriding even the contractual duty to act in the employer's financial interests where the employer is a university. The second is to keep it to himself and his commercial sponsor so that other commercial interests in competition may not get wind of it.[22]

Honest, ordinary scientists express concerns over these tensions, for scientists are only too familiar with this type of conflict and there are indications that the scientific community would welcome ethical and practical guidelines. It is certainly not a matter which can be left unresolved where universities enter wholesale or as institutions into arrangements creating such fundamental conflicts of interest for their research scientists.

The University of Oxford has published guidelines which embody the principle that the University is a distinct entity which may, or whose employees may, explore 'links' with outside interests. Where that happens, the University must protect its integrity as an institution which 'seeks to promote the advancement, preservation, and dissemination of knowledge; the instruction of undergraduate, graduate and postdoctoral students; and the advancement of the public interest'. It must also ensure that there are no improprieties of the sort which would conflict with the Nolan principles on standards in public life. Oxford intends to require its employees to get its express authority before they hold executive directorships and that authority will be given only exceptionally. 'Consent will be given only if the appointing authority is satisfied that the appointment will comply with the general conditions relating to the holding of other appointments.' The code's provisions are geared to clarifying where the University ends and other enterprises begin and to ensuring that the integrity (in the widest sense of wholeness) of the University is not compromised. It is also designed to ensure that there is a consciousness.[23]

A project signalled in the *Times Higher Education Supplement* of 15 June 2001 may prove to be helpful in making this kind of thing practicable. A website (www.integrityinscience.org) was being set up on which could be found details of the other 'interests' of scientists, university researchers and non-profit organizations 'whose work is being underwritten by the private sector'. The newspaper records the comment on behalf of the Centre for Science in the Public Interest that 'corporations increasingly are funding academic scientists to conduct research . . . and provide advice. Too frequently, neither the scientists nor the corporations disclose that.' The effect of the existence of this site is likely to be to make it less easy to avoid making disclosures and more shameful to be found not to have done so.

Packham and Tasker's basic rules stand up very well still. Something like them applied informally suggested a way forward in a situation of a type which appears to be becoming worryingly common. In the *Times Higher Education Supplement* of 16 April 1999, Sir David Weatherall, Regius Professor of Medicine in the University of Oxford, commented that 'mounting pressures on scientists by government and funding bodies to develop links with industry and to pursue work likely to be of commercial value are generating a research environment fraught with pitfalls'. Weatherall gives examples of 'just how badly things can go wrong'. The Canadian pharmaceutical company Apotex sought to suppress research results in a project it had funded involving scientists at the University of Toronto. In principle, such action ought to be able to be countered by pressure within the academic community to 'share' the results of research through the normal routes of publication, and the giving of papers at conferences. In this example, these peer review processes also went wrong, in that 'one international scientific society accepted research papers' written and submitted without being shown to the head of the project, in which outcomes were 'reinterpreted'.[24] There is also a danger to freedom of speech in reprisal against academics who fall foul of such interests.[25] Olivieri, the scientist in question, was 'removed as director of the highly successful Toronto Haemoglobinopathies programme'. Only direct intervention by the president of the university, the hospital and Sir David Weatherall himself got her reinstated.

David Weatherall approaches this situation in exactly the spirit of constructive rule-making which now seems the only practical way forward. He sets out a list of desiderata, adding elements to the Packham and Tasker list (numbered 2 and 4 here). (1) 'Companies that disagree with academic collaborators should do so under conditions of open scientific debate.' (2) There should be an expectation that the academic community will support a scientist suffering 'harassment' from such commercial funders. (3) 'And learned societies must carefully investigate the origin of research papers offered to them and make sure there are no conflicts of interest among those involved in collecting and writing up the data.' Such conflicts must also be addressed within the local academic community where the work is being undertaken. There must be no compromising of the freedom to publish the truth which is at the heart of the academic endeavour and the ultimate guarantee of quality. (4) Where there is a safety factor there is additional responsibility to be open about risk. 'In any agreement involving research on patients between a clinical scientist and a company, the scientist must have the freedom to tell the patients and the scientific community about any concerns they have regarding the damaging effects of the drug or procedure.'

Awareness of context: the benefits to the science itself of its industrial development

These protective principles should not have as their aim the prevention of all funding liaisons with industry and commerce, or even all shared work. In some branches of applied science, the science itself benefits from being tried out in industry or commerce; indeed it may need it. 'A science is growing up which will underpin software engineering.'[26] 'Some of the foundations of this science exist.' Its applications are already 'diverse' and cover 'a huge range'. The argument put forward in one instance was that the task of mapping the territory could not progress without the feedback from the experience gained in attempting to make 'applications'. 'Industrial experience in these activities feeds back into the science and even leads us to modify our scientific foundations.'[27] It was further suggested that 'the strategy for developing this science' is 'experimental'. 'It can only be developed on the basis of engineering experiment.' To that end, it is argued, 'controlled experiment in the academic laboratory is not enough'.[28] That last assertion is important and it had to be justified. 'Scale,' said Professor Milner, 'is an essential part of the software problem.' So the development of rules of 'scientific good conduct' for academic science needs to take place in awareness that it is not necessarily always desirable or possible to treat the academic and the commercial scenes as though they were quite separate.

The problem of ensuring compliance

The greatest problem is to find a way of ensuring compliance with any set of rules which may be devised. The industrial partner has to be brought to accept and adhere for its part to any such code. The university has to be persuaded to consider it a nationally (or internationally) recognized set of norms, and the autonomy of universities may make that a difficulty in practice. One way of encouraging such habits of thought is for the government to use 'conditions of grant' sanctions and withhold public funding from institutions found out in bad practice. But that in its turn requires a political will which is not visible in the UK at the beginning of the third millennium.

The other way is to change the climate of expectation. That might be achieved by the setting up of a watchdog on standards in the commercial exploitation of academic science. It would require the political will, and a U-turn on the part of recent governments, which have put first the putative saving to the public purse of getting private funding to do what otherwise would fall to the public funder, and have turned a blind eye to adverse consequences to the integrity and credibility of the resulting scientific findings. The climate was right in the 1990s to maintain a national Committee on Standards in Public Life. The climate has not been right to set up a committee on standards in the conduct of publicly funded scientific research, perhaps because so much of it is now partly funded by industrial and commercial interests, and it has not been government policy to discourage that by setting high hurdles of propriety in its administration. The suggestion that such a body be set up has been made, however, by Herbert Arst and Mark Caddick. They call for 'the creation of an independent body dedicated to ensuring scientific integrity that would: have an enforceable set of rules; offer protection for those making accusations in good faith; have resources and powers to conduct or oversee investigations; ensure that conclusions of misconduct are reported and acted upon'.[29] If, as they suggest, 'receipt of research funding, taking up a post in an academic institution, or the publication of work were dependent on acceptance of the authority of such a body, it would be possible for [that body] to receive and impartially investigate complaints and act on any significant instance of misconduct', this would, in effect, restore the 'buffer' thought essential to the protection of academic freedom and integrity during the twentieth century. Some such requirement (again perhaps backed by 'conditions of grant' sanctions), would be essential in order to get universities to accept what might otherwise look like an intrusion on their autonomy. But this too would require government will. Perhaps only a major disaster consequent upon the failure to police the integrity of research will create that will.

Personal accountability?

Developing good habits

Universities are now actively engaged in providing courses for staff development. They are rarely as comprehensive on the side of the development of administrators as of academic staff. Seminars 'to support educational development' might include admissions interviewing, tutorial teaching, small group learning, gender in teaching, feedback to enhance student learning, negotiating conflict in educational relationships, lecturing and student learning, approaches to learning: practice sessions, performance matters: voice, posture, and relaxation, voice coaching, supervising PhD students, new approaches to assessment, departmental seminars as an introduction to teaching and learning. A series of seminars might be designed to support research: writing research grant applications, writing research papers, advanced biomedical communications, managing research projects, descriptive statistics for research, introductory statistical modelling for research. The next sequence is of 'seminars to support professional development': managing appraisal, appraisal training for departments and teams. Then there is 'personal effectiveness': dealing with stress, assertiveness. There is 'time management', directed, it seems, chiefly at administrative underlings, though there is a seminar for 'those who manage their own time' (including 'managers'). There are possibilities of seminars on presentation skills and on written communication. Finally comes the series of 'seminars to promote effective management' for 'heads of department; those who lead research teams; technical, clerical, library and secretarial staff with supervisory responsibilities; and administrators', covering financial management, managing induction, management of contract research staff, team leadership, managing administrative projects, dealing with harassment, with a section of seminars for personal recruitment, manual handling, equality and diversity, disability matters, managing employee absence, managing employee conduct and performance, coaching skills. A final area provides for introduction to the university and its governance.[30]

What sort of training is really required here? Internalization of basic rules would do more than anything else to improve performance rapidly. That means getting into the heads of those with authority or powers in a university so thorough a knowledge of the rules of fairness and of the proper exercise of discretion that they cannot make the elementary mistakes which are so frequent without noticing.

Personal liability

Another route by which accountability may conceivably be ensured within existing statutory provision is through bringing home the personal liability of individual governors as members of the corporation. Palfreyman argues that members of the boards of governors of the post-1992 universities, members of the council of the 'old' chartered universities and the fellows of Oxford and Cambridge colleges[31] 'may become personally liable to compensate the institution for any financial losses resulting from mismanagement and for any damages and legal costs arising from successful claims brought against the institution and even the Members personally by a third party for breach of contract or in tort', though it is admittedly unlikely.

Palfreyman lists the fiduciary duties of the members of a governing body as: acting solely in the best interests of the institution; not confusing its interest with theirs; not using confidential information to their personal advantage; not voting to their personal benefit; acting prudently with skill and care (on the 'reasonably competent' test); and acting *intra vires*, with proper authority given by duly convened and quorate meetings, ensuring that any delegation of power or decision-making is legitimate.[32] But most of this would be likely to provide a realistic basis for calling to account through the courts only where the result of the mismanagement or misconduct was financial loss. It would be likely that the institution's indemnity insurance would protect such members from being forced to face the consequences of their actions and omissions in any personally telling way. Perhaps that should change.

This does not necessarily touch the spot (with the exception of the governing bodies of Oxford and Cambridge colleges), since the problem area of poor-quality administration characteristically lies at the level of the detailed running of the institution's affairs, and not round the table where the governors meet. But it could 'move' so as to lie on that table when the institution failed to put it right.

What is the individual responsibility of the senior officers of universities and what follows from that by way of accountability? One of the grounds on which a member of staff may be removed from office under the Model Statute drawn up following the Education Reform Act of 1988, is (to take the form adopted by the University of Wales at Swansea) 'failure . . . of the person concerned to perform the duties of his office or to comply with the conditions of tenure of his office'. That must include observing the subordinate legislation of the institution, and most conspicuously so in the case of the vice-chancellor as chief executive, or the senior administrative officers and management. But in case after case when those entrusted with responsibility under the subordinate legislation of an institution fail to follow its requirements there are no repercussions for themselves. They break the domestic laws and the rules of natural justice. They dismiss members of staff without due process. They discipline students without telling them that they have a right to know of accusations against them and to be given an opportunity to defend themselves. Perhaps the member of staff or the student succeeds in litigation against the university, but the individual or individuals guilty of the breach of the internal regulations are unlikely to be called to account. A case in point is the criminal prosecution of the University of Cambridge in 1999, on eight counts, over the loss of a radioisotope. The university had to plead guilty on several of the counts, but no senior head rolled. A laboratory technician or other relatively lowly member of staff may get the blame in court and be sacked from his job. The head of department's formal responsibility for health and safety in the department is not in dispute. But it is not (with one or two notable exceptions, such as the Qureshi case at Manchester where a head of department was found personally liable over racial discrimination) his head that rolls or he who pays the damages.

Accountability and responsibility

'I had better tell you about it,' says the minister; 'I must admit fault,' says the civil servant. The practical effect of the Butler doctrine that a minister is accountable while a civil servant is responsible 'is to diminish ministerial responsibility without increasing official responsibility'.[33] In short, if something goes wrong, the minister owns up to it, takes responsibility and resigns (in theory), but the civil servant has responsibility thrust upon him and is subjected to internal discipline.

The attempts in the literature of recent civil service reform to clarify the difference between accountability and responsibility are confused. The problem is more difficult still in the arena of the 'management' of a university where it may be by no means clear who is playing minister and who is playing civil servant. Sir Richard Scott himself provided a paper for a collection published by the Chartered Institute of Public Finance and Accountancy in 1996 in the wake of the Scott Report.[34] He drew out two 'vital elements' upon which the system of ministerial accountability depends: clarity about who can be held to account and held responsible when things go wrong; confidence that Parliament is able to gain the accurate information required to hold the Executive to account and to ascertain where responsibility lies. There is no difficulty in this context with asserting that the decision is the minister's. But there is a difficulty over the role the advice plays when it is given by persons possessing information which is not under the minister's eye.

The Public Service Committee had a great deal of difficulty with the distinction between accountability and responsibility. Sir Michael Quinlan thought there was a distinction, indeed 'a valid and significant distinction'. He cast it in terms of a delegation of powers in which those to whom the powers are lent carry the blame for any misapplication of them: 'Accountability means "I have the authority and the power to give directions and I can, therefore, be questioned about whether I gave directions or whether I will give them"'. He takes responsibility to be 'about whether praise or blame attaches'.[35]

The general view accepted in the evidence before the Public Service Committee was in line with this, that accountability merely means explaining yourself, while responsibility involves the possibility that blame will attach, and punishment follow. 'I think accountability is an obligation, as I understand it, to explain, to say what happened, to be accountable for it; responsibility implies some more potentially disciplinary response for it.'[36]

A minister and a senior civil servant will not be much dissimilar perhaps in intelligence or in educational attainment. If something goes badly wrong, the minister may resign, but he will not have to face a disciplinary tribunal. But the civil servant may be blamed and disciplined.

Yet Sir Michael Quinlan conceded that there was no tidy dividing line, and the lack of a sharp distinction between accountability and responsibility proves to be both conceptual and practical. One of the problems is the subtlety with which the one shades into the other at precisely the point where it matters who knew what. Despite the Scott Report's criticisms, 'in the end it would seem that Ministers are not to blame, because they did not knowingly mislead Parliament, civil servants are not to blame, because they were the servants of the Ministers, and, therefore, we are left in a sort of area where nobody is really to blame for anything that happened, and does not that rather confuse the position of accountability?' it was asked on behalf of the Public Service Committee.[37] This phenomenon is not unknown in the world of higher education. The comment in the Robbins Report (p. 24) on 'the general obscurity in which so many of their administrative and financial arrangements are shrouded' was restricted to Oxford and Cambridge, but it is of wider application, and as well-founded a criticism as it was 40 years ago.

So one of the ways forward in improving the present glaring flaws in the running of universities is to do some hard thinking about personal accountability, who should carry it, where it should rest, and redressing the present imbalances of power which mean that the student or ordinary member of staff is usually helpless to get wrongs righted because the university protects its senior figures as though they *were* the university.

A *higher education audit commission?*

> Accountability can only be meaningful if it involves some form of
> meaningful external scrutiny by agents independent of the institution
> concerned, who are themselves clearly accountable to some body, and
> who produce a public report that can have important and clear con-
> sequences, positive or negative, for the institution or academic unit
> concerned.[38]

A series of reports of the National Audit Office and the Public Accounts
Committee have appeared. One after another, Huddersfield University,
Swansea Institute of Higher Education, Portsmouth University, Glasgow
Caledonian University, Southampton Institute of Higher Education, Thames
Valley University, have all had serious problems. The problems have often
concerned the behaviour of a chief executive acting as though he were a
potentate and acting in secrecy, with a small clique of complaisant governors
and no real awareness among the others that matters for which they had
formal responsibility were not being dealt with in an appropriate way, or
sometimes even lawfully. Staff can suffer overloading or job insecurity;
students may suffer from a consequent drop in standards. The Further and
Higher Education Act 1992 put into statute an ideological assumption that
it was appropriate for the new universities which were being created out of
the former polytechnics to have boards of governors, most of whom were
not working in the institution and whose chief qualification for serving lay
in, for example, their local 'industrial experience'. They were to be 'persons
appearing to the appointing authority to have experience or, and to have
shown capacity in industrial, commercial or employment matters or the
practice of any profession'.[39]

This has not been a decision without its adverse consequences. 'Governors
are expected to underwrite the cost of projects, the educational rationale
for which they are discouraged from questioning. Equally, however, the
Academic Board may well put forward suggestions of proposals without
having any sense of the resource implications.'[40] Such governors have not
always proved effective watchdogs, as the series of reports from the National
Audit Office and the Public Accounts Committee shows.

Against this background of warning signals, we come again to ways and
means. It ought to be possible to find routes not only to requiring accountability but also to providing remedies for 'not following the governing instruments' of a university or acting against its interests.

Yet it is not easy to circumvent vested interest in being free of real scrutiny,
especially on the part of the old, rich and powerful universities. Various things
were hinted at in the House of Lords debates of December 1991, before the
finalizing of the terms of the Act of 1992, and of course before its drawbacks
could become apparent in the light of experience.

The first hint was of direct government intervention to change the statutes
of universities. Lord Renfrew was disturbed at the suggestion:

The Committee will perceive that it is a serious matter. Each of the existing universities in Britain was established either by a specific Act of Parliament or by a Royal Charter, under which procedures are laid down for making statutes. Any new statutes are proposed by the universities in question and have to be approved by the Privy Council . . . Clause 71 of the present Bill will allow an order of the Privy Council to modify the governing instrument after consultation . . . so this clause would set aside at a stroke the procedures built up over the years for all existing universities whereby their statutes may be changed. It would annul at a stroke the degree of independence conferred over the centuries by various Acts of Parliament and by Royal Charters. I should be astonished and dismayed if that were the considered intention of the Government.

A head of a Cambridge college, he proposed an amendment to exempt 'the existing and long-established universities', with that focus on 'local interest' which so often weakens the arguments universities could make so much more powerfully if they stuck together.

The thrust of this argument was that exceptions should be made to any regulatory framework which might make possible some direct calling to account, in favour of the old and established universities.[41] There is a familiar ring to this special pleading. It bears a resemblance to the arguments put forward from 1999 by some of the old and elite institutions that they should be left out of the teaching assessment plans because their track record was so strong, and they did not need to be held accountable. It remains to be seen how well they will stand up to quality assessment of the administration which supports their provision of teaching.

One route to improving the accountability of universities would be to strengthen the powers of the Quality Assurance Agency to conduct institutional audits in ways already touched on.[42]

Another, the setting up of a higher education audit commission has been mooted in a series of articles by Roger Brown, formerly chief executive of the Quality Assurance Agency, and subsequently principal of the Southampton Institute of Higher Education.[43] (The Southampton Institute had been the subject of National Audit Office and Public Accounts Committee reports as a result of events in the time of its previous principal/director.) Such a commission might be parallel to a committee charged with protecting standards and integrity in academic scientific research. It would, as Brown points out, be something of a paradox, in that it would appear to impose a further bureaucracy and to constitute a further threat to autonomy; yet properly managed it need not do so, and would indeed be protective against those things. 'I believe that my proposals would, if implemented effectively, lead to much greater public support for these institutions and those who govern and manage them, something which is badly needed if the sector is to retain public confidence in its activities.'[44] A key question here once more is the political will.

6

Conclusion: the University and Social Commentary

The law in England since the late 1980s has said that academic freedom of speech ought to enjoy a freedom beyond the general freedom of speech of other members of society. That assumes that there is a public interest, for one of the problems about the official countenancing of a special freedom of speech is that it necessitates holding open a space in which some very silly and self-indulgent things can be said. It is inherently a risky enterprise, for only if things can be tried out in public with some ease can others test and explore them. Only after that has happened does it begin to become clear what is worth having and may lead somewhere. And it may not emerge for a considerable time what that is. We need to consider here first the reasons for a special statutory protection of academic freedom of speech and secondly the 'political' role academics may usefully play as commentators.

The modern legislative framework in the UK

It is remarkable in the face of the pervasive recognition that intellectuals are likely to be as troublesome as they are useful to society, that English law was prepared to recognize in the late twentieth century that unless this intellectual endeavour is protected, society will suffer.[1] As Northrop Frye puts it: 'There's an immense difference between a professor's being able to speak his mind and get away with it and hold his job, and his finding himself in a concentration camp.'[2] The question is whether there is a profession which does not merely require but actually is itself the exercise of a special freedom of speech.

'Academic freedom consists in the right to choose one's own problem for investigation, to conduct research free from any outside control, and to teach one's subject in the light of one's own opinions.'[3] These academic exercises are forms of speech. Polanyi went further. He argued that such freedom, collegially exercised, is necessary to the fulfilment of the common purposes of scholarship; that in the academic arena 'freedom is an efficient form of organisation . . . efforts will be efficiently coordinated if only each is left to follow his own inclinations'.[4]

The parameters have changed since these remarks were made in 1951. The academic staff employed by the new (post-1992) universities in the UK are commonly working under contracts which limit the speech of researchers even about their specialist areas of work. There is a trend, even in the old universities, towards line management structures, which run on the master–servant principle, and counter to collegiality. The current statutory protections of academic freedom of speech date from the period when these changes began to be felt, yet discussion of the intention of the legislation at the time it was enacted reflected no conscious desire to effect the changes which have come about. They appear to be unconnected with the question whether academic freedom of speech is necessary for a university to fulfil its scholarly function. For that must, presumably, be the main reason for affording it a special statutory protection.

The Education (No. 2) Act 1986, s. 43(1) requires that 'freedom of speech within the law' be 'secured for members, students and employees of the establishment and for visiting speakers'. The need for this legislation had been created by a series of episodes in which militant students had sought to silence invited speakers.[5] The 1986 Act sought to provide for a protected academic environment for freedom of speech. It seems that remarks on any subject at all are covered, providing they are made on the premises, and in some formal connection with the university. Once there, anyone becomes a 'protected speaker'.

On 15 February 1986, Baroness Cox spoke in the House of Lords on two issues which she conjoined under 'the politicisation of education'. She called for 'the guardians of our academies' to 'make freedom of speech their overriding commitment, however unpalatable the views of the speaker may be to them or to their militant students', on the 'Polanyi' grounds that freedom of speech is 'essential for the pursuit of truth and knowledge which lies at the heart of education as we know it'.[6] On the other hand (and here she was thinking of the then current trends in schools), she argued that it was important to prevent 'the politicisation of teaching and curricula'. These conflicting messages, that in the educational arena one must be able to say what one pleases (within the law), and that certain types of speech ought to be banned, she drew together in one breathless sentence crowding together the interests and purposes of schools and universities: 'Education in a free society should enshrine the principles of freedom of speech, freedom to pursue the truth and freedom to develop views and interests not predetermined by the political commitments of local authorities or of teachers.'[7]

A clause in the Education Reform Act 1988 provides a protection which was again prompted by circumstances of the moment: 'Academic staff have freedom of speech within the law to question and test received wisdom, and to put forward new ideas and controversial or unpopular opinions, without placing themselves in jeopardy of losing their jobs or privileges they enjoy at their institutions.' This provision was never explicitly extended to short-term contract research scientists or to academic-related staff, and it remains uncertain how far it applies to them. It was primarily directed at those in the type of appointment which had previously been tenured. So it cannot be argued that its primary intention was the protection of academic freedom of speech as such. It lacked the comprehensiveness of scope of s. 43 of the 1986 Act.

'I note and respect your commitment to freedom of speech and expression and can confirm that the university is also committed to those principles,' wrote the Vice-Chancellor of Middlesex University to a member of his academic-related staff, his head of media relations.[8] Almost immediately afterwards she was sacked 'for alleged misdemeanours, which included the charge that she "sought to assert her independence", and maintained a tradition of free speech, as editor of the University in-house newspaper, *North Circular*'. The member of the academic staff who actually wrote the offending article, but who was protected by s. 202 of the 1988 Act, did not suffer the same fate.

In the House of Commons debates of 1987 there are nervous scratchings-about on this point. On 26 October: 'The Government recognise the importance of maintaining academic freedom, and the provisions [of the Act] will be framed with that objective in mind.'[9] It proved necessary in the House of Commons debates of 20 November 1987 to ask a question to focus attention on the precise relationship between tenure and academic freedom: 'on the means by which the provisions of the Education Reform Bill will strengthen the protection of academic freedom'.[10]

The answer Mr Baker received from Mr Jackson cited the wording of s. 202 of the Act and added, sidestepping the question: 'The precise content of the idea of academic freedom in any particular situation depends, however, among other things, on the type of institution and the subject taught or researched; we do not believe that it can be said to have a single clear definition applicable in all circumstances.'[11] The plan was to hive off to the University Commissioners the task of clarifying this point.[12] This seems to imply that the protections might properly vary from institution to institution, thus echoing the localization of academic freedom in the 1986 Act. It runs counter to any presumption that there exists a type of academic freedom of speech to be protected as a general good. And in any case the half-promised work was never done.

The answer in Hansard continues: 'The existence of suitable and disinterested appeals arrangements will represent an important element of protection for academics from victimisation on account of their views.'[13] This, too, was never 'delivered'. There is no appeal in the Model Statute from the findings under a grievance procedure, and no protection against reprisal.

A Model Statute *was* drawn up.[14] It does not go into these matters and merely reproduces the provision in s. 202. That too does not appear to have been what was intended, indeed half-promised, by Parliament: 'It will be for the Privy Council, in considering whether to recommend to Her Majesty that amendments to university statutes put forward by the commissioners should be confirmed, to satisfy itself that the Government's objective of protecting academic freedom has been properly met.'[15]

It was optimistically asserted that, because employment matters were being taken out of the jurisdiction of the visitor: 'the fact that academics will no longer be precluded from actions in the courts against their employers for wrongful dismissal will represent a further strengthening of academic freedom, in addition to the access they have to industrial tribunals over claims of unfair dismissal'.[16] That leaves out of account the fact that the academic has still lost his job, and probably any future career prospects, and that the courts are notoriously reluctant to consider reinstatement.

'Are we not getting into difficulties because we are confusing prevention with punishment?' asked Mr Williams, in his evidence to the Joint Committee on Parliamentary Privilege.[17] The two may, however, be conjoined, and here we have the first principle common to Parliament and other 'free speech environments'. Speech impeded by fear of reprisal ceases to be free speech at all. In *Pepper v Hart*, Lord Browne-Wilkinson took it that Article 9, at the time of its enactment, was designed to ensure that Members of Parliament did not suffer any penalty for speaking freely and could oppose their views to the wishes of the monarch with impunity.[18] This notion, in spirit, informs s. 202 of the Education Reform Act 1988, which allows members of the academic staff to 'question and test received wisdom' without being in jeopardy of losing their jobs or privileges at their institutions.

At issue in the Middlesex case involving the editor of the *North Circular* was an apparent conflict of the Vice-Chancellor's wishes (for the newspaper to be a marketing instrument which he would take with him on journeys abroad to try to win overseas students for the university), and the editor's ambition for it to become a real newspaper, which could report negative as well as positive news. But the matter became a cause célèbre and drew in the lives and careers of other employees and a student who happened to be doing research on whistleblowing for a PhD at the time.[19] This episode showed up the gaps in a protection of freedom of speech which contained express protection against reprisal, for the 1988 legislation was primarily designed to quiet anxieties about the implications of the loss of tenure for that diminishing proportion of those who worked in universities who had previously had it. Because it does not expressly cover academic-related staff or (probably) short-term contract scientists and others, and does nothing to protect students if their supervisors or institutions seek to limit their freedom to 'question and test received wisdom', it would be understandable for those not expressly included at s. 202 to 'confuse' prevention and punishment.

On the British scene the question of campus speech codes has not presented itself as yet with any urgency. The US intention is, on the face of it, benevolent. The assumption is that the weak, the underdogs, need protecting from the full blast of the freedom of speech of the strong and articulate. It then becomes necessary to set up a 'safe speech area' rather than a 'free speech area'. A lesson is perhaps that external control intended to create a balance may be more malign than letting speech go on without restraint. In the USA, political correctness can exercise a certain tyranny. In that country, a university as a free speech environment can regulate the time, place and manner of speech, but not its content. Thus it might be possible to exclude classrooms from a campus speech code, so that what might be offensive if said in the campus bookshop would not be an offence if discussed with serious academic purpose in a class.[20] *Papish v Board of Curators,* 410 US 667 (1973) concerned an attempt to stop distribution of a student newspaper containing an obscene headline.[21] But it was noticed that that meant that universities might be tempted to use the powers they did have as a device for barring the content of speech. That point was attended to in *Clark v Community for Creative Non-Violence* 468 US 288 (1984).[22] If a student organization is 'recognized' by a university, the university then has no right to determine what it can say.[23] A campus speech code is not allowed to be unreasonably broad,[24] so as to prohibit all manner of speech.

Freedom of scholarly discourse and the changing political context

Academic freedom of speech has not always been seen as a good, and in the world of thought of earlier centuries modern preoccupations might have had no place. In the centuries when Oxford and Cambridge were communities of masters who ran their affairs like any trade guild, they were also protective of certain orthodoxies. Scholars who tried to teach otherwise were not to be allowed to make the university a 'school for heretics' (*gymnasium haereticorum*). In 1358, a recanting holder of unauthorized opinions at Oxford was required to say that he recognized that 'our mother the venerable University is catholic, founded on sound teaching and protective of sound faith'.[25] What was being 'protected' was not freedom of speech but the true faith, and those whose belief might be shaken by teaching which challenged it. In 1411, various articles were condemned with the assertion that the University would not allow any doctor, master, bachelor or scholar of the University to teach or defend or even purposefully to hold (*docere, defendere, vel efficaciter tenere*) any such conclusion.[26] Parallel examples can be furnished from Europe, in the form of the lists of banned opinions at the University of Paris during the thirteenth century. So the principle of the 1986 Act is relatively modern.

The present notion that it is in the public interest that academe be allowed freedom to think and write and speak derives from the post-medieval development of a realization that the policing of thought is politically undesirable in the interests of discouraging tyranny. Ideas seeking free expression may be not 'merely' academic: there is a balancing act of public interest in the dissemination of ideas which can go the either way in different political climates. Justice Black in *Burenblatt v United States* 1959 (dissenting) spoke of:

> the unarticulated premise that this Nation's security hangs upon its power to punish people because of what they think, speak or write about, or because of those with whom they associate for political purposes. The Government, in its brief, virtually admits this proposition when it speaks of the 'communication of unlawful ideas'. I challenge this premise, and deny that ideas can be proscribed under our Constitution.[27]

There exists in the USA a notion of 'un-American activities' for which there is no exact British equivalent. The Federal Espionage Act of 15 June 1917 covers 'whoever . . . shall wilfully cause or attempt to cause insubordination, disloyalty, mutiny, or refusal of duty' in a military context, but with a wider hinterland behind it. Justice Sanford recognized in *Gitlow v New York*, 1925, that 'utterances' may:

> threaten breaches of the peace and ultimate revolution. And the immediate danger is none the less real and substantial, because the effect of a given utterance cannot be accurately foreseen. . . . A single revolutionary spark may kindle a fire that, smouldering for a time, may burst into a sweeping and destructive conflagration.[28]

Comparatively recent is the recognition that scholarly inquiry (or, in modern parlance, research) may lead to discoveries which will be of practical benefit to the citizenry, so that it is in the public interest for yet another reason to safeguard the freedom of that inquiry. But once we move down that road, we rapidly move outside the campus and into the worldwide arena in which research is conducted and reported, and the forum becomes still less a literal place. After the terrorist attacks in the USA on 11 September 2001, the American Council of Trustees and Alumni issued a report naming academics who had been unpatriotic in criticising the American response.

Bringing the institution into disrepute

When someone criticizes the conduct of a university, he may 'bring it into disrepute'. In many ordinary employment situations that would be a sacking offence. The Nolan (later Neill) Committee on Standards in Public Life produced its Second Report in 1996, and included in it strictures against gagging of staff in universities: 'Institutions of higher and further education should make it clear that the institution permits staff to speak freely and without being subject to disciplinary sanctions or victimisation about academic standards and related matters, providing that they do so lawfully, without malice, and in the public interest' (Recommendation 7). That expressly allows for the principle that academic freedom of speech need not be confined to the specialist scholarship of the speaker and it does not specify only academic staff. On the other hand, this remained an 'employment' protection in the minds of the Nolan Committee members; it did not include students or visiting speakers, like the Education (No. 2) Act 1986, s. 43, and does not enshrine the principle that a university is an environment within which anyone should be able to speak freely. The employee of a university faces a conflict between the duty of loyalty to the employer under the contract and the public interest in speaking out in its higher academic interests. The Model Statute (which in theory provides protections before dismissal where free speech issues arise) is binding under the 1988 Act only on the 'old' universities and not upon the former polytechnics, and we have been noting that it does not by any means cover all employees of universities.

The framework has been further altered by the Public Interest Disclosure Act 1998. This provides protection for all employees who raise issues of concern in the public interest and through the appropriate channels. It is again primarily a protection against reprisal in employment and does not assist students or visiting speakers. The full effect of European human rights legislation and the Human Rights Act which came into force in the UK in October 2000 has probably not yet been felt at the time of writing.

The UK has not yet fully engaged on the British scene with the problems that American universities encounter over campus speech codes,[29] although the UK's 'harassment' codes are likely to take us increasingly into that area. 'Multicultural curricula, affirmative action, sexual harassment, women's studies' clutter the academic scene in the USA with stumbling-blocks to academic freedom of speech, so that 'one person's freedom is . . . always another person's restriction'.[30] In the USA the 'balancing exercise' between freedom and harm has tended to concentrate on such issues of political correctness.

In *Rigg v University of Waikato* (Commissaries' Report [1984] 1 NZLR 149) the balance struck was between freedom and responsibility. This too is an area where little systematic testing has taken place. The Chris Brand case at the University of Edinburgh in the late 1990s raised questions about the freedom of an academic to make assertions on the basis of his research about the acceptability of paedophilia or the intellectual superiority of whites.[31] Robert Slack won a case for unfair dismissal against the University of North London, over his attempt to raise concerns about the quality of a course in the business school.[32] The Suzi Clark case at Middlesex University led to dismissal of a member of the academic-related staff in March 1999.[33] We are short of case law testing the 'Polanyi' principle that academic freedom of speech must have special protection, but these examples suggest that outcomes are likely to be variable and the core principles by no means always consistently identified.

Political speech, censorship and the public interest: the balancing act

It is in fact remarkable that s. 202 of the 1988 Act and s. 43 of the 1986 Act remain in force. A government acts against what appears to be its natural interest in policing thought, and legislates to protect freedom of speech only in societies where it is recognized that that in its turn protects against tyranny and abuse of power. That has not been the message of recent UK government policy, or the implication of recent UK government pressure. In the ancient Greek world, Isocrates draws attention in his address to the general assembly of Athens (the *Areopagiticus*)[34] to the fact that states which think they are in the best circumstances commonly adopt the worst policies;[35] that those with responsibility for public welfare can be surprisingly blind about the problems the state is facing.[36] There has therefore long been a recognized value in political speech bold enough to draw attention to these faults.

Milton's *Areopagitica* of seventeenth-century England prompted his biographer Dr Johnson to reflect: 'He published . . . his *Areopagitica*, a Speech of Mr John Milton for the liberty of unlicensed Printing.' 'The danger of such unbounded liberty, and the danger of bounding it, have produced a problem in the science of government which human understanding seems hitherto unable to solve. If nothing may be published but what civil authority shall have previously approved, power must always be the standard of truth; if every dreamer of innovations may propagate his projects, there can be no settlement; if every murmurer at government may diffuse discontent, there can be no peace; and if every sceptic in theology may teach his follies, there can be no religion.' Dr Johnson knew that the response of those in power is characteristically to try to enforce silence: 'The remedy against these evils is to punish the authors; for it is yet allowed that every society may punish, though not prevent, the publication of opinions, which that society shall think pernicious';[37] He also knew that attempted repression may be counterproductive: 'but this punishment, though it may curse the author, promotes the book; and it seems not more reasonable to leave the right of printing unrestrained, because writers may be afterwards censured, than it would be to sleep with doors unbolted, because by our laws we can hand a thief.'[38]

Thomas Paine spoke in the eighteenth century with equal vigour of the difficulty of keeping a balance in the public interest between the need to stir things by speaking out, and the routine response of blockage on the part of those in power:

> The people of England, wearied and stunned with parties, and alternately deceived by each, had almost resigned the prerogative of thinking. Even curiosity had expired, and a universal languor had spread itself over the land. The opposition was visibly no other than a contest for power, whilst the mass of the nation stood torpidly by as the prize.[39]

In the same period, William Paley was concerned that the duty to speak out should not be construed to mean that every hiccough ought to lead to 'resistance':

> Not every invasion of the subject's rights, or liberty, or of the constitution; not every breach of promise, or of oath; not every stretch of prerogative, abuse of power, or neglect of duty by the chief magistrate, or by the whole or any branch of the legislative body; justifies resistance, unless these crimes draw after them public consequences of sufficient magnitude to outweigh the evils of civil disturbance.[40]

That is again to say (in another way) that the exercise of a freedom should be tempered by the consideration whether it is in the public interest. 'To do what we will, is natural liberty; to do what we will, consistently with the interest of the community to which we belong, is civil liberty.'[41] Thomas de Quincey also recognized that there was a balance to be struck by governments, between allowing freedom of speech and the silencing of speech in the public interest, that in the generations before him, 'the great principles of representative government and the rights of conscience were passing through the anguish of conflict and fiery trial'.[42]

It could be a fiery trial for individuals too. In 1794, Kant received a letter from the King of Prussia instructing him to curb his tongue: 'We do ... expect that in the future, to avoid our highest disfavour, you will ..., in keeping with your duty, apply your reputation and your talents to the progressive realisation of our paternal purpose; if not, then you must infallibly expect unpleasant measures for your continuing obstinacy.' Kant gave in. He said that he would in future 'refrain altogether from public discourses on religion, in both lectures and writings, whether natural or revealed'. Kant said later that he had undertaken to do this only during the King's lifetime. Nevertheless, he allowed his tongue to be bridled.[43]

In his *On the Duty of Civil Disobedience*, Thoreau proposes it as a duty of government to maintain intellectual space for the citizen: 'Government is an expedient by which men would fain succeed in letting one another alone; and ... when it is most expedient, the governed are most let alone by it.'[44] But that view is rare. From a government's point of view, conformity to the rules society lays down is highly desirable in a subject: 'A common and natural result of an undue respect for law is, that you may see a file of soldiers, colonel, captain, corporal, privates, powder-monkeys and all, marching in admirable order over hill and dale to the wars, against their wills, aye, against their common sense and consciences, which makes it very steep marching indeed.'[45] The citizenry can thus become mere 'small movable forts and magazines', as Thoreau puts it,[46] and the consequence of that, he suggests, may be to diminish the community: 'Under the name of order and civil government, we are all made at last to pay homage to and support our own meanness.'[47]

To bring these examples up to the present day is to recognize that these fundamentals have not changed; the price of freedom has not ceased to be

eternal vigilance. There is no need to suppress speech no one will listen
to. Nadine Gordimer comments on the situation under apartheid in South
Africa: 'The measure of freedom of expression is the measure of a writer's
freedom. It's as simple as that.' She describes the Publications Act of South
Africa, with its more than 90 clauses: 'under which a writer's individual
works could be banned; in addition, a ban on a writer for her or his political
activity meant that the writer could not publish anything, of whatever nature,
not even a fairy tale for children'. 'If a black writer's book was banned, it
was assumed that since he or she was articulate that writer must be a security
risk.'[48]

In a study of local government in 1972 it was still apparent that: 'The
exercise of power precludes discussion. It restricts the partners to the debate
to fellow officials and colleagues; and in so doing immunises the official or
councillor to the clarity of thought and logic of argument that characterises
policies that have to be justified in the face of scepticism.'[49]

It is important for universities not to fail to keep their end up in this
debate. 'Spin', the falsification of, or 'economy with' the truth by press
offices in the interests of 'protecting the reputation' of a university which
has behaved badly, should not be regarded as an acceptable use of public
money. Honesty and openness, the truth and integrity of their work, are
essential to the survival of the university 'project'.

Mechanisms of censorship

In *On Liberty,* John Stuart Mill stated: 'The time, it is to be hoped, is gone
by, when any defence would be necessary of the "liberty of the press" as one
of the securities against corrupt or tyrannical government. No argument
... can now be needed, against permitting a legislature ... to prescribe
opinions to [the people], and to determine what doctrines or what arguments they shall be allowed to hear.'[50] One of the supreme justifications
of universities is that they should do some of the talking which protects
this liberty.

Yet academe, that 'free speech environment', has its own mechanisms of
censorship. Academic communities have ways of discouraging courageous
speech.

> There are limitations, there are constraints, there are – I wouldn't say
> censorship – but ways of limiting the propagation of these questions.
> That's what interests me: the ways in which liberal industrial societies
> do not censor in the literal sense, but through many mechanisms –
> institutional mechanisms, or commercial mechanisms, or technical
> mechanisms – limit this questioning activity.[51]

As things stand, those academic-related staff denied the protection of s. 202
of the Education Reform Act 1988, with its right to 'question and test received

wisdom', may suffer dismissal. The head of media relations at Middlesex University, Suzi Clark, wrote to the *Times Higher Education Supplement*:

> My refusal to be part of a cover-up from the board of governors is the reason, I believe, that trust and confidence in me 'wavered'. I ask whether it is reasonable to expect someone to display corporate loyalty when this is personally and professionally unethical and contrary to public interest. I would also like to know whether an employee who refuses to be party to 'censorship by the back door' can be considered a 'whistleblower'. If not, then what protection can they expect? None whatsoever, if one looks at the price paid, in terms of career, by the John Pickerings[52] of this world, for having taken a principled stand in the public interest . . . Finally, since when has it been 'insubordinate' to offer professional advice that, had it been taken, would have spared the University vast embarrassment and reputational damage?[53]

'It is time surely for David Blunkett [then Secretary of State] to intervene and remind the University that sacking people for expressing opinions is not what is expected in what should be a diverse and pluralistic society.'[54]

The student community is also vulnerable to 'censorship' of free expression of opinion:

> Employment legislation prohibits bullying at work, but because PhDs are not salaried or contracted, they are not legally 'employees' and so are vulnerable to capricious supervisors . . . I regret to say that the conduct of my PhD supervisor was tantamount to bullying. Corroborative complaints by peers and by me proved futile, culminating in my supervisor misappropriating corresponding authorship after editorial review of our manuscript. Although nebulous commitments to PhD supervision published in guidelines are welcome, they are merely cosmetic unless enforced impartially against the occasionally aberrant supervisor . . . My university . . . is ostensibly content to usurp . . . authorship and confidence by allowing vulnerable PhDs to be bullied . . . Reform is required to make possible equitable adjudication in alleged cases of supervisor misconduct . . . To ensure scientific integrity, postgraduate students need adequate protection from the repercussions of 'speaking out'. PhDs should surely be protected from bullying and unfair termination of studentships in the same way as 'employed' researchers are protected by legislation and contracts.[55]

Patronage and reprisal commonly go together and it may be hard to separate the effect of the one from the effect of the other. This is especially true in the client–patron relationships fostered in modern academic scientific research, as we saw in Chapter 3. The author who submits to peer review is at 'the mercy of the malignant jealousy of an anonymous rival'.[56] The perception of that danger can have destructive consequences. The suicide of Jason Altom, a graduate student at Harvard, prompted correspondence in *Nature* on the problem of the degree to which scientists are at the mercy of the patronage of their seniors: 'It is surprising how much control super-visors can exert over their students' careers . . . Throughout a postgraduate scientific career, recommendations are required. This system is inherently biased and subjective. As long as one has a friendly and objective supervisor, all is well. But . . . I know of many students who cannot speak out against their mentors . . . largely because they will need references in the future.'[57] 'Bias is a fact of science . . . If scientists are open-minded and objective why . . . have so many major scientific discoveries only been accepted after bitter and at times brutal resistance?'[58]

A danger now increasingly familiar was signalled as early as 1951 by Michael Polanyi: 'Broadly speaking, you must choose between dedication to the advancement of a system of knowledge which requires freedom, or the pursuit of applied science which involves subordination.'[59] The idea here is that for a scientific discovery effectively to be applied in, for example, a manufacturing process, it must be exploited within a struc-ture where it can be 'handled' by persons who will do what they are told. Increasingly these relatively inescapable imperatives of applied science are being moved into other kinds of scientific inquiry, in a process we explored in Chapter 3.

In 1951, Michael Polanyi saw the internal 'economy' of the scientific research process in a quite different way, which did not differentiate between applied science and 'blue skies' research. 'The co-ordinative principle of science . . . consists in the adjustment of each scientist's activities to the results hitherto achieved by others.'[60] On this view, the scientist is intel-lectually autonomous, but conscious at the same time that he belongs to a great and continuing tradition. It is the tradition which regulates, not an individual in a position of authority. 'Whenever a scientist wrestles with his intellectual conscience, whether to accept or reject an idea, he should be taken to be making contact with the whole tradition of science, in fact with all scientists',[61] past, present and future. This is a notion not far removed from that of the *consensus fidelium* in Christian tradition, with its assumption that there is a 'continuity of community' in every age.[62] It is striking that this seemed self-evident to a scientist, for it is easier on the face of it to see how it would apply to the study of history or literature. But he was making a point about the nature of the scholarly enterprise, and one which went to the heart of its efficiency in achieving its purposes.

> The existing practice of scientific life embodies the claim that freedom is an efficient form of organisation. The opportunity granted to mature scientists to choose and pursue their own problems is supposed to result in the best utilisation of the joint effects of all scientists in a common task . . . It is assumed that their efforts will be efficiently coordinated if only each is left to follow his own inclinations.[63]

On this view, there is a 'unity between personal creative passion and willing-ness to submit to tradition and discipline',[64] with 'the liberty to assert one-self'[65] remaining paramount.

Conformity and compliance

Sextus Empiricus saw the sceptic's as a balancing act, designed to spare him intellectual discomfort. For him, the task of the sceptic is to arrive at a state of mental suspension.[66] For it is disturbing to encounter contradictoriness in things. The 'empirical' ideal is both to arrive at quietude and to avoid going the way of the 'dogmatizers' by taking a view.[67] The sceptic sets out to deal with this disruption to his tranquillity by devising an opposition to every opinion so that argument is met by counterargument and a steady state is achieved. But the very idea that detachment is a scholarly good is itself a position. Sextus Empiricus is aware than in proposing his agenda for the sceptic he is, paradoxically, himself asserting something which looks very like a dogma.[68] He also realizes that the sceptic's mode of life, if taken to its logical conclusion, would make it impossible for him to live an ordinary life at all. He says that the sceptic must simply live according to the ordinary rules of life, but undogmatically, without committing himself.[69]

Another approach is to take a view, even to oppose another view, but to remain deliberately tolerant. 'Choice has to be respected even when it is wrong, as it certainly often is,'[70] says Northrop Frye.

But whatever the motivation, refraining from comment is not the way to press scholarly inquiry. There has to be critical speech. There can be honest difference of opinion among scholars even about what a given work is, how it is to be categorized.

> Critical estimates of Apuleius' book vary greatly, as do opinions about its form and function. At one extreme it has been viewed as an ill-organised collection of scabrous tales . . . solely for the entertainment of the reader; at the other extreme, as the serious confession of an Apuleius saved from the errors of the flesh by the grace of Isis . . . It can be . . . read as Platonic allegory, psychic authobiography, Bildungsroman, and literary parody.[71]

It follows that academic challenge is generally to be regarded as a good: 'We are ascertaind (sic) of all disputable doubts, only by arguing and differing in opinion,' says John Donne.[72] And: 'Discord is never so barren that it affords no fruit.'[73]

The difficulty is to separate critical evaluation driven solely by intellectual considerations from evaluation in which there is some element of pique or self-interest or rivalry. Richard Baxter, the seventeenth-century Puritan, thought religious toleration an evil. He regarded it as 'soul murder'. And, if you reminded him that the want of this toleration had been his own capital grievance, he replied, 'Ah, but the cases were very different: I was in the right; whereas the vast majority of those who will benefit by this new-fangled toleration are shockingly in the wrong.'[74]

Freedom of speech thus perhaps has to allow people to do a great deal of damage to one another's reputations. It would not be fair to say that this was anything new. A similar acerbity is to be found among the scholars of the ancient world. The Greater Hippias opens with Socrates teasing Hippias on how busy and important he is.[75] Then in the eighteenth century Gibbon tersely dismissed the *Autobiography* of Libanius, the fourth-century teacher in Constantinople, as 'the vain, prolix, but curious narrative of his own life. . . . Vain and idle compositions . . . the productions of a recluse student.'[76] But in a twenty-first century university it is different perhaps in its implications because it can inhibit academic freedom of speech in complex way and on a far grander scale. C. P. Snow gives a fictional example:

> If you do plunge in, you've got to be ready for certain consequences to yourself. You're bound to make yourself conspicuous. You're bound to say things which people don't want to hear. The odds are that it will damage your chances. Look, let me be brutal. I know you want your Fellowship renewed, when it runs out . . . But if you make too much of a nuisance of yourself . . . there's going to be a cloud round the name of Skeffington. I don't mean that they'd do anything flagrantly unjust, or that they thought was unjust. . . . With most of us there is a perfectly genuine area of doubt about whether we're really any better than the next man . . . So, if they have anything against us, the net result is liable to be that Skeffington is out, and M. F. Eliot doesn't get promotion.[77]

This is the form of censorship now threatening universities. The shifts of structure and expectation we have been looking at mean that 'big leading players', both academic and administrative, now pose a considerable threat to academic freedom of speech. A form of subtle peer-control coupled with managerial control of the consequences work actively against that courage and outspokenness which are the academic's job. Both discourage the honest expression of opinion.

So the first need if universities are to do their necessary job in society as critics, is for universities themselves to be run more openly, with genuine opportunities for those connected with them to have their say. The Robbins Report of the early 1960s included in academic freedom 'a right to some participation in the formulation of common policy'. Robbins saw the academic staff of universities primarily as 'members', the 'owners' of the institution, and custodians of its purposes. The presumption of collegiality still obtains in some places, but the reality is otherwise: the reality is the increasing exclusion of the academics by the management, especially of the new universities, from policy and decision-making.

'The university represents the freedom that is the only genuine product of social concern . . . I belong, or am trying to belong, to the one real university, the community of freedom where all the genuinely human acts of civilisation take place.'[78] To prepare citizens only for work and the making of money is to condemn them to an inward poverty which ultimately devalues all outward wealth. A younger generation with nothing more interesting to engage it than the possession of the most fashionable mobile phone and little to say which cannot be put into a text message are not being well served by their educational system. They are cut off from a huge range of possibilities of sheer interest in life. Accustomed to respond to the simple manipulations of advertising, they are dangerously unprepared to be critical of the next piece of demagogery, whether it proceeds from the state or from a new Hitler.

Universities have to find the confidence to act and speak and 'be in the real world' on their own terms. They must become more comfortable in it and more confident about their powers to influence it, open it up and shake it free of the shackles of the present state- and commercially driven threat of progressive intellectual impoverishment. That probably means a few individuals taking the risk of saying what they really think, and saying it persistently until the emperor's lack of new clothes is frankly admitted.

Notes

Introduction (pp. 1–4)

1. John Henry Newman ([1852] 1898) *The Idea of a University Defined and Illustrated in Nine Discourses Delivered to the Catholics of Dublin.* London: Longmans.
2. I. Salusinszky (1987) *Criticism in Society* (interview with Northrop Frye), p. 38. London: Routledge.
3. Education Reform Act 1988, s. 202, and see Chapter 6.
4. Education (No. 2) Act 1986, and see Chapter 6.
5. Reported in *Times Higher Education Supplement,* 7 May 1999.
6. Donald Kennedy (1997) *Academic Duty.* Boston, MA: Harvard University Press.
7. Robert Aspland (1817) *An Inquiry into the Nature of the Sin of Blasphemy and into the Propriety of Regarding it as a Civil Offence,* Three Sermons, p. 76. London.
8. Ibid., p. 72.
9. Northrop Frye ([1969] 1990) The community of freedom, in Robert D. Denham (ed.) *Reading the World: Selected Writings, 1935–76,* p. 116. New York: Peter Land Publishing.

Chapter 1   The Academic Project: Driving Forces (pp. 5–37)

1. *The Times,* 10 October 1991: F. Kinsman describing a remark of Ivan Boetsky to students at the University of California, before Boetsky was sent to prison.
2. R. K. Merton ([1942] 1973) The normative structure of science, in N. W. Storer (ed.) *The Sociology of Science: Theoretical and Empirical Investigations,* pp. 267–78. Chicago: Chicago University Press. Also R. K. Merton (1968) *Social Theory and Social Structure,* p. 606. New York: The Free Press.
3. See, for example, David Packham and Mary Tasker (1997) Industry and the academy – a Faustian contract?, *Industry and Higher Education,* April: 85–90.
4. C. P. Snow ([1959] 1993) *The Two Cultures.* Cambridge: Cambridge University Press.
5. I. Salusinszky (1987) *Criticism in Society* (interview with Jacques Derrida), p. 19. London: Routledge.

6. Xenophon (1968) *Constitution of the Lacedaemonians*, I.1, in E. C. Marchant and G. W. Bowerstock (eds and trans) *Scripta Minora*. London: Heinemann.
7. Aristotle, *On Dreams*, II. 459b.
8. R. Courant and H. Robbins (1996) *What is Mathematics*, 2nd edn (Foreword by Ernest D. Courant). Oxford: Oxford University Press.
9. Aristotle, *On Length and Shortness of Life*, 464b.
10. Ibid., 465a.
11. Ibid., 466a.
12. Ibid., 465b.
13. Aristotle, *On Respiration*, 471b–472b.
14. Plato, *Republic*, I.x, 336B–D.
15. Cicero, *Letter*, xii.20.
16. David Weatherall (1995) *Science and the Quiet Art*. Oxford: Oxford University Press.
17. Leon Ellenbogen (ed.) (1981) *Controversies in Nutrition*, p. 1. New York: Churchill Livingstone.
18. Lucretius, *De rerum natura*, lines 21–80.
19. Plato, *Republic*, I.xi, 337B–C.
20. See, for example, Gag on food scientist is lifted as gene modification row hots up, *Nature*, 397, 18 February 1999: 457, and GM foods debate needs a recipe for restoring trust, *Nature*, 398, 22 April 1999: 639.
21. Carl Bode (ed.) ([1851] 1980) *The Selected Journals of Henry David Thoreau*, p. 135. New York: New American Library.
22. Manilius (1977) in G. P. Goold (ed.) *Astronomica*, I.65. Leipzig: Teubner.
23. Plutarch, *Lives*, Theseus I.1.
24. I. Thomas (ed. and trans) (1967) *Greek Mathematics*, 2 vols, p. 154. Boston, MA: Loeb Classical Library, Harvard University Press.
25. Diodorus of Sicily (1968) *Library of History*, I.i, 3–4, in C. H. Oldfather (trans). London: Loeb Classical Library, Harvard University Press.
26. S. T. Coleridge (1983) *Biographia literaria*, vol. I, ch. 9, in James Engell and W. Jackson Bate (eds) *Collected Works*, p. 141. Princeton, NJ: Princeton University Press.
27. Theophrastus (1968) in A. Hort (ed.) *Enquiry into Plants*, I.iii, 1–4. London: Heinemann.
28. Theophrastus (1968) in A. Hort (ed.) *On Odours*, I.1, II.4. London: Heinemann.
29. G. R. Evans (1983) *Old Arts and New Theology*. Oxford: Oxford University Press.
30. Theophrastus, *Enquiry into Plants*, op. cit., I.iv. London: Heinemann.
31. Ibid., I.ii, 3–5.
32. Ibid., I.iii.
33. Plato, *Republic*, I.xii, 338C.
34. Bode (ed.), op. cit., p. 135.
35. Ibid., p. 105.
36. Seneca, *Natural Questions*, 1 Preface 1.
37. In his book *On the Trinity*, Boethius divides philosophy into physics, mathematics and theology.
38. See Evans (1983), op. cit.
39. On the *accessus*, see R. B. C. Huygens (1970) *Accessus ad auctores*. Hingham, MA: Leiden.
40. 'The Pythagoreans . . . thought that [the] principles [of mathematics] must be the principles of all existing things.' Aristotle, *Metaphysics*, A5, 985b23–6.

41. *Quae in morbis communia sunt.* Celsus (1960) in W. G. Spencer (ed.) *De medicina*, Proemium, 57. London: Heinemann.
42. 'It is sensible to spend one's youth planting for the future. Only then, in maturity, should one turn one's attention to building. When you do build, build storage, so that wine and oil can be kept until they will fetch a good price.' Cato (1967) in W. D. Hooper and H. Boyd Ash (eds) *De agri cultura*. London: Heinemann.
43. Henry James (1948) The art of fiction, in M. Roberts (ed.) *The Art of Fiction and Other Essays by Henry James*, p. 3. Oxford: Oxford University Press.
44. The blockage James was referring to was not of intellectual snobbery, but of a moral kind: 'Art, in our protestant communities . . . is supposed in certain circles to have some vaguely injurious effect upon those who make it an important consideration.' Ibid.
45. See p. 54.
46. J. A. Peacock, A. F. Heavens and A. T. Davies (1990) *Physics of the Early Universe*, p. 51. Bristol: The Institute of Physics.
47. Ibid., p. 50.
48. Ibid., p. 59.
49. Ibid., p. 1.
50. This is 'a generalised "Copernican principle": our location in the universe is typical, and is not distinguished in any fundamental way from any other'. Ibid., p. 2.
51. Ibid.
52. Ibid., p. 18.
53. Tamsyn S. Barton (1994) *Power and Knowledge: Astrology, Physiognomies, and Medicine under the Roman Empire*, pp. 27–8. Ann Arbor, MI: University of Michigan Press.
54. Cicero, *De finibus*, 1.30, on Epicurus.
55. Aristotle, *On Dreams*, I.462b.
56. Seneca, op. cit., 1.iii.9.
57. Ibid., 1.iii.7.
58. Richard Sorabji (1998) Is Theophrastus a significant philosopher?, in Johannes M. van Ophuijsen and Marlein van Raalte (eds) *Theophrastus, Reappraising the Sources*, pp. 203–21, 206. Somerset, NJ: Transaction Publishers.
59. R. Courant and H. Robbins, op. cit., Preface to 2nd edn.
60. Dionysius of Halicarnassus (1968) in E. Gray (ed.) *The Ancient Orators*, I.i, Preface. Boston, MA: Loeb Classical Library, Harvard University Press.
61. Celsus, *De medicina*, op. cit., Proemium.
62. Lucis Junius Moderatus Columella (1960) in H. B. Ash (ed.) *Res rustica*, I. Preface, 3–4. London: Heinemann.
63. *Tam discentibus egeat quam magistris. Agricolationis neque doctoris, qui se profiterentur, neque discipulos cognovi.* Ibid.
64. Ibid.
65. Caroline Jean Archer (1995) From all purpose anodyne to maker of deviance: opiates in the US 1890–1940, in Roy Porter (ed.) *Drugs and Narcotics in History*, pp. 114–32. Cambridge: Cambridge University Press.
66. Ibid., pp. 168–86.
67. Hugh Freeman (ed.) (1984) *Mental Health and the Environment*. London: Churchill Livingstone.
68. T. V. Ramabhadron (ed.) (1994) *Pharmaceutical Design and Development: A Molecular Biology Approach*. New York: Taylor & Francis.

69. Freeman (ed.), op. cit., p. 5, Introduction.
70. Bode (ed.), op. cit., p. 34.
71. Varro (1967) in W. D. Hooper and H. Boyd Ash (eds) *Rerum rusticarum.* London: Heinemann.
72. Ibid., I.ii.2.
73. Ibid., I.v.2.
74. Jonathan Barry and Bernard Harris (eds) *Studies in the Social History of Medicine,* Series preface. London: Routledge.
75. Cicero, *Academica,* I.iv.13.
76. E. R. Dodds (1973) *The Ancient Concept of Progress,* p. 2. Oxford: Clarendon Press.
77. Cf. discussion in Sextus Empiricus, *Adversus logicos,* I.27.
78. Cf. forbidden questions, pp. 9–10.
79. Northrop Frye, The developing imagination, in Denham (ed.), op. cit., p. 81.
80. Weatherall, op. cit., p. 21.
81. Ibid., p. 57.
82. Don Fawcett (ed.) (1994) *A Textbook of Histology,* 12th edn, Preface. London: Arnold.
83. Ibid.
84. Freeman (ed.), op. cit., p. 6.
85. Stress at Thamesmead, in Freeman (ed.), op. cit., Introduction, p. 367.
86. Archer, op. cit., pp. 114–32.
87. Paul Hoyningen-Huene (1993) *Reconstructing Scientific Revolutions: Thomas S. Kuhn's Philosophy,* p. 14 (trans from German, 1989). Chicago: University of Chicago Press.
88. S. Kuhn, in Paul Hoyningen-Huene, op. cit., p. xii, Foreword.
89. Ibid.
90. Ibid., p. xvi, Foreword.
91. Sextus Empiricus, *Outlines of Pyrrhonism,* I.i.1.
92. Northrop Frye, The developing imagination, in Denham (ed.), op. cit., p. 81.
93. Simon Schaffer (1994) in Margaret A. Boden (ed.) *Dimensions of Creativity,* p. 14. London: MIT Press.
94. Ibid., p. 15.
95. M. B. Strauss (1968) *Familiar Medical Quotations.* Philadelphia, PA: Lippincott Williams and Wilkins.
96. John J. Winkler (1985) *Auctor and Actor: A Narratological Reading of Apuleius's Golden Ass,* pp. vii–viii. Berkeley, CA: University of California Press.
97. Ibid., p. ix.
98. Barton, op. cit., p. 1.
99. To use the terminology of the Dearing Report of the 1990s.
100. Barton, op. cit., pp. 27–8.
101. Curtis L. Meinert and Susan Tonascia (1986) *Clinical Trials: Design, Conduct and Analysis,* p. 3. Oxford: Oxford University Press.
102. Freeman (ed.), op. cit., p. 23.
103. The Greeks do not have a word for progress, merely for increase (*epidosis*). In Latin there is *progressio/progressus.* Dodds, op. cit., p. 1.
104. Ibid., p. 27.
105. Ibid., p. 28.
106. Ibid., pp. 26–7.
107. Ibid., p. 27.

108. A. W. B. Simpson (1987) *Legal Theory and Legal History: Essays on the Common Law*, p. 172. London: Hambledon.
109. Courant and Robbins, op. cit., Preface to 2nd edn.
110. Wayne R. Hedrick, David L. Hykes and Dale E. Starchman (eds), (1995) *Ultrasound Physics and Instrumentation*, 3rd edn. St Louis: Mosby International.
111. Northrop Frye, The developing imagination, in Denham (ed.), op. cit., p. 83.
112. Bode (ed.), op. cit., p. 127.
113. Ammianus Marcellinus's *Rerum gestarum libri qui supersunt* lacked the chapter headings with which it is now supplied, which provide the reader with signposts. Those were added by the editor. Ammianus Marcellinus (1963) in John C. Rolfe (ed.) *Rerum gestarum libri qui supersunt*, 3 vols. London: Heinemann.
114. Plutarch, *Moralia, De liberis educandis*, 2.
115. Courant and Robbins, op. cit., Preface to 2nd edn.
116. Bode (ed.), op. cit., p. 140.
117. F. R. Japp (1898) Kekulé Memorial Lecture, *Journal of the Chemical Society*, 73: 97–138.
118. Bode (ed.), op. cit., p. 28.
119. Schaffer, op. cit., p. 17.
120. Salusinszky (interview with Northrop Frye), op. cit., p. 41.
121. Bode (ed.), op. cit., p. 23.
122. Michael Polanyi ([1951] 1998) *The Logic of Liberty: Reflections and Rejoinders*, p. 37. Indianapolis, IN: Liberty Fund.
123. Gregory Orr (1993) *Richer Entanglements: Essays and Notes on Poetry and Poems*, p. 24. Ann Arbor, MI: University of Michigan Press.
124. Ibid., p. 25.
125. Henry James, op. cit., p. 4.
126. Ibid., p. 16.
127. Ibid., p. 12.
128. Orr, op. cit., p. 25.
129. C. H. Sisson (1974) *In the Trojan Ditch*, p. 13. Chester Springs, PA: Dufour Editions.
130. Luce himself has another tactic, also involving a conscious playing with hypotheses. He puts forward an argument about Atlantis 'based on the circumstantial evidence of archaeology, history and legend' and 'tries to use this evidence to limit the number of admissible hypotheses until one emerges as the most credible'. J. V. Luce (1969) *The End of Atlantis*, pp. 13, 15. London: Flamingo, HarperCollins.
131. Henry David Thoreau (1928) *On the Duty of Civil Disobedience*, p. 2. New Haven, CT: Avon.
132. Bode (ed.), op. cit., p. 55.
133. Ibid.
134. Dionysius of Halicarnassus, op. cit., I.iv.
135. Bode (ed.), op. cit., p. 175.
136. Ibid., p. 126.
137. *Quid mea cum pugnat sententia secum, quod petit spernit, repetit quod nuper omisit, aestuate et vitae disconvenit ordine tot, diruit, aedificat, mutat quadrata rotundis.* Horace (1978) in H. Rushton Fairclough (ed.) *Satire*, 1.1.97. Boston, MA: Loeb Classical Library, Harvard University Press.
138. *Quaecumque libido est incedo solus.* Ibid., 1.6.111–12.
139. Manilius, op. cit., Preface.
140. Bode (ed.), op. cit., p. 42.

141. Roger Porter (1992) Series foreword, in John G. Nutt, John P. Hammersad and Stephen T. Gaucher, *Parkinson's Disease: 100 Maxims*, p. vii. London: Arnold.
142. Freeman (ed.), op. cit., p. 25.
143. Seneca, op. cit., 1 Preface 1.
144. Thomas Paine (1995) Letter addressed to the addressers, on the late proclamation, in Mark Philp (ed.) *Rights of Man, Common Sense and other Political Writings*, p. 335. Oxford: Oxford University Press.
145. H. H. Wilson (1956) in Corliss Lamont (ed.) *Freedom is as Freedom Does: Civil Liberties Today*, p. xv. New York: USA Press.
146. Boden (ed.), op. cit., p. 11.
147. Bode (ed.), op. cit., p. 40.
148. Professor G. D. S. Kirk (1980–81) *Cambridge University Reporter*, p. 346.
149. S. Kuhn, in Paul Hoyningen-Huene, op. cit., p. xii, Foreword.
150. Ibid., p. xv.
151. Manilius, op. cit., Preface.
152. Stephen Guest (1992) Profiles in legal theory, *Ronald Dworkin*, p. viii. Edinburgh: Edinburgh University Press.
153. Ibid., p. 1.
154. Ibid.
155. James Tully (ed.) (1988) *Meaning and Context: Quentin Skinner and his Critics*, p. 3. Oxford: Polity Press.
156. Richard T. Vann (1998) The reception of Hayden White, *History and Theory*, 37: 146–7.
157. Meinert and Tonascia, op. cit., Preface.
158. For example, Sextus Empiricus (1997) in R. Bell (ed.) *Adversus mathematicos*, p. xi. Oxford: Clarendon Press. And see also below.
159. Thomas (ed. and trans), op. cit., pp. 146–8: using the text of G. Friedlein (1873) *Proclus on Euclid*, p. 64ff. Leipzig: Teubner.
160. Thomas (ed. and trans), op. cit., p. 156.
161. Diogenes Laertius (1966) in R. D. Hicks (ed.) *Lives of Eminent Philosophers*, I.13–4. London: Heinemann.
162. Ibid., p. xv.
163. Ibid.
164. *Nulli clari viri medicinam exercuerunt.*
165. *Donec maiore studio litterarum disciplina agitari coepit.* Celsus, op. cit., Proemium, 5–6.
166. Dionysius of Halicarnassus, op. cit., I.iv.
167. A. W. B. Simpson, op. cit., p. 175.
168. Ibid.
169. House of Commons Select Committee on Science and Technology (1999) Minutes of evidence, February, Sir Alec Broers.
170. Salusinszky (interview with Northrop Frye), op. cit., pp. 40–1.
171. Jan Gorak (1991) *The Making of the Modern Canon*, p. ix. London: Continuum International.
172. Ibid., p. viii.
173. Ibid., p. ix.
174. F. R. Leavis (1943) *Education and the University*, p. 106. London: Chatto and Windus.
175. John Fletcher (1968) *New Directions in Literature*, p. 35. London: Marion Boyars Publishers.
176. Courant and Robbins, op. cit., Preface to 2nd edn.

177. Coleridge, op. cit., vol. I, ch. 3, p. 57.
178. Salusinszky (1987) *Criticism in Society* (interview with Frank Kermode), p. 118. London: Routledge.
179. Ibid., p. 117.
180. Richard Stoneman (1982) *Daphne into Laurel: Translations of Classical Poetry from Chaucer to the Present*, p. 2. London: Duckworth Press.
181. Winkler, op. cit., p. vii.
182. Donald Laming, unpublished paper commenting on D. V. Cicchetti (1991) The reliability of peer review for manuscript and grant submission: a cross-disciplinary investigation, *Behavioural and Brain Sciences*, 14: 119–86.
183. S. Jasanoff (1995) *Science at the Bar: Law, Science and Technology in America*, p. 53. London: Harvard University Press.
184. Jasanoff, *Science at the Bar*, op. cit., p. 55.
185. Ibid., pp. 42–9, 52.
186. Ibid., p. 54.
187. F. R. Leavis (1986) Valuation in criticism, in R. Singh (ed.) *Valuation in Criticism and Other Essays*, p. 276. Cambridge: Cambridge University Press.
188. C. P. Snow (1960) *The Affair*, p. 12. London: Macmillan.
189. Ibid., p. 19.
190. Ibid., p. 40.
191. David Vincent (1988) *The Culture of Secrecy*, p. 65. Oxford: Clarendon Press. See also H. D. Traill (1860) The anonymous critic, *Saturday Review*, 10: 11.
192. Vincent, op. cit., p. 65.
193. C. E. C. B. Appleton (1870) Our first year, *Academy*, 22 October, p. 1.
194. Richard Cumberland (1809) *London Review*, p. 19.
195. George Saintsbury (1922) The charm of journalism, *A Scrap Book*, p. 11 and note. London.
196. David Edwards (1995) *Free to be Human*, pp. 202–3. Totnes: Resurgence Books.
197. R. J. Johnson (1996) Who's gatekeeping the gatekeepers?, *The Professional Geographer*, 48: 91–4.
198. Mark A. Gillman (1966) *Envy as a Retarding Force in Science*, p. 10. Aldershot: Avebury.
199. Coleridge, op. cit., vol. I, ch. 3, p. 59.
200. Ibid., vol. II, ch. 21 and vol. VII, p. 107.
201. Northrop Frye, The developing imagination, in Denham (ed.), op. cit., p. 81.
202. Quoted in Leavis, *Education and the University*, op. cit., pp. 108–9.
203. F. R. Leavis (1982) in G. Singh (ed.) *The Critic as Anti-Philosopher*, p. 166. London: Chatto and Windus.
204. Ibid.
205. Leavis, *Education and the University*, op. cit., p. 106.

Chapter 2   Teaching (pp. 38–58)

1. Cicero, *Academica*, I.ii.7.
2. Samuel Johnson (1905) in George Birbeck Hill (ed.) *Milton: Lives of the Poets*, 3 vols. Oxford: Oxford University Press.
3. John Henry Newman (1979) *Letters and Diaries* (to Henry Lee Warner, 6 January 1829), vol. 2, p. 113. Oxford: Clarendon Press.

4. Newman, *Letters and Diaries*, vol. 2, p. 207, in H. Tristram (ed.) (1956) *John Henry Newman, Autobiographical Writings*, pp. 99–100. Oxford: Oxford University Press.
5. Newman, *The Idea of a University*, op. cit.
6. There is a good deal of discussion of that idea in the submissions to the Royal Commissions on Oxford and Cambridge, particularly the ones which reported in 1877 and 1922.
7. Newman, *The Idea of a University*, op. cit., p. xiii.
8. Ibid., p. xi.
9. Ibid., p. xiii.
10. Henry A. Giroux (1996) Towards a postmodern pedagogy, in Lawrence Cahoon (ed.) *From Modernism to Postmodernism*, pp. 687–97.
11. Northrop Frye, The university of the world, in Denham (ed.), op. cit., p. 91.
12. Northrop Frye (1967) *The Morality of Scholarship*, p. 9. Ithaca, NY: Cornell University Press.
13. Michael Kearns (1999) *Rhetorical Narratology*. Lincoln, NE: University of Nebraska Press.
14. David Bridges (2000) Back to the future: the higher education curriculum in the 21st century, *Cambridge Journal of Education*, 30: 37–55.
15. Ibid., pp. 44–5.
16. Julian, Letter 36, rescript on Christian teachers, in W. Cave (ed.) (1923) *Works*, vol. 3, p. 117. London: Heinemann. Fourth-century nephew of the Constantine who turned the Roman Empire officially Christian, studied philosophy and was a sufficiently educated pagan to be prepared to return the Empire to its old ways.
17. Salusinszky (interview with Northrop Frye), op. cit., p. 40.
18. Northrop Frye, The larger university, in Denham (ed.), op. cit., p. 79.
19. Northrop Frye, *The Morality of Scholarship*, op. cit., p. 8.
20. Northrop Frye, Universities and the deluge of cant, in Denham (ed.), op. cit., p. 117.
21. Cmnd 2154, p. 7.
22. Ibid., p. 6.
23. See pp. 38, 40–2.
24. Elizabeth A. Fones-Wolf (1994) *Selling Free Enterprise*, p. 193. Chicago: University of Illinois Press.
25. Ibid.
26. Ramabhadron (ed.), op. cit.
27. Keith Harry (ed.) (1999) *Higher Education through Open and Distance Learning.* London: RoutledgeFalmer.
28. Northrop Frye, The developing imagination, in Denham (ed.), op. cit., p. 83.
29. Plutarch, *Moralia*, I.2.
30. *Nec indocti intellegere possent nec docti legere curarent.* Cicero, *Academia*, II.ii.4.
31. Cicero, *Academia*, I.ii.5.
32. *Ut possemus aliquando qui et ubi essemus agnoscere.* Cicero, *Academia*, I.iii.9.
33. *Verbis . . . novis cogimur uti.* Cicero, *Academia*, I.ii.5.
34. Oscar B. Garfield (ed.) (1990) *Current Concepts in Cardiovascular Physiology*, Preface, p. ix. London: Academic Press.
35. This article first appeared in the *Oxford Magazine*, Trinity term, 1999.
36. Coleridge, op. cit., vol. I, ch. 3, p. 59.
37. Northrop Frye, Education and the humanities, in Denham (ed.), op. cit., p. 75.
38. Anthony Hopwood, *Times Higher Education Supplement*, 2 February 2001.

39. *Learning and Teaching in History, Classics and Archaeology* (2001), 2: 1.
40. House of Commons Select Committee on Science and Technology (1998) Minutes of Evidence, 7 December, HC 17-iii, Sir Peter Williams.
41. Ibid.
42. *The Innovation–Exploitation Barrier*, Cm 3786, p. 8, para. 18. Cf. the Treasury's *Report on Financing of High Technology Business* (1998) p. 2, which stresses the value of management experience.
43. HC 17-i, 25 November 1998, p. 119, Question 549.
44. *The Innovation–Exploitation Barrier*, op. cit., para. 20.
45. HC 17-iii, 7 December 1998, p. 138.
46. HC 17-v, 16 December 1998, p. 165.
47. Ibid., p. 180.
48. Ibid., p. 171.
49. *The Innovation–Exploitation Barrier*, op. cit., p. 9, para. 21.
50. 'Confusion' has been 'caused by the large number of Government initiatives designed to promote research collaboration between industry and academia'. The government's response to the Science and Technology Committee's *First Report: The Implications of the Dearing Report for the Structure and Funding of University Research*, 1997–98, p. vii.
51. HC 17-iii, 7 December 1998, p. 141.
52. HC 17-i, 25 November, p. 117.
53. Ibid., p. 112.
54. HC 17-iii, 7 December, p. 141.
55. Stephen Court (2000) University staff and the knowledge-based economy, *Higher Education Review*, 33: 3–16.

Chapter 3   The Control of Research (pp. 59–91)

1. A. Kornberg (1995) *The Golden Helix: Inside the Biotech Venture*, p. 14. Basingstoke: University Science Books.
2. Colin Tudge (1999) London School of Economics, *Times Higher Education Supplement*, 21 May.
3. A. Milner (1999) *Cambridge University Reporter*, 27 January, p. 309.
4. Ibid.
5. Ibid.
6. HC 17-v, 16 December 1998, p. 171, Question 812.
7. White Paper (1993) *Realizing our Potential: A Strategy for Science, Engineering and Technology*, Cm 2250, 3.12, 3.13. London: HMSO.
8. HC 17-iii, 27 January 1999, pp. 200–1.
9. HC 303-II, *First Report: The Implications of the Dearing Report for the Structure and Funding of University Research*, 21 January 1998, p. 158.
10. HC 17-iii, 7 December 1998, p. 144, Sir Peter Williams.
11. Cf. 'climate' in the response to the House of Lords' report, *The Innovation–Exploitation Barrier*, op. cit., p. 20, para. 5.
12. 'The fact that Wellcome have put so much money into the science base alongside the Government has stimulated the investment recently. There must be tremendous confidence in the scientists in universities.' HC 17-iii, 7 December 1998, p. 139.

13. In Germany the government matches venture capitalist's funding. Ibid., p. 140.
14. Kornberg, op. cit., p. ix.
15. HC 888-I (1997–98) Fifth Report, *British Biotech*, para. 11.
16. Ibid., para. 14.
17. HC 17-v, 16 December 1998, p. 65.
18. HC 17-iii, 7 December 1998, pp. 136–7, Sir Peter Williams.
19. HC 17-viii, 1 February 1999, p. 236, Sir Alec Broers.
20. Raymond Spiers (1996) Ethical issues in research relationships between universities and industry: conference review (Baltimore 1995), Center for Biomedical Ethics, University of Maryland), *Science and Engineering Ethics*, 2: 115–20.
21. G. R. Evans (2001) The integrity of UK academic research under commercial threat, *Science as Culture*, 10: 97–111.
22. Raymond Spiers (1998) Ethics and the funding of research and development at universities, *Science and Engineering Ethics*, 2: 375–84.
23. As with the GKN Chair at Cambridge in 2000.
24. *The Innovation–Exploitation Barrier*, op. cit.
25. Established by Act of Parliament on 2 July 1998 and endowed with £200m of funds from the National Lottery, NESTA is primarily designed to assist with projects needing relatively modest funding and to provide fellowships for creative individuals.
26. *The Innovation–Exploitation Barrier*, op. cit., p. 12ff.
27. HC 17-vii, 27 January 1999, p. 201.
28. HC 888-I, op. cit., p. viii, para. 15.
29. I. Feller (1991) Issues for the HE sector – lessons from US experience with collaboration. Symposium on the true price of collaborative research, Royal Society, London, 22 January, cited in David Packham and Mary Tasker (1997) Industry and the academy – a Faustian contract?, *Industry and Higher Education*, April: 85–90.
30. *Cambridge University Newsletter* (2001) April/May.
31. Oxford University in a statement published on 9 December 1999.
32. *Oxford University Gazette* (1999) 9 December.
33. Cm 3786, para. 7.
34. Sir Michael Davies (1994) *The Great Battle at Swansea*. Bristol: Thoemmes Press.
35. HC 17-vii, 27 January 1999, p. 203.
36. Kornberg, op. cit., p. 2.
37. HC 17-viii, 1 February 1999, p. 230.
38. Sir Alec Broers wrote in the Cambridge University alumni magazine, *Cam*, in the autumn of 1999, of the West Cambridge site of so much planning dispute: 'Its innovative mix of university departments and charitable and commercial research centres could easily materialise even faster than we now imagine.'
39. HC 17-viii, 1 February 1999, p. 236, Sir Alec Broers.
40. HC 17-vii, 27 January 1999, p. 210.
41. Cm 3786, p. 4, para. 8.
42. Such as the one in which Glaxo became involved with the Department of Pharmacology at Cambridge University.
43. As in the Fishel case at Nottingham University.
44. Oxford has done a good job here. Oxford University (2000) *Statutes, Decrees and Regulations*, pp. 811–12. Oxford: Oxford University Press.

45. 'The University participates in seed capital funds, including the Quantum Fund and Cambridge Research and Innovation Ltd.' HC 17-viii, 1 February 1999, p. 223.
46. *Guardian* (2001) 29 May.
47. HC 17-viii, 1 February 1999, p. 236.
48. There are good, clear outline guidelines in Oxford. *Oxford University Gazette* (1999) 9 December.
49. HC 17-vii, 27 January 1999, p. 210.
50. Ibid., p. 204.
51. Ibid., p. 206.
52. I am indebted here to remarks made by Professor N. Steneck in a paper given in Cambridge on 29 May 2001.
53. Scientific Advisory System: Genetically Modified Foods, Science and Technology Committee (1999) HC 286-ii, 8 March, pp. 35–6.
54. HC 303-II, 5 November 1997, p. 10.
55. HC 286-i, 3 March 1999.
56. Gregory Palast (1999) *Index on Censorship*, 3 May: 62.
57. Ibid., p. 64.
58. Scientific Advisory System: Genetically Modified Foods, Science and Technology Committee (1999) HC 286-ii, 10 March, pp. 79, 80.
59. Hilary D'Cruz (1998) The whistleblower's bill, *The Company Lawyer*, 19: 120–2.
60. On this point see D. Lewis, K. Schroder and Stephen Homewood (1998) *A Short Guide to the Public Interest Disclosure Act 1998*. Middlesex: Middlesex University.
61. Senate Select Committee on Public Interest Whistleblowing (1994). See D. Lewis (1996) Employment protection for whistleblowers: on what principles should Australian legislation be based?, *Australian Journal of Labour Law*, 9: 158–9.
62. David Lewis (1995) Whistleblowers and job security, MLR 208.
63. Ibid., at 209, and cf. Nancy Hauserman (1986) Whistleblowing: individual morality in a corporate society, *Business Horizons*, 29.
64. Lewis (1995), op. cit. at 210.
65. *Walton v. T.A.C. Ltd* (1981) IRLR 357.
66. Lewis (1995), op. cit. at 219.
67. Ibid., at 210.
68. Ibid.
69. Principle 4.1.3, paras 11, 12.
70. Lewis (1995), op. cit. at 211.
71. Sir Douglas Wass (1996) *Scott and Whitehall*, PL 461.
72. Ibid., at 462.
73. Ibid.
74. Ibid.
75. In the USA the Civil Service Reform Act, as amended by the Whistleblower Protection Act 1989 prohibits personnel actions in retaliation for disclosures of 'gross mismanagement, a gross waste of funds, an abuse of authority, or a substantial and specific danger to public health or safety' (5 USC, para. 2302(b)(8) (1978) and 5 USC, para. 1201ff (1989)).
76. Peter Poon (1995) Legal protections for the scientific misconduct whistleblower, *Journal of Law, Medicine and Ethics*, 23: 88–95.
77. Definition of good faith: 'an honest belief, the absence of malice and the absence of design to defraud or to seek an unconscionable advantage'. A US Public

Health Service Regulation (42 CFR, para. 50.102 (1993)) defines misconduct in science as 'fabrication, falsification, plagiarism, or other practices that seriously deviate from those that are commonly accepted within the scientific community for proposing, conducting, or reporting research. It does not include honest error or honest differences in interpretations or judgements of data.' Issues: (1) standard for proving misconduct; (2) the definition of retaliation; (3) how the burden of proving retaliation should be equitably distributed; (4) the appropriate remedies for retaliation; (5) immunity of the whistleblower from defamation suits. See Poon, op. cit., p. 88.

78. Poon, op. cit., 92.
79. Ibid., pp. 92–3.
80. Letter from Michael Driscoll, Vice-Chancellor of Middlesex University, sent to all University staff, 27 November 1998.
81. *Open Government*, 4.21: 36.
82. Dawn Oliver and Gavin Drewry (eds) (1998) *The Law and Parliament*. London: Butterworths.
83. *Open Government*, op. cit., pp. 36–7.
84. Wass (1996), op. cit., at 468.
85. Ibid.
86. Ibid., at 463.
87. Ibid.
88. Ibid., at 468.
89. *Open Government*, Cmnd 2290, 8.43: 60.
90. K. C. Davis (1971) *Discretionary Justice in Europe and America*, ch. 4. Urbana, IL: University of Illinois Press and J. L. Jowell (1973) *The Legal Control of Administrative Discretion*, PL 179. See too R. Baldwin and J. Houghton (1986) *Circular Arguments: The Status and Legitimacy of Administrative Rules*, PL 239.
91. Robert Baldwin (1995) *Rules and Government*, p. 85. Oxford: Clarendon Press.
92. Davis, op. cit., ch. 4 and Jowell, op. cit.
93. Baldwin, op. cit., p. 177.
94. Ibid., p. 180.
95. E. Bardach and R. Kagan (1982) *Going by the Book: The Problem of Regulatory Unreasonableness*, p. 67. Philadelphia, PA: Temple University Press.
96. Lord Howe of Aberavon (1996) *Procedure at the Scott Inquiry*, PL 445.
97. *Open Government*, 5.1: 38.
98. HC 17-vii, 27 January 1999, p. 200.
99. *The Government's Response to the Science and Technology Committee's First Report: The Implications of the Dearing Report for the Structure and Funding of University Research* (1997–98) p. v.
100. HC 17-v, 16 December 1998, p. 166.
101. Cm 3786, p. 4, para. 8.
102. HC 17-i, 25 November 1998, p. 113.
103. HC 17-v, 16 December 1998, p. 180.
104. *The Government's Response to the Science and Technology Committee's First Report*, op. cit., pp. vi–vii.
105. Ibid., p. xxxix.
106. Raymond E. Spier (1998) Ethics and the funding of research and development at universities, *Science and Engineering Ethics*, 4: 375–84.
107. Ibid.
108. Ibid., p. 378.

109. Company researchers battle over data access (2000) *Science*, 10 November, 290: 1063.
110. Gag on food scientist is lifted as gene modification row hots up (1999) *Nature*, 18 February, 397: 457.
111. Cm 3786, p. 11, para. 26.
112. F. M. Abbot and David J. Gerber (eds) (1997) *Public Policy and Global Techno-logical Integration*, p. 27. Dordrecht: Kluwer Law International.
113. Peter Drahos (1996) *A Philosophy of Intellectual Property*, p. 9. Aldershot: Dartmouth.
114. B. Sherman (1997) Remembering and forgetting: the birth of modern copyright law, in David Nelken (ed.) *Comparing Legal Cultures*, pp. 237–66. Aldershot: Dartmouth.
115. Abbot and Gerber (eds), op. cit., p. 12.
116. Ibid.
117. Kornberg, op. cit., p. 252.
118. HC 17-vii, 27 January 1999, p. 204.
119. HC 17-i, 25 November 1998, Memorandum for Dr Bruce Smith.
120. Cm 3786, p. 11, para. 26.
121. HC 17-vii, 27 January 1999, p. 200.
122. Colin Tudge, London School of Economics (1999) *Times Higher Education Supplement*, 21 May.
123. Ibid.
124. Ibid.
125. Gordon Stewart, University of Glasgow (1999) *Times Higher Education Supplement*, 21 May.
126. *Index on Censorship* (1999) 3: 47.
127. *Times Higher Education Supplement*, 21 May 1999.
128. *Index on Censorship*, op. cit.

Chapter 4   Politics, Administration and the Real World (pp. 92–105)

1. This chapter, with some differences, was published as an article (Academics and the real world) in the *Higher Education Review* (32 (2000)) and is reproduced here with permission.
2. HL Deb, 16 December 1991, col. 1023, Lord Renfrew.
3. Ibid., col. 1052.
4. Lord Hatch of Lusby was concerned about 'interference with staff'. Ibid., col. 1045.
5. Ibid., col. 1048.
6. Ibid., cols 1048 and 1050. Lord Pearson supplied further examples of ideological tyranny; ibid., col. 1054.
7. Ibid., col. 1050.
8. Ibid., col. 1051.
9. Nancy L. Thomas (1998) The attorney's role is on campus, *Change*, May/June, pp. 35–42.
10. HL Deb, 16 December 1991, col. 1023, Lord Renfrew.
11. Ibid., col. 1039. Cf. col. 1022.

12. Baroness Young, moving Amendment 253. Ibid., col. 1022.

13. Ibid., col. 1036, Baroness Blackstone.

14. Baroness Blackstone added, 'I do not find credible the suggestion that the funding council might go off the rails at the same time.' Ibid., col. 1037.

15. House of Commons Committee of Public Accounts (1998–99) *Twenty-sixth Report, Minutes of Evidence, Overseas Operations, Governance and Management at Southampton Institute*, p. 4, Question 29.

16. Ibid., p. 9, Question 94.

17. Ibid., pp. 9, 10, Question 108.

18. Ibid., p. 10, Questions 116, 117.

19. I speak on the basis of dozens of cases throughout the UK of which I have direct knowledge as Public Policy Secretary for the Council for Academic Freedom and Academic Standards. The next question is whether there is a problem of any scale here. I have encountered at many levels in government and in universities the confident assertion that although there may be occasional lapses, the system is, on the whole, working well. Nolan took the same view. One can speak only of what one knows. Week after week, I am approached by staff and students.

20. HL Deb, 16 December 1991, col. 1047, Baroness Blackstone.

21. John Griffith (1990) The Education Reform Act: abolishing the independent status of the universities, *Education and the Law*, 2(3): 97.

22. Lord Belstead explained that 'the way in which my right honourable friend has sought to exercise influence in this field has been through holding back grant to the funding councils until a satisfactory settlement has been reached . . . It is an approach known as setting conditions precedent.' HL Deb, 16 December 1991, col. 1033.

23. Ibid., cols 1033–4.

24. As Lord Renfrew pointed out: 'For the first time, the Secretary of State would have the ability to intervene in the affairs of an institution. He may, for example, decide he does not like a particular course and that he is not willing to fund it.' Lord Dainton warned that 'as the Bill now stands [the Secretary of State] would have the power to prescribe criteria for the admission of students, what subjects should be taught or not taught, who would be thought fit or unfit to teach or conduct research in a particular subject, how candidates should be examined and other matters.' HL Deb, 16 December 1991, col. 1025, Lord Dainton.

25. Ibid., col. 1036, Baroness Blackstone; col. 1034, Lord Belstead.

26. Neville Harris (1993) *Law and Education: Regulation, Consumerism and the Education System*, p. 97. London: Sweet & Maxwell.

27. HL Deb, 16 December 1991, col. 1040, Earl Russell.

28. Davies (1994), op. cit., cited by the Second Report of the Committee on Standards in Public Life.

29. These are set out conveniently in Harris, op. cit., p. 94.

30. Schedule 7, 3(1)(b).

31. House of Commons Committee of Public Accounts, op. cit., p. 16, Questions 173, 174.

32. Ibid., p. 16, Question 174.

33. HL Deb, 16 December 1991, cols 1135, 1138.

34. Ibid., cols 1135, 129.

35. The following is taken from O. Hyams (1998) *Law of Education*, pp. 522–4. London: Sweet & Maxwell.

36. *R v Board of Governors of Sheffield Hallam University ex parte R* (1995) ELR 267 and *R v Manchester Metropolitan University ex parte Nolan* (1994) ELR 380.
37. *Pearce v University of Aston in Birmingham* (No. 2) (1991) 2 All ER 469 at 475.
38. An institution designated by the 1992 Act but not established by Royal Charter and conducted not by a company but by a corporation would, Hymans argues, be analogous to a maintained voluntary school before the incorporation of the governing bodies of such schools. 1992 Act, ss. 238, 239.
39. *R v University of Cambridge ex parte Evans* (1997), J. Sedley and (1998) J. Turner went opposite ways on this point.
40. HL Deb, 16 December 1991, col. 1039.
41. Ibid., col. 1026.
42. 1992 Act, s. 83(2)(a), (b).
43. HL Deb, 16 December 1991, col. 1069.
44. J. Jowell and Dawn Oliver (eds) (1994) *The Changing Constitution*, 3rd edn, p. 121. Oxford: Clarendon Press.
45. House of Commons Public Service Committee (1996) Second Report, *Ministerial Accountability and Responsibility*, vol. III, p. 38, Sir Michael Quinlan.
46. Wass (1984), op. cit., p. 49.
47. *Open Government*, Cm 2290, 3.16, p. 25.
48. HC Deb, 2 December 1987, 573w.
49. House of Commons Public Service Committee, op. cit., vol. III, p. 38, Sir Michael Quinlan.
50. Peter Barberis (1997) The concept of public duty, *The Civil Service in an Era of Change*, pp. 82–94. Aldershot: Dartmouth.
51. Mark J. Rozell (1994) *Executive Privilege*, pp. 18–19. Baltimore: Johns Hopkins University Press.
52. Supreme Court in *US v Nixon* (1974) 483 US 683, 705–6, 708.
53. *The Public Papers of the Presidents: Dwight D. Eisenhower* (1954) pp. 483–4. Pittsburgh, PA: United States Government.
54. Cm 2290, 3.14, p. 24.
55. House of Commons Public Service Committee, op. cit., vol. III, p. 80, Sir Richard Scott.
56. See examples discussed in Jowell and Oliver (eds), op. cit., p. 124.
57. House of Commons Public Service Committee, op. cit., vol. III, p. 131.
58. Ibid.
59. Ibid., vol. III, p. 45, Peter Shore MP.
60. Cm 2290, 1.9, p. 2.
61. The practice of keeping academic research to oneself until it has reached a stage where it can be released by publication in a sufficiently matured state is another matter.
62. House of Commons Public Service Committee, op. cit., vol. III, p. 143, Sir Robin Butler.
63. Ibid., p. 144.
64. *Burma Oil Co. Ltd v Bank of England* (1980) AC 1090; *Air Canada v Secretary of State for Trade* (1983) 2 AC 394.
65. Report of the Public Inquiry into the Disposal of Land at Crichel Down (1954) Cm 9176; Fourth Report, Defence Committee (1985–86) HC 519.
66. Some examples of occasions when the department as a whole has been blamed are to be found in Jowell and Oliver (eds), op. cit., p. 124.
67. Ibid.

68. Public Finance Foundation Report (1996) A civil servant's view of accountability, *Government Accountability: Beyond the Scott Report*, Kenneth Bloomfield, pp. 11–14.
69. Public Finance Foundation Report (1996) Clarifying responsibility and accountability, op. cit., pp. 21–5, Graham Mather.
70. Ibid.
71. House of Commons Public Service Committee, op. cit., vol. III, p. 121, Graham Matthew MEP, Memorandum.

Chapter 5 What is to be Done? (pp. 106–122)

1. Duke Maskell and Ian Robinson (2001) *The New Idea of a University*. London: Haven Books.
2. Mary Tasker and David Packham (1993) Industry and higher education: a question of values, *Studies in Higher Education*, 18: 127–36.
3. *Cambridge University Reporter* (1969–70) pp. 370–6.
4. Tasker and Packham, op. cit., pp. 127–36.
5. Cm 3786, p. 20, para. 50.
6. HC 17-v, 16 December 1998, Question 841.
7. Ibid., p. 176.
8. Ibid.
9. HC 17-iii, 7 December 1998, p. 138, Cooksey.
10. Ibid., p. 139, Williams.
11. Ibid., p. 138.
12. Salusinszky (interview with Northrop Frye), op. cit., p. 38.
13. Kornberg, op. cit., p. x.
14. For example in HC 17-iii, 7 December 1998.
15. See House of Commons Select Committee on Science and Technology (1998) Fifth Report, *British Biotech*, vol. II, Appendices to Minutes of Evidence, HC 888-II, 17 June, letter from J. Wilson Carswell.
16. *Government Statement on the Report of the Committee under the Chairmanship of Lord Robbins* (1963–64) Cm 2165.
17. See *Sunday Times*, 14 November 1999, on internal warfare in the Cabinet over the Cambridge–MIT funding.
18. Moving Amendment 253, HL Deb 1991, col. 1023, 16 December.
19. Notice in the *Cambridge University Reporter*, 10 November 1999.
20. I. Feller (1991) Issues for the HE sector – lessons form the US experience with collaboration, Symposium on the True Price of Collaborative Research, Royal Society, London, 22 January, cited in David Packham and Mary Tasker (1997) Industry and the academy – a Faustian contract?, *Industry and Higher Education*, April: 85–90.
21. In the UK it may have no choice, under s. 202 of the Education Reform Act 1988.
22. Abbot and Gerber, op. cit., pp. 9, 115.
23. 'For the purpose of this guidance, an executive directorship is one involving an active management role, whether or not including research, in the company concern.' Administrative officers are to be restricted thus: 'Unless formally nominated by the University to do so, no administrative officer shall serve in a

personal capacity as director or other officer of a company or commercial enterprise, the establishment of which arose out of or was connected with work done in the University, or any company or commercial enterprise in a contractual relationship with the University where the administrative officer was concerned or connected with the placing or negotiation of the contract in question. [Administrative officers] shall decline to accept any director's fee [and] shall be deemed to accept the nomination in the discharge of his or her duties as an employee of the University.' Administrative officers are not to hold shares in any company 'which arose out of or was connected with work done in the University' unless they buy them in the normal way after they have been listed on the stock exchange. Oxford's guidelines on conflict of interest point: to 'the use of the University's research or administrative facilities to pursue personal business, commercial or consulting activities' (2(a)); to 'any attempt to restrict rights governing the timing and content of publications, save in circumstances properly approved by the University to protect privacy, commercially sensitive proprietary information, and patentable inventions' (2(b)); to 'involvement in externally funded activity which might infringe the right of a student engaged in the activity to complete the degree for which he or she is registered and/or to publish freely his or her findings (save in the circumstances referred to in (b) above)' (2(c)); to 'a financial interest held by an individual (or by his or her immediate relative/s or household member/s) in an external enterprise engaged in activities closely related to that individual's line of research in the University: examples of such interests are paid consultancies, paid service on a board of directors or advisory board, equity holdings in or royalty income from the enterprise' (2(d)); to 'a personal involvement in any company or commercial enterprise which is in a contractual relationship with the university or which is in the process of negotiating the terms and conditions of a contract' (2(e)).

24. On this widespread problem, see *Times Higher Education Supplement*, 12 June 1999.
25. An excellent code addressing this difficulty was in use by the Mayo Clinic in 1999.
26. A Milner, *Cambridge University Reporter*, 27 January 1999, p. 309.
27. Ibid.
28. Ibid.
29. *Times Higher Education Supplement*, July 2001 and www.liv.ac.uk.
30. *Oxford University Gazette*, 4571, 17 January 2001.
31. Though not, apparently, the governing bodies of Oxford and Cambridge as universities.
32. David Palfreyman (1998) Unlimited personal liability for fellows, *Oxford Magazine*, 4th week, Michaelmas Term, pp. 4–8.
33. Public Finance Foundation Report (1996), op. cit., pp. 21–5, Kenneth Bloomfield.
34. Public Finance Foundation Report (1996), op. cit., pp. 5–10, Sir Richard Scott.
35. House of Commons Public Service Committee (1996) *Second Report, Ministerial Accountability and Responsibility*, vol. III, p. 35, Sir Michael Quinlan.
36. Ibid., vol. III, p. 53, Lord Howe.
37. Ibid., vol. III, p. 143, Sir Robin Butler.
38. Roger Brown (2000) Accountability in higher education: have we reached the end of the road? The case for a Higher Education Audit Commission. Lecture given at University of Surrey, Roehampton, 24 October.
39. Further and Higher Education Act 1992, Schedule 7, 3(2)(a).
40. Roger Brown (2001) The governance of the new universities: do we need to think again?, *Perspectives*, 5: 42–7.

41. HL Deb, 16 December 1991, cols 1042–3.
42. See pp. 48–50.
43. Brown (2001), op. cit., pp. 42–7.
44. Ibid., p. 47.

Chapter 6   Conclusion: the University and Social Commentary (pp. 123–137)

1. See pp. 124–5.
2. Salusinszky (interview with Northrop Frye), op. cit., p. 39.
3. Michael Polanyi ([1951] 1998) *The Logic of Liberty: Reflections and Rejoinders*, p. 33. London: Routledge.
4. Ibid., p. 34.
5. See Philip Schlesinger and John Griffith (1980) *Free Speech for All? The Banning of Tony Benn at Bristol University and Sir Keith Joseph at the LSE.* London: Council for Academic Freedom and Democracy.
6. HL Deb 1986, vol. 470, 1138.
7. It was the second of the Baroness's themes which the other speakers in the debate took up, and no one pointed to the inherent contradictoriness of what she had said. HL Deb 1986, vol. 470, 1138–46. The government issued a Green Paper, *The Treatment of Politically Controversial Issues in Schools and Colleges* (1986) PL 331. Section 44 of the same Act covers separately protections against the second of Baroness Cox's concerns, political indoctrination in schools. There is a clear understanding in the 1986 Act that special protections of academic freedom of speech are appropriate only to tertiary education. The paradox remains unresolved. A student in a final summer term in a school has a right to be protected from politically partisan influence, presumably because he still has a tender young mind, while the same student having moved on in the subsequent term to a university is exposed by the same statute to all speech. He has moved into a 'protected speech environment', where the overriding consideration is that a university cannot fulfil its purpose unless people can speak freely there.
8. See pp. 129–30.
9. HC Deb, 26 October 1987, 6w.
10. On 20 November 1987, the date when the bill was published, Kenneth Baker stated in the House that: 'In the case of universities, the Government's policy is that newly appointed staff should no longer be given "tenure", that is, special protection against dismissal on grounds of redundancy or financial exigency.' The Bill provides (Clause 132) that staff currently in post who have tenure should retain it as long as they continue in their present posts. These appointed after 20 November 1987 should no longer have this special protection.' HC Deb, 20 November 1987, 678w.
11. HC Deb, 20 November 1987, 679w.
12. 'The Government therefore consider it more appropriate for the requirements of academic freedom to be taken into account by the university commissioners, in consultation with individual universities and colleges, when statutes are amended to provide appropriately for the definition of good cause for dismissal and for arrangements for appeal against dismissal.' HC Deb, 20 November 1987, 679w.
13. HC Deb, 20 November 1987, 679w.

14. This Model Statute has been varied little from university to university, since it can only be added to, not subtracted from.
15. HC Deb, 20 November 1987, 680w.
16. Ibid.
17. Joint Committee on Parliamentary Privilege, Minutes of Evidence, 10 March 1998, p. 3, Question 539, Mr Williams.
18. *Pepper v Hart* (1993) AC 593 HL at 638.
19. See a series of articles in the *Times Higher Education Supplement* of spring 1999.
20. Laurence R. Markus (1996) *Regulation of Speech on Campus*, p. 127. Westpoint, VA: University Press.
21. Ibid., p. 120.
22. Ibid., p. 121.
23. Ibid., pp. 121–2.
24. Ibid., p. 125. *Doe v University of Michigan* (1989) 721 F. Supp. 852 (E. D. Michigan).
25. *Quod istam matrem nostram Universitatem venerabilem scio Catholican esse, in doctrina sana fundatam et sanae fidei protectricem.* H. Anstey (ed.) (1857) *Munimenta academica*, vol. I, p. 210. Rolls Series. London: HMSO.
26. Ibid., vol. I, p. 269.
27. Leo Hurwitz (1985) *Historical Dictionary of Censorship in the US*, p. xxiv. Westport, CT: Greenwood Press.
28. Ibid., p. xx.
29. For a recent study and citations of earlier work, especially Sunstein, see Markus, op. cit.
30. Louis Menand (1996) *The Future of Academic Freedom*, p. vii, 3. Chicago: University of Chicago Press.
31. 'A professor who believes in the value and the possibility of unconstrained intellectual inquiry, and in the importance of protecting that inquiry with the concept of academic freedom, is in no position to condemn the activities of colleagues who see knowledge as principally political, since that would mean interfering with those colleagues' own freedom of inquiry.' Menand, op. cit., pp. vii, 12.
32. *Guardian*, 6 April 1999.
33. G. R. Evans (1998) More beans, *Oxford Magazine*, 159, Michaelmas Term. Suzi Clark (1998) The canker of corporatism, *Oxford Magazine*, 160, Michaelmas Term and editorial ibid.
34. Isocrates (1968) *Areopagiticus*, 140, in G. Norlin (ed.) *Works*, vol. II, p. 105. London: Heinemann.
35. Ibid.
36. Ibid.
37. Samuel Johnson, op. cit.
38. Ibid.
39. Thomas Paine (1995) Common sense, in Philp (ed.), op. cit., p. 3.
40. Wiliam Paley (1877) Origin of civil government, 3, *Moral and Political Philosophy, Paley's Works*, p. 130. London.
41. Ibid., 5, p. 134.
42. Thomas de Quincey ([1821] 1949) *Confessions of an English Opium Eater*, p. 19, London: Folio Society.
43. I. Kant (1979) *The Conflict of the Faculties (Der Streit der Facultäten)* Mary J. Gregory (trans), Preface 10–19 (A XII-XXIII). New York: Abaris Books. Quoted in William J. Hoye (1997) The religious roots of academic freedom, *Theological Studies*, 58: 409–29.

44. Thoreau (1928), op. cit., pp. 2–3.
45. Ibid., p. 4.
46. Ibid., p. 5.
47. Ibid., pp. 14–15.
48. Nadine Gordimer (1996) The measure of freedom, *Index on Censorship*, 25 September, pp. 115–21.
49. J. G. Davies (1972) *The Evangelistic Bureaucrat: A Study of a Planning Exercise in Newcastle upon Tyne*, p. 227. London.
50. J. S. Mill, *On Liberty*, ch. II.
51. Salusinszky (interview with Jacques Derrida), op. cit., p. 21.
52. John Pickering was Pro-Vice-Chancellor of the University of Portsmouth, who lost his job after he made a public interest disclosure.
53. Letter from Suzi Clark, *Times Higher Education Supplement*, 16 April 1999.
54. Letter from Keith Flett, ibid.
55. Letter in *Nature*, 393 (4 June 1998). This letter cites the Beg case as of importance because it seemed to provide a way to deal with problems which cross the staff–student boundary. It failed in the High Court in 1999.
56. Quoted in *Lancet* (1989) p. 1116.
57. Letter from Sadhanshu Dole, Cologne, *Nature*, 397 (25 February 1999), p. 644.
58. Gillman, op. cit., p. 9.
59. Polanyi, op. cit., p. 43.
60. Ibid., p. 34.
61. Ibid., p. 39.
62. See G. R. Evans (1994) *The Church and the Churches*. Cambridge: Cambridge University Press.
63. Polanyi, op. cit., p. 34.
64. Ibid., p. 40.
65. Ibid., p. 43.
66. Sextus Empiricus, *Outlines of Pyrrhonism*, I.iv.8.
67. Ibid., I.iv.12.
68. Ibid., I.vii.13.
69. Ibid., I.xi.23.
70. Northrop Frye, Universities and the deluge of cant, in Denham (ed.), op. cit., p. 120.
71. Apuleius ([1972] 1989) in J. Arthur Hanson (ed.) *Metamorphoses*, p. xii. London: Heinemann.
72. John Donne (1980) in Helen Peters (ed.) *Paradoxes and Problems*, Paradox IX, p. 20. Oxford: Oxford University Press.
73. Ibid.
74. Quincey, op. cit., p. 19, note.
75. Probably not an authentic work of Plato.
76. Libanus (1992) in A. F. Norman (ed.) *Autobiography and Selected Letters*, p. 7. London: Heinemann.
77. Snow, op. cit., p. 85.
78. Northrop Frye, The community of freedom, in Denham (ed.), op. cit., p. 116.

Bibliography

Abbot, F. M. and Gerber D. J. (eds) (1997) *Public Policy and Global Technological Integration.* Dordrecht: Kluwer Law International.

Barberis, P. (1997) The concept of public duty, *The Civil Service in an Era of Change*, pp. 82–94. Aldershot: Dartmouth.

Barton, T. (1994) *Power and Knowledge: Astrology, Physiognomies, and Medicine under the Roman Empire.* Ann Arbor, MI: University of Michigan Press.

Bloomfield, K. (1996) A civil servant's view of accountability, *Government Accountability: Beyond the Scott Report*, Public Finance Foundation Report.

Bode, C. (ed.) (1980) *The Selected Journals of Henry David Thoreau*, p. 135. New York: New American Library.

Boden, A. (1994) in M. A. Boden (ed.) *Dimensions of Creativity.* London: MIT Press.

Brown, R. (2001) The governance of the new universities: do we need to think again?, *Perspectives*, 5: 42–7.

Clark, S. (1998) The canker of corporatism, *Oxford Magazine*, 160, Michaelmas Term.

Coleridge, S. T. (1983) *Biographia literaria*, vol. I, ch. 9, in J. Engell and W. Jackson Bate (eds) *Collected Works.* Princeton, NJ: Princeton University Press.

Courant, R. and Robbins, H. (1996) *What is Mathematics*, 2nd edn (Foreword by E. D. Courant). Oxford: Oxford University Press.

Davies, J. G. (1972) *The Evangelistic Bureaucrat: A Study of a Planning Exercise in Newcastle upon Tyne.* London.

Davies, Sir M. (1994) *The Great Battle at Swansea.* Bristol: Thoemmes Press.

Dodds, E. R. (1973) *The Ancient Concept of Progress.* Oxford: Clarendon Press.

Evans, G. R. (1998) More beans, *Oxford Magazine*, 159, Michaelmas Term.

Evans, G. R. (2001) The integrity of UK academic research under commercial threat, *Science as Culture*, 10: 97–111.

Freeman, H. (ed.) (1984) *Mental Health and the Environment.* London: Churchill Livingstone.

Frye, N. ([1969] 1990) The community of freedom, in Robert D. Denham (ed.) *Reading the World: Selected Writings, 1935–76.* New York: Peter Lang Publishing.

Frye, N. ([1963] 1990) The developing imagination, in Denham (ed.) *Reading the World: Selected Writings, 1935–76.* New York: Peter Lang Publishing.

Frye, N. ([1972] 1990) Universities and the deluge of cant, in Denham (ed.) *Reading the World: Selected Writings, 1935–76.* New York: Peter Lang Publishing.

Government Statement on the Report of the Committee under the Chairmanship of Lord Robbins (1963–64) Cm 2165. London: HMSO.

Harris, N. (1993) *Law and Education: Regulation, Consumerism and the Education System*. London: Sweet & Maxwell.

House of Commons Public Service Committee (1996) *Second Report, Ministerial Accountability and Responsibility*. London: HMSO.

Johnson, R. J. (1996) Who's gatekeeping the gatekeepers?, *The Professional Geographer*, 48: 91–4.

Jowell, J. and Oliver, D. (eds) (1994) *The Changing Constitution* (3rd edn). Oxford: Clarendon Press.

Kornberg, A. (1995) *The Golden Helix: Inside the Biotech Venture*. Basingstoke: University Science Books.

Leavis, F. R. (1943) *Education and the University*. London: Chatto and Windus.

Manilius (1977) in G. P. Goold (ed.) *Astronomia*. Leipzig: Teubner.

Markus, L. R. (1996) *Regulation of Speech on Campus*. Westpoint, VA: Cambridge University Press.

Maskell, D. and Robinson, I. (2001) *The New Idea of a University*. London: Haven Books.

Meinert, C. L. and Tonascia, S. (1986) *Clinical Trials: Design, Conduct and Analysis*. Oxford: Oxford University Press.

Menand, L. (1996) *The Future of Academic Freedom*. Chicago: University of Chicago Press.

Moodie, G. and Eustace, R. (1974) *Power and Authority in British Universities*. London: George Allen & Unwin.

Newman, J. H. ([1852] 1898) *The Idea of a University Defined and Illustrated in Nine Courses Delivered to the Catholics of Dublin*. London: Longmans.

Packham, D. and Tasker, M. (1997) Industry and the academy – a Faustian contract?, *Industry and Higher Education*, April: 85–90.

Palfreyman, D. (1998) Unlimited personal liability for fellows, *Oxford Magazine*, 4th week, Michaelmas Term.

Polanyi, M. ([1951] 1998) *The Logic of Liberty: Reflections and Rejoinders*. London: Routledge.

Poon, P. (1995) Legal protections for the scientific misconduct whistleblower, *Journal of Law, Medicine and Ethics*, 23: 88–95.

Realizing our Potential: A Strategy for Science, Engineering and Technology (1993) Cm 2250. London: HMSO.

Salusinszky, I. (1987) *Criticism in Society*. London: Routledge.

Schaffer, S. (1994) in M. A. Boden (ed.) *Dimensions of Creativity*. London: MIT Press.

Snow, C. P. (1960) *The Affair*. London: Macmillan.

Spiers, R. (1998) Ethics and the funding of research and development at universities, *Science and Engineering Ethics*, 4: 375–84.

Thomas, I. (ed. and trans) (1967) *Greek Mathematics*, 2 vols. Boston, MA: Loeb Classical Library, Harvard University Press.

Thoreau, H. D. (1928) *On the Duty of Civil Disobedience*. New Haven, CT: At the Sign of the Chorofates.

Wass, Sir D. (1996) *Scott and Whitehall*, PL 461.

Weatherall, D. (1995) *Science and the Quiet Art*. Oxford: Oxford University Press.

Winkler, J. J. (1985) *Auctor and Actor: A Narratological Reading of Apuleius's Golden Ass*. Berkeley, CA: University of California Press.

Index

The Society for Research into Higher Education

The Society for Research into Higher Education (SRHE) exists to stimulate and coordinate research into all aspects of higher education. It aims to improve the quality of higher education through the encouragement of debate and publication on issues of policy, on the organization and management of higher education institutions, and on the curriculum, teaching and learning methods.

The Society is entirely independent and receives no subsidies, although individual events often receive sponsorship from business or industry. The Society is financed through corporate and individual subscriptions and has members from many parts of the world.

Under the imprint *SRHE & Open University Press*, the Society is a specialist publisher of research, having over 80 titles in print. In addition to *SRHE News*, the Society's newsletter, the Society publishes three journals: *Studies in Higher Education* (three issues a year), *Higher Education Quarterly* and *Research into Higher Education Abstracts* (three issues a year).

The Society runs frequent conferences, consultations, seminars and other events. The annual conference in December is organized at and with a higher education institution. There are a growing number of networks which focus on particular areas of interest, including:

Access	Learning Environment
Assessment	Legal Education
Consultants	Managing Innovation
Curriculum Development	New Technology for Learning
Eastern European	Postgraduate Issues
Educational Development Research	Quantitative Studies
FE/HE	Student Development
Funding	Vocation at Qualification
Graduate Employment	

Benefits to members

Individual

- The opportunity to participate in the Society's networks
- Reduced rates for the annual conferences

- Free copies of *Research into Higher Education Abstracts*
- Reduced rates for *Studies in Higher Education*
- Reduced rates for *Higher Education Quarterly*
- Free copy of *Register of Members' Research Interests* – includes valuable reference material on research being pursued by the Society's members
- Free copy of occasional in-house publications, e.g. *The Thirtieth Anniversary Seminars Presented by the Vice-Presidents*
- Free copies of *SRHE News* which informs members of the Society's activities and provides a calendar of events, with additional material provided in regular mailings
- A 35 per cent discount on all SRHE/Open University Press books
- Access to HESA statistics for student members
- The opportunity for you to apply for the annual research grants
- Inclusion of your research in the *Register of Members' Research Interests*

Corporate

- Reduced rates for the annual conferences
- The opportunity for members of the Institution to attend SRHE's network events at reduced rates
- Free copies of *Research into Higher Education Abstracts*
- Free copies of *Studies in Higher Education*
- Free copies of *Register of Members' Research Interests* – includes valuable reference material on research being pursued by the Society's members
- Free copy of occasional in-house publications
- Free copies of *SRHE News*
- A 35 per cent discount on all SRHE/Open University Press books
- Access to HESA statistics for research for students of the Institution
- The opportunity for members of the Institution to submit applications for the Society's research grants
- The opportunity to work with the Society and co-host conferences
- The opportunity to include in the *Register of Members' Research Interests* your Institution's research into aspects of higher education

Membership details: SRHE, 3 Devonshire Street, London
W1N 2BA, UK Tel: 020 7637 2766. Fax: 020 7637 2781.
email: srhe@mailbox.ulcc.ac.uk
world wide web: http://www.srhe.ac.uk./srhe/
Catalogue: SRHE & Open University Press, Celtic Court,
22 Ballmoor, Buckingham MK18 1XW. Tel: 01280 823388.
Fax: 01280 823233. email: enquiries@openup.co.uk

CALLING ACADEMIA TO ACCOUNT
RIGHTS AND RESPONSIBILITIES

G. R. Evans

- If universities are of value to the community, that value needs to be defined and constantly monitored. What are they for?
- Universities are complex organizations. How can they be run so as to provide an environment within which students and staff can work and think and write to best effect?
- Academic judgements decide the class of degrees, and the appointments and promotions prospects of academic staff. How should such judgements be formulated, and how tested for fairness and accuracy?

The very purpose of universities is being called into question by recent changes in the ways they are run and funded, the way their standards are maintained, and the assumptions upon which they do their teaching and research. Calling big institutions to account is not easy. It takes a sharp eye for detail and both boldness and persistence on the part of the whistleblower. But it is important that universities should be accountable, and *Calling Academia to Account* explores this issue comprehensively.

Contents

Introduction – Part 1: Calling to account in the wider world – Values and the world of scholarship – Rights and responsibilities: academic freedom and professional ethics – Value for money – The public interest – Part 2: Calling to account within universities – Structure and purpose – Institutional autonomy: academics and managers – Membership, employment, office – Making the rules: internal legislation – The rights of the subordinate and the insubordinate – Resolving disputes – Part 3: Standards: accounting for academic decisions – The value of a 'degree' – Peer review and appraisal – Forming academic judgements – Ensuring sound procedures – Reasonableness – Conclusion – Notes and references – Index – The Society for Research into Higher Education.

256pp   0 335 20194 6 (paperback)   0 335 20195 4 (hardback)

THE STATE OF UK HIGHER EDUCATION
MANAGING CHANGE AND DIVERSITY

David Warner and David Palfreyman (eds)

In *The State of UK Higher Education* a team of experienced university managers explores the strengths and weaknesses of the various elements and sectors of the UK higher education system. Their chapters illustrate the rich diversity of responses within different institutions to similar drivers of change. The contributions are personal and punchy but also enjoy a shared perspective as all but one of the authors have spent part of their careers at the University of Warwick. The exception, Peter Scott, draws together a number of important threads in an overarching and powerful final chapter. Overall, this book examines the changing concept and nature of higher education; provides a comprehensive analysis of UK higher education today; and points to how it might develop in the early years of the twenty-first century.

Contents
Introduction: Setting the scene – Part 1: The institutions – The ancient collegiate universities: Oxford and Cambridge – The big civics – Exeter University: going back to the future? – The 1960s new universities – Old and new: Durham and Stockton – Higher education in Scotland: diversity, distinctiveness and devolution – Higher education in Wales – The modern English universities – Part 2: Outsiders and insiders – The funding Councils: governance and accountability – The admissions system: Expansion, inclusion and the demands of diversity – The cuckoo in the nest? The business school in a university – The changing fortunes of continuing education: from margins to mainstream . . .? – An unsuitable job for a woman? – A view from the market place – Part 3: The Warwick way – Managing transformation – Academic development – Conclusion: triumph and retreat – Appendix: M.L. Shattock: A bibliography of major published works and unpublished reports 1969–2000, compiled by Jonathan Nicholls – Bibliography – Index – The Society for Research into Higher Education.

Contributors
Suzanne Alexander, Allan Bolton, Robert Burgess, David Caldwell, Steve Cannon, John Gledhill, Philip Harvey, John Hogan, David Holmes, Anthony McLaren, Russell Moseley, Jonathan Nicholls, David Palfreyman, Tony Rich, Jim Rushton, Peter Scott, Rosemary Stamp, David Warner.

256pp   0 335 20833 9 (Paperback)   0 335 20659 X (Hardback)